The Landlord's Book of Forms and Agreements

Cliff Roberson, LLM, Ph.D.

McGraw-Hill

New York   Chicago   San Francisco   Lisbon
London   Madrid   Mexico City   Milan   New Delhi
San Juan   Seoul   Singapore   Sydney   Toronto

The McGraw·Hill Companies

1 2 3 4 5 6 7 8 9 0   DOC/DOC   0 9 8 7 6 5

ISBN 0-07-146121-3
Part of ISBN 0-07-146914-1

This publication is designed to provide accurate and authoritative information in regard to the subject matter covered. It is sold with the understanding that the publisher is not engaged in rendering legal, accounting, or other professional service. If legal advice or other expert assistance is required, the services of a competent professional person should be sought.

—From a Declaration of Principles Jointly Adopted by a Committee
of the American Bar Association and a Committee of Publishers and Associations

McGraw-Hill books are available at special quantity discounts to use as premiums and sales promotions, or for use in corporate training programs. For more information, please write to the Director of Special Sales, McGraw-Hill Professional, Two Penn Plaza, New York, NY 10121-2298. Or contact your local bookstore.

 This book was printed on recycled, acid-free paper containing a minimum of 50% recycled, de-inked fiber.

Library of Congress Cataloging-in-Publication Data

Roberson, Cliff
  The landlord's book of forms and agreements / Cliff Roberson. — 1st ed.
     p. cm.
  Includes index.
  ISBN 0-07-146121-3 (book : alk. paper) — ISBN 0-07-146915-X (cd-rom) — ISBN 0-07-146914-1 (set : alk. paper) 1. Landlord and tenant—United States—Forms. 2. Leases—United States. I. Title.
  KF588.1.R62 2006
  346.7304'34–dc22

                                                                                    2005025275

06-07-1021 BT

Contents

6. Collecting Delinquent Rent   151

Preface

The goal of this book is to make you a successful landlord. No one becomes a landlord for fun; you do it for financial reasons. Accordingly, a successful landlord always keeps this goal as the most basic reason for his or her actions. All actions should be evaluated as to both their short-range and long-range financial impact. By following this course of action and the guidance provided in the book, you can make money as a landlord.

> A successful landlord makes money from two sources: the rent and the appreciation of his or her property (increase in value of the property). To be successful, maximize both sources.

The book is a guide to ensure your success as a landlord. It covers most key laws affecting landlords in all 50 states. The book is designed so that each chapter is semi-independent of the others. This allows a landlord to focus on the problems at hand and not have to search through the entire book. Every effort was made to make the explanations relevant, accurate, and success-focused. I want you, as a landlord, to feel confident in dealing with the various problems inherent in landlording.

Renting residential property appears to be complicated, but with the guidance contained in this book, it is not. In the book, you are provided guidance on how to

- Choose good tenants
- Avoid deadbeats as tenants
- Write appropriate and legal rental agreements
- Deal with and eliminate problems with tenants and problem tenants
- Understand and handle your responsibilities as a landlord regarding repair, maintenance, and security issues
- Limit your civil and criminal liability as a landlord
- Comply with landlord–tenant laws involving discrimination, security deposits, eviction of tenants, and habitability of your rental units.

Included with the book is a CD that has all the forms and leases contained in the book and many additional forms and letters. We live in a society that is changing constantly. To keep the material in the book current, a Web site has been developed and updated material will be posted at the Web site. Because the law often changes without notice, updates to the material in the book will be posted on the Web site. I will also post selected questions submitted by other landlords and the answers to those questions. You may submit questions to the Web site. If your question and its answer are posted on the site, your personal identity will not be revealed. The Web site may be accessed at www.rentforprofit.com. To sign up for a free subscription to the monthly landlord newsletter *Rent for Profit*, delivered by e-mail, visit the Web site.

> For recent developments, updates, and other useful information on being a profitable landlord, visit www.rentforprofit.com.

The Landlord's Book of Forms and Agreements focuses on residential property only, not on commercial leases. There are significant differences between a lease for a business and a lease for an apartment or residence. The book also does not cover the renting of hotel rooms.

The book is not intended as the substitute for personalized professional advice from a knowledgeable real estate attorney. If you need legal help, consult a real estate attorney who is licensed to practice law in your state. If you are a manager of government-owned project housing, make sure to check the regulations governing those units. In addition, if your property participates in the federally subsidized programs commonly referred to as Section 8 property, use the leases provided by the housing authority that administers the program. In summary, to be successful as a landlord, be knowledgeable, be professional, evaluate the opportunities, and plan ahead.

> The accompanying CD contains a copy of each form discussed in the book. These forms may be loaded on to your computer and edited or modified to fit your particular need.

List of Forms

Chapter 1: The Successful Landlord

Form 1-1 Descriptive handout for prospective residents.

Form 1-2 Move-in information for new residents.

Form 1-3 Thank-you letters to tenants moving in.

Chapter 2: Calculating the Rent

Form 2-1 Rental market survey.

Form 2-2 Calulating the rent.

Chapter 3: Selecting the Right Tenants

Form 3-1 Rental application.

Form 3-2 Written authorization to check credit, references, and other background information.

Form 3-3 Law enforcement report consent form.

Form 3-4 Employment verification.

Form 3-5 Credit reference verification.

Form 3-6 Bank verification.

Form 3-7 Reference from former landlord (option 1).

Form 3-8 Questions for previous landlord (option 2).

Form 3-9 Objective point system for resident selection.

Form 3-10 Denial of rental application based on credit report information.

Form 3-11 Reason for nonacceptance.

Form 3-12 Cosigner agreement.

Chapter 4: The Lease

Chapter 5: Managing the Property

Chapter 6: Collecting Delinquent Rent

Acknowledgments

While I am listed as the sole author, I could not have written this book without the assistance and support of many people—including but not limited to my editor, Melissa Scuereb, the copy editor, Eric Lowenkron, and Patty Wallenburg of TypeWriting.

1

The Successful Landlord

Getting Your Feet Wet

The art of being a landlord and investing in rental property is more than a matter of simply investing in real estate and people. Renting residential units is a hands-on project, unlike investing in stocks and mutual funds. How do you get started? I and many other landlords became real estate investors by renting out the property we knew best: our former homes. Others started by buying property for future use and renting it out until they needed it. Many landlords started by purchasing one rental unit and then adding to that number as they gained wealth and experience in the art of landlording.

To maximize your chances of success, the decision to buy property for residential renting purposes should be made only after careful planning. You need to determine how much you can pay for a property. Although this determination is subject to many factors, probably the most important is the projected rental income. In your projections, you must include insurance, property taxes, mortgage payments, routine maintenance, landscaping, and other costs associated with owning rental property. This sounds scary, but it is not. Start small, learn your lessons, and build your wealth.

Making a Profit

This book is designed to help you maximize your profits. Being a landlord is a difficult task; there is little fun in it, especially if you are losing money. With this in mind, the book has been designed to help you maximize your profits. By using the methods recommended in the book you will

- Find suitable tenants faster
- Keep your tenants longer
- Foster greater cooperation between you and the tenants
- Keep rental deficiencies to a minimum
- End the landlord–tenant relationships in a positive manner

Attitude

Successful landlords are those who keep the primary goal of making a profit in mind and conduct their business in a professional manner. Although there are only so many ways a lease may be written, how you conduct yourself is completely under your control. Your tenant is your customer, not your "buddy" or your enemy. Establish a professional relationship with the tenant so that the tenant understands that you expect him or her to comply with the terms of the lease. A tenant should not be allowed to extract favors from you on the basis of friendship. You should always conduct yourself as a professional landlord and property owner. Being a professional landlord also means treating the tenant in a respectful and courteous manner. There is no excuse for a landlord to be a totalitarian dictator.

Communications

Having been involved in legal proceedings between landlords and tenants as a property owner, an attorney, and a small claims judge, I have noticed that most landlords and tenants try to do what's right and that the problem in many cases is a failure to communicate. Communication is far more than just telling tenants what you expect them to do. It includes a complete understanding of the agreements, rights, and duties of the landlord and the tenant. One way to cut down on miscommunication between tenants and landlords is to use standardized forms, as recommended in this book. Get in the habit of putting all important agreements and understandings between you and your tenants in writing. Oral agreements are an invitation to a disagreement as to terms and meaning. Require that all agreements between you and your tenants be in writing.

Make it a policy to return all tenant or prospective tenant calls by the next business day. Prompt answering of tenant questions often defuses situations before they become hostile. This policy also lets those individuals know that you consider their calls important.

Cliff's Rules Necessary to be a Successful Landlord

- Conduct your business in a professional manner.
- Know the law.
- Take care in selecting your tenants.
- Get it in writing—oral agreements are an invitation for disputes.
- Return telephone calls from your tenants before the end of the next business day.
- Ensure that your actions are always legal and beyond what is required by the law.
- Establish a business relationship with an experienced landlord–tenant lawyer.
- Keep current by visiting www.rentforprofit.com.

Using a Rental Agency

The simplest and easiest way to be a landlord is to use a rental agency. I acquired my first rental property when I was in the military service. Shortly after buying a new home, I was transferred to another coast. I used a rental agency to handle the property. The agency took half the first month's rent for securing a new tenant and 7 percent each month after that. When there were repairs or maintenance problems, the agency took care of them and billed me for the cost of the repair or maintenance items plus a 10 percent handling fee. The tenants never knew who the landlord was. The agency acted as the manager. The problem with using an agency is simple: Its fees are generally what you consider as your profit.

As noted in Chapter 3, the most important decision you will make in being a landlord is to recruit and select the right tenant. The right tenant generally makes the difference between a profit and a loss. Accordingly, another option is to use an agency to help with the selection of a tenant. These agencies, often referred to as "lease-up" agencies, will advertise your property and screen the prospective tenants. Some agencies will even negotiate the lease for you. After they have selected the best available tenant, you take over and maintain the tenancy. Although this is cheaper than using a full-time professional management agency, it still cuts into your profit. Normally, the lease-up agency will charge you part of the first month's rent you receive from the tenant.

The third approach is to be your own agent but use a tenant screening agency. Using this method, you obtain prospective tenants and then have them screened by the screening company. This approach is discussed in Chapter 3. The screening agency will, for a one-time fee, obtain credit reports, references, and other background checks on the prospective tenant. After you have read Chapter 3, you will see why I recommend using a screening agency rather than trying to do everything yourself. The agency can take a lot of the problems in selecting the right tenant from you, yet you do not lose too much of your profit. Depending on the type of screening, agencies normally charge $40 to $80 per applicant to do the screening.

Nature of Landlord–Tenant Relationship

Although a tenant under a lease has a temporary right to occupy the premises, you as the property owner retain ownership of the property, which is the superior legal title to the property. Conduct your relationships with your tenant under this premise. You are the owner, and he or she is only temporarily occupying the property and has a duty to respect that property. Although you are the owner, when the tenant is in possession of the property, you have only limited rights of entry.

The right to use leased premises during the term specified in the lease is transferred from the landlord to the tenant and, during the existence of the lease, the tenant has control over the rental unit for all practical purposes for the term granted, with the landlord's rights being confined to a reversionary interest. In the absence of an express or necessarily implied covenant to the contrary, a tenant may put the leased premises to any lawful purpose that is consistent with the design and construction of the property and is not injurious to the property. Accordingly, while the tenant's right to occupation and use of the leasehold is exclusive, it is not unlimited: The concept of exclusive use does not extend to acts that destroy the owner's interest in the property and is limited to lawful use. The landlord, moreover, is free to attach restrictions to the leasing of the property that, if clearly stated and not illegal or unconscionable, are fully enforceable. The restrictions should be incorporated into the lease agreement to prevent misunderstanding.

Entry to the Rental Unit by the Landlord

An unauthorized entry by a landlord into a tenant's premises constitutes a trespass to the same extent as does an entry or intrusion by a stranger. In most states, there are well-defined purposes for which a landlord has the right to enter on the premises, such as the right to enter to repair the rental unit or, at a reasonable hour, to demand payment of the rent, when the lease does not fix a place at which the rent is payable and the tenant has not brought it to the landlord on the due date.

> Always include provisions in the lease that allow the landlord to enter the premises for certain purposes, such as making repairs and checking the condition of the unit. The lease forms included in this book provide for the right to enter the premises.

After a tenant abandons the demised premises, leaving them vacant and without anyone to look after them, generally the landlord may, without affecting the landlord's rights against the tenant or incurring any liability to the tenant, enter for the purpose of taking care of the premises. The Uniform Residential Landlord and Tenant Act recognizes the landlord's right to enter the rental unit without consent in an emergency.

> The entry by a landlord, maids, and plumbers, into a tenant's room during the tenant's seven months' absence was not a breach of the lease or an illegal trespass, where entry was required to fix a leak in the pipes. (*St. Joseph's Immigrant Homes, Inc., for St. Agnes Residence v. Seaman*, 53 Misc 2d 1095, 281 NYS 2d 143.)

In most states, the landlord has a right during the tenancy to enter and make such repairs as are necessary to prevent waste. However, in the absence of a clause or agreement stating otherwise, the landlord does not have, during the term of a lease, a right to enter the premises to make alterations and improvements or to investigate as to the need of repairs. Accordingly, in the absence of a reserved right of the landlord to enter for the purpose of making repairs, a person employed by the landlord to perform work on the leased premises is a trespasser if the worker enters or remains on the premises without the consent of the tenant. If the right of entry to make repairs is not given to the landlord in the lease, neither the landlord nor the landlord's employees are trespassers when they enter the premises to make proper repairs.

> Where a tenant left his apartment vacant for five or six days in the winter, the landlord had the right to enter to take such action as was necessary to prevent the freezing of the water pipes. *Rammell v. Bulen* (App, Franklin Co) 51 Ohio L Abs 125, 80 NE2d 167.

Right of Other Persons to Enter the Rental Unit

The right of third persons to enter the premises depends on the renter and not the landlord, and such entry does not affect any of the landlord's rights, provided that those persons do not commit a trespass amounting to an injury to the reversion. A landlord has only limited rights to prevent or prohibit persons from coming on the premises at the invitation of the tenant. In addition, the landlord cannot legally give third persons any right to interfere with the tenant's proper use and enjoyment of the premises.

Showing the Property

A landlord has the right to show a rental unit to prospective tenants after receiving notice by the present tenant of termination of the tenancy, provided that the right is exercised in a reasonable manner. For example, when a month-to-month tenant gives the required 30-day notice of termination, the tenant is under a duty to allow the landlord reasonable opportunities to show the premises to prospective tenants and is liable for an unreasonable refusal to do so. Under the Uniform Residential Landlord and Tenant Act, a tenant cannot unreasonably withhold consent to the landlord to enter the dwelling unit to exhibit the unit to prospective or actual purchasers, tenants, workers, or contractors.

Adversarial Relationship

Your ultimate goal as a landlord is to make a profit. The tenant's ultimate goal is to obtain rental property that meets his or her needs for the lowest possible price. Accordingly, the bilateral agreement between you and the tenant is inherently an adversarial relationship. It is normal for both you and the tenant to attempt to obtain the best advantages possible and to incorporate those advantages into the lease. The professional approach to use in negotiating a lease is a no-nonsense approach. After the lease has been executed, conduct your business on the premise that you will uphold your part of the bargain and expect your tenants to uphold their part.

Often, tenants believe that they are not treated well by their landlords, and many dislike their landlords. This is your opportunity to elevate the landlord–tenant relationship to a professional level. Although you are not their buddies, you should strive to maintain a caring business relationship with the tenants. Treat them as valued customers.

General Rules Regarding Upkeep of the Premises

States by statute, regulations and court decisions have placed certain requirements on landlords. Typical is the statutory requirement placed on Florida landlords by that state. Listed below are general obligations taken from the Florida Landlord Tenant Act.

Landlord's obligation to maintain premises—
(1) The landlord at all times during the tenancy shall:

(a) Comply with the requirements of applicable building, housing, and health codes; or

(b) Where there are no applicable building, housing, or health codes, maintain the roofs, windows, screens, doors, floors, steps, porches, exterior walls, foundations, and all other structural components in good repair and capable of resisting normal forces and loads and the plumbing in reasonable working condition. However, the landlord shall not be required to maintain a mobile home or other structure owned by the tenant.

The landlord's obligations under this subsection may be altered or modified in writing with respect to a single-family home or duplex.

(2)(a) Unless otherwise agreed in writing, in addition to the requirements of subsection (1), the landlord of a dwelling unit other than a single-family home or duplex shall, at all times during the tenancy, make reasonable provisions for:

1. The extermination of rats, mice, roaches, ants, wood-destroying organisms, and bedbugs. When vacation of the premises is required for such extermination, the landlord shall not be liable for damages but shall abate the rent. The tenant shall be required to temporarily vacate the premises for a period of time not to exceed 4 days, on 7 days' written notice, if necessary, for extermination pursuant to this subparagraph.
2. Locks and keys.
3. The clean and safe condition of common areas.
4. Garbage removal and outside receptacles therefore.
5. Functioning facilities for heat during winter, running water, and hot water.

(b) Unless otherwise agreed in writing, at the commencement of the tenancy of a single family home or duplex, the landlord shall install working smoke detection devices. As used in this paragraph, the term "smoke detection device" means an electrical or battery operated device which detects visible or invisible particles of combustion and which is listed by Underwriters Laboratories, Inc., Factory Mutual Laboratories, Inc., or any other nationally recognized testing laboratory using nationally accepted testing standards.

The landlord may provide in the rental agreement that the tenant is obligated to pay costs or charges for garbage removal, water, fuel, or utilities. The landlord is not responsible to the tenant under this section for conditions created or caused by the negligent or wrongful act or omission of the tenant, a member of the tenant's family, or other person on the premises with the tenant's consent.

Tenant's obligation to maintain dwelling unit—The tenant at all times during the tenancy shall:

(1) Comply with all obligations imposed upon tenants by applicable provisions of building, housing, and health codes.

(2) Keep that part of the premises which he or she occupies and uses clean and sanitary.

(3) Remove from the tenant's dwelling unit all garbage in a clean and sanitary manner.

(4) Keep all plumbing fixtures in the dwelling unit or used by the tenant clean and sanitary and in repair.

(5) Use and operate in a reasonable manner all electrical, plumbing, sanitary, heating, ventilating, air-conditioning and other facilities and appliances, including elevators.

(6) Not destroy, deface, damage, impair, or remove any part of the premises or property therein belonging to the landlord nor permit any person to do so.

(7) Conduct himself or herself, and require other persons on the premises with his or her consent to conduct themselves, in a manner that does not unreasonably disturb the tenant's neighbors or constitute a breach of the peace.

Freedom to Choose Your Tenants

At one time, a landlord had a right to choose who his or her tenants would be. This freedom to refuse to enter into the landlord–tenant relationship has been limited by federal and state legislation designed to afford protection against invidious discrimination. For example, the Federal Fair Housing Act prohibits (1) refusal to sell or rent or to negotiate a rental or sale of a dwelling on the basis of race, color, religion, sex, national origin, familial status, or disability, (2) discrimination in the terms, conditions, or privileges of sale or rental or in the provision of services in connection therewith on the basis of race, color, religion, sex, national origin, familial status, or disability, (3) advertising that one intends to discriminate on the basis of these categories, and (4) claiming that a dwelling is not available when in fact it is.

It is handy to have a descriptive handout for individuals who inquire about your rental units. The handout should look like Form 1-1.

Rent

Rent is a normal but not an essential incident of the relationship of a landlord and a tenant. The payment of rent to the owner by one in occupancy of premises generally indicates that there is a landlord–tenant relationship between such persons, but the fact that a payment is referred to as a payment of rent does not establish the existence of a landlord–tenant relationship between the parties when other facts negate the existence of that relationship.

In ordinary use, the term "rent" refers to the return made by a person who occupies real estate under an express or implied contract with the owner for the occu-

Address: _____

Subdivision: _____

School district:_____

Elementary:

Private elementary in the area:

Middle/high school:_____

Private middle/high school: _____

Home (Apartment) includes:

Total livable space in square feet:_____

_____ Bedrooms

_____ Baths

_____ Living room

_____ Dining room/den

Family/additional room with _____

Type of heat: _____

Appliances:_____

Additional/optional features: _____

Parking/garage: _____

Landscaped lot/yard: _____

All of this for only $_____ per month/biweekly plus $_____ deposit.

Date available: _____

Call for more information: _____

FORM 1-1 Descriptive handout for prospective residents.

pation of the premises and is defined as the benefits in money, provisions, chattels, or services paid or given in exchange for the use and occupation of real estate. Rent is distinguishable from the "room rates" paid by a hotel guest, which constitute payments for the temporary use of a portion of real property for a limited time and purpose. Rent also may be distinguished from miscellaneous charges such as unreasonable wear and tear penalties, late charges, and security deposits.

The parties to a lease may agree that items such as late fees and the attorney's fees incurred by a landlord in proceeding against a tenant will be treated as additional rent. The words "royalties" and "rents" are used interchangeably to describe the compensation that the occupier pays the landlord for that species of occupation that the contract between them allows. Rent also may include consideration in the form of services provided by the tenant.

Residential Security Deposits

All states regulate the handling of rental security deposits. The state requirements are generally similar to those set forth below for the state of New Jersey.

The security deposit generally must be deposited in an interest-bearing account in a bank or saving and loan association in New Jersey at the time the lease is signed. The tenant must give written notice of where the money has been deposited within 30 days of receipt by the landlord.

If the landlord does not return the security deposit within 30 days from the date the tenant moves out of the premises, the tenant may sue to recover double the amount due, plus court costs. If the amount sought is $2,000 or less, the tenant may sue in the small claims section. If the amount sought does not exceed $10,000, the tenant may sue in the special civil part. If the amount sought exceeds $10,000, the tenant must sue in the law division.

The landlord must notify the tenant of the amount of the security deposit being retained and the nature and cost of the repairs.

If the amount of any damage caused by a tenant plus any unpaid rent is more than the security deposit, the landlord may sue for the additional money.

If a residential building is sold, the seller must turn over each security deposit plus any interest to the buyer and notify each tenant by registered or certified mail.

States that require the landlord to pay interest on security deposits include

Connecticut	District of Columbia	Illinois	Maryland
Massachusetts	Minnesota	New Hampshire	New Jersey
New Mexico	North Dakota	Ohio	Pennsylvania
Virginia			

Florida, Iowa, and New York require the payment of interest on certain rentals.

Liability of Landlord for Tenant's Illegal Use of the Property

Generally, the relation of landlord and tenant does not render the landlord criminally liable for any illegal use of the premises by a tenant. However, the landlord is criminally liable if he or she aids or assists the tenant in illegal use of the premises. In some jurisdictions, statutes are directed against landlords who let the property be or know that the property is being used for particular illegal purposes, such as prostitution, illegal sale of liquor, and gambling.

Landlord's Obligation to Act in Good Faith

The courts uniformly hold that every rental agreement or duty imposes an obligation of good faith in its performance or enforcement on both the landlord and the tenant. If a court, as a matter of law, finds a rental agreement or any provision of a rental agreement to have been unconscionable at the time it was made, the court may refuse to enforce the rental agreement, enforce the remainder of the rental agreement without the unconscionable provision, or so limit the application of any unconscionable provision as to avoid any unconscionable result.

When it is claimed or appears to a court that the rental agreement or any provision thereof may be unconscionable, the parties shall be afforded a reasonable opportunity to present evidence as to meaning, relationship of the parties, purpose, and effect to aid the court in making the determination.

Welcoming the New Tenant

To start the tenancy off in a professional yet friendly manner, the landlord should take affirmative steps to welcome the tenant to the neighborhood. You may wish to place a small welcome basket in the unit where the tenant will see it when he or she moves in. You also may provide the new tenant with an information sheet with information regarding the neighborhood. I also would include move-in information for the new tenant. Form 1-2 may be used to provide useful information to the tenant.

Dear_____:

The below information is provided to assist you in getting settled in your new home.

Police: emergency–911   nonemergency _____

Fire: emergency–911   nonemergency _____

Post office is located at_____

Your property address:

The Property Manager is _____

Office Hours: _____ Phone Number:_____

Management's E-Mail Address: _____

Send Rent Payments to:

Utilities: _____

Electric:_____

Gas company:_____

Water company:_____

Telephone company: _____

Other: _____

continued

FORM 1-2 Move-in information for new residents.

Trash pickup information:_____

School Information:

Elementary: _____

Junior high/middle:_____

High:_____

Day care: _____

Pest control:_____

Other: _____

Other: _____

Your water shut-off is located: _____

Your electrical shut-off is located at: _____

Your gas shut-off is located at:_____

Other important items and their locations: _____

FORM 1-2   Move-in information for new residents (continued).

It is important to start the tenancy on a good footing. Many landlords use a thank-you letter similar to the one in Form 1-3 to start the relationship.

Residential Landlord and Tenant Statutes

The renting of residential property is governed primarily by state and local law. That's why it is important to check your local laws before taking action as a landlord. A number of states have adopted the Uniform Residential Landlord and Tenant Act (URLTA) or the Model Residential Landlord–Tenant Code. Those states include

Dear_____

I want to inform to you how grateful I am to have you as a tenant. In the years that I have owned this property, I have had some very loyal and dedicated residents. And it is residents like you who deserve a good share of the credit for making this possible. I'm sure that, over the years, I will hold your support and your friendship as a very special blessing.

Sincerely,

_____

Owner

FORM 1-3   Thank-you letter to tenants moving in.

- Alaska
- Arizona
- Florida
- Hawaii
- Iowa
- Kansas
- Kentucky
- Montana
- Nebraska
- New Mexico
- Oregon
- Rhode Island
- South Carolina
- Tennessee
- Virginia

Other states have adopted essential parts of the URLTA. The Uniform Residential Landlord and Tenant Act is one of the "uniform laws" written by the Commission on Uniform State Laws. The uniform laws are not real laws but recommendations to the states about what the law should be. Generally, most states eventually adopt a major portion of the uniform laws. The uniform laws were written for the purpose of reconciling the hodgepodge of conflicting and "incorrect" state laws across the county. The commission is made up of lawyers and law professors who give painstaking attention to creating a fair and workable law. The uniform laws become real laws when they are adopted by the states and enacted as those states' law.

Except as noted in the text, the principles set forth in this book are based on requirements contained in the URLTA. There are some common terms used by the URLTA, as set forth in the Tennessee statute:

- "Action" includes recoupment, counterclaim, set-off, suit in equity, and any other proceeding in which rights are determined, including an action for possession;
- "Building and housing codes" includes any law, ordinance, or governmental regulation concerning fitness for habitation, or the construction, maintenance, operation, occupancy, use, or appearance of any premises, or dwelling unit;
- "Dwelling unit" means a structure or the part of a structure that is used as a home, residence, or sleeping place by one (1) person who maintains a household or by two (2) or more persons who maintain a common household;

- "Good faith" means honesty in fact in the conduct of the transaction concerned;
- "Landlord" means the owner, lessor, or sublessor of the dwelling unit or the building of which it is a part, and it also means a manager of the premises who fails to disclose that the manager does not own the property;
- "Organization" includes a corporation, government, governmental subdivision or agency, business trust, estate, trust, partnership or association, two (2) or more persons having a joint or common interest, and any other legal or commercial entity;
- "Owner" means one (1) or more persons, jointly or severally, in whom is vested: All or part of the legal title to property; or All or part of the beneficial ownership and a right to the present use and enjoyment of the premises;
- "Owner" also includes a mortgagee in possession;
- "Person" includes an individual or organization;
- "Premises" means a dwelling unit and the structure of which it is a part and facilities and appurtenances therein and grounds, areas, and facilities held out for the use of tenants generally or whose use is promised to the tenant;
- "Rental agreement" means all agreements, written or oral, and valid rules and regulations embodying the terms and conditions concerning the use and occupancy of a dwelling unit and premises;
- "Rents" means all payments to be made to the landlord under the rental agreement;
- "Security deposit" means an escrow payment made to the landlord under the rental agreement for the purpose of securing the landlord against financial loss due to damage to the premises occasioned by the tenant's occupancy other than ordinary wear and tear and any monetary damage due to the tenant's breach of the rental agreement;
- "Security deposit" is advance rentals; and "Security deposit" shall in no way infer that the landlord is providing any service for the personal protection or safety of the tenant beyond that prescribed by law;
- "Tenant" means a person entitled under a rental agreement to occupy a dwelling unit to the exclusion of others;
- "Nuisance vehicle" means any vehicle that is incapable of operating under its own power and is detrimental to the health, welfare, or safety of persons in the community;
- "Unauthorized vehicle" means a vehicle that is not registered to a tenant, an occupant or a tenant's known guest, and has remained for more than seven (7) consecutive days on real property leased or rented by a landlord for residential purposes; and
- "Vehicle" means any device for carrying passengers, livestock, goods, or equipment that moves on wheels and/or runners.

Summary of the Model Act Provisions

The office of the state of Washington's attorney general provides the following summary of the model act.

Who Is Covered by the Law?

Most tenants who rent a place to live come under the state's Residential Landlord and Tenant Act. However, certain renters are specifically excluded from the law.

Those who are generally not covered by the Residential Landlord–Tenant Act are:

- Renters of a space in a mobile home park. They are usually covered by the state's Mobile Home Landlord-Tenant Act (RCW 59.20). However, renters of both a space and a mobile home are usually covered by the residential law.
- Residents in hotels and motels.
- Residents of public or private medical, religious, educational, recreational, or correctional institutions.
- Tenants who have exercised an option to buy the dwelling.
- Tenants who have signed a lease option agreement but have not yet exercised that option are still covered.
- Residents of a single family dwelling that is rented as part of a lease for agricultural land.
- Residents of housing provided for seasonal farmwork.
- Tenants who are employed by the landlord, when their agreement specifies that they can only live in the rental unit as long as they hold the job (such as an apartment house manager).
- Tenants who are leasing a single family dwelling for one year or more, when their attorney has approved the exemption.
- Tenants who are using the property for commercial rather than residential purposes.

Rights of All Tenants

Renters who are not covered by the Landlord–Tenant Act have the following basic rights under other state laws:

- Right to a livable dwelling
- Protection from unlawful discrimination
- Right to hold the landlord liable for damage caused by the landlord's negligence
- Protection against lockouts and seizure of personal property by the landlord

Types of Rental Agreements

A rental agreement between the landlord and the tenant sets down the terms that will be followed while the tenant lives in the rental unit.

The following is a description of the two most common types of rental arrangements: leases and month-to-month rental agreements. Whatever a rental agreement is called, it's important to read the document carefully to learn its exact terms.

Month-to-month agreement.   This agreement is for an indefinite period, with rent usually payable on a monthly basis. The agreement can be in writing or oral, but if any type of fee or refundable deposit is being paid, the agreement must be in writing. A month-to-month agreement continues until either the landlord or the tenant gives proper notice to end it.

The rent can be raised or the rules changed at any time, provided that the landlord gives the tenant proper notice.

Lease.   A lease requires the tenant to stay for a specific amount of time and restricts the landlord's ability to change the terms of the rental agreement. A lease must be in writing to be valid.

During the term of the lease, the rent cannot be raised or the rules changed unless both landlord and tenant agree. Leases of one year or more are exempt from the Landlord and Tenant Act, but only if the tenant's attorney has approved such an exemption.

Illegal Provisions in Rental Agreements

Some provisions that may appear in rental agreements or leases are not legal and cannot be enforced under the law. They include the following:

- A provision that waives any right given to tenants by the Landlord and Tenant Act
- A provision that tenants give up their right to defend themselves in court against a landlord's accusations
- A provision that limits the landlord's liability in situations in which the landlord normally would be responsible
- A provision allowing the landlord to enter the rental unit without proper notice
- A provision requiring a tenant to pay for all damage to the unit even if it is not caused by tenants or their guests
- A provision stating the tenant will pay the landlord's attorney's fees under any circumstances if a dispute goes to court

- A provision that allows the landlord to seize a tenant's property if the tenant falls behind in rent

Deposits and Other Fees

When a new tenant moves in, the landlord often collects money to cover such things as cleaning and damage. The money collected may be refundable or non-refundable.

Refundable Deposits

Under the Landlord–Tenant Act, the term "deposit" can be applied only to money that can be refunded to the tenant.

If a refundable deposit is being charged, the law requires that the rental agreement must be in writing. It must say what each deposit is for and what the tenant must do to get the money back:

- The tenant must be given a written receipt for each deposit.
- A checklist or statement describing the condition of the rental unit must be filled out. The landlord and the tenant must sign it, and the tenant must be given a signed copy. (The attorney general's office offers a free sample checklist for this purpose.)
- The deposits must be placed in a trust account in a bank or escrow company. The tenant must be informed in writing where the deposits are being kept. Unless some other agreement has been made in writing, any interest earned by the deposit belongs to the landlord.

Nonrefundable Fees

These fees will not be returned to the tenant under any circumstances. If a non-refundable fee is being charged, the rental agreement must be in writing and must state that the fee will not be returned. *A nonrefundable fee cannot legally be called a "deposit."*

Landlord's Responsibilities

Under the Landlord and Tenant Act, the landlord must do the following:

- Maintain the dwelling so that it does not violate state and local codes in ways that endanger tenants' health and safety.
- Maintain structural components, such as roofs, floors, and chimneys, in reasonably good repair.

- Maintain the dwelling in reasonably weather-tight condition.
- Provide reasonably adequate locks and keys.
- Provide the necessary facilities to supply heat, electricity, and hot and cold water.
- Provide garbage cans and arrange for the removal of garbage, except in single-family dwellings.
- Keep common areas such as lobbies, stairways, and halls reasonably clean and free from hazards.
- Control pests before the tenant moves in. The landlord must continue to control infestations, except in single-family dwellings or when the infestation was caused by the tenant.
- Make repairs to keep the unit in the same condition as it was when the tenant moved in (except for normal wear and tear).
- Keep electrical, plumbing, and heating systems in good repair and maintain any appliances that are provided with the rental.
- Inform the tenant of the name and address of the landlord or landlord's agent.
- Set water heaters at 120 degrees when a new tenant moves in.
- Provide smoke detectors, and ensure that they work properly when a new tenant moves in. (Tenants are responsible for maintaining detectors.)

Important note: A landlord is not responsible for the cost of correcting problems that were caused by the tenant.

Tenant's Responsibilities

Under the Landlord and Tenant Act, a tenant is required to do the following:

- Pay rent and any utilities agreed upon
- Comply with any requirements of city, county, or state regulations
- Keep the rental unit clean and sanitary
- Dispose of garbage properly
- Pay for fumigation of infestations caused by the tenant
- Properly operate plumbing, electrical, and heating systems
- Not intentionally or carelessly damage the dwelling
- Not permit "waste" (substantial damage to the property) or "nuisance" (substantial interference with other tenants' use of their property)
- When moving out, restore the dwelling to the same condition it was in when the tenant moved in, except for normal wear and tear

If the Landlord Wants to Make Changes

Below are generalizations about the two most common types of rental agreements. Be sure to consult your rental documents to find out how changes can be made in the terms of the agreement.

Month-to-month agreements.   If the landlord wants to change the provisions of a month-to-month rental agreement, such as by raising the rent or changing the rules, the tenant must be given at least 30 days' notice in writing. (Less notice is not allowed under the law.) These changes can become effective only at the beginning of a rental period (the day the rent is due).

If the landlord wishes to convert the unit to a condominium, the tenant must be given a 90-day notice.

The Landlord and Tenant Act does not limit how much rent can be raised or how often. However, the landlord cannot raise the rent to retaliate against a tenant.

Leases.   Under a lease, in most cases, changes cannot be made unless both the landlord and the tenant agree to the proposed change.

If the Property Is Sold

The sale of the property does not automatically end a lease or month-to-month rental agreement.

When a rental unit is sold, tenants must be notified of the new owner's name and address either by certified mail or by a revised posting on the premises.

All deposits paid to the original owner must be transferred to the new owner, who must put them in a trust or escrow account. The new owner must notify tenants promptly where the deposits are being held.

Landlord's Access to the Rental

The landlord must give the tenant at least a two-day notice of his or her intent to enter at reasonable times. However, the law says that tenants must not unreasonably refuse to allow the landlord to enter the rental when the landlord has given at least one day's notice of intent to enter at a specified time to show the dwelling to prospective or actual purchasers or tenants.

Any provision in a rental agreement that allows the landlord to enter without such notice is not valid under the law. The law says that tenants shall not unreasonably refuse the landlord access to repair, improve, or service the dwelling. In case of an emergency, or if the property has been abandoned, the landlord can enter without notice.

If the Rental Needs Repairs

Required notice.   When something in the rental unit needs to be repaired, the first step is for the tenant to give written notice of the problem to the landlord or the person who collects the rent. The notice must include the address and apartment number of the rental; the name of the owner, if known; and a description of the problem.

It's a good idea to deliver the notice personally or to use certified mail and get a return receipt from the post office. After giving notice, the tenant must wait the required time for the landlord to begin making repairs. Those required waiting times are

- 24 hours for no hot or cold water, heat, or electricity or for a condition that is imminently hazardous to life
- 72 hours for repair of the refrigerator, range, oven, or a major plumbing fixture supplied by landlord
- 10 days for all other repairs

Tenant's options.   What can the tenant do if repairs are not started within the required time? If the tenant is paid up in rent and utilities, the following options can be used:

1. The tenant can move out. After tenants wait the required time, the law allows them to give written notice to the landlord and move out immediately. Tenants are entitled to a prorated refund of the rent as well as the deposits they normally would get back.
2. Litigation or arbitration can be used to work out the dispute. A tenant can hire an attorney and go to court to force the landlord to make repairs. (These kinds of suits cannot be brought in small claims court.) Or, if the landlord agrees, the dispute can be decided by an arbitration service. Arbitration is usually less costly and quicker than going to court.
3. The tenant can hire someone to make the repairs. In many cases the tenant can have the work done and then deduct the cost from the rent. (This procedure cannot be used to force a landlord to provide adequate garbage cans.)

Before having any repairs made by a licensed or registered tradesperson, if one is required, or by any person capable of doing the work, the tenant must submit a good faith estimate to the landlord. To speed the repair process, the estimate can be given to the landlord along with the original written notice of the problem. When the required waiting period has ended, and the landlord has not begun repairs, the tenant can contract with the lowest bidder to have the work done. **Important note:** If the repair is one that has a 10-day waiting period, you cannot contract to have the work done until 10 days after the landlord receives notice or 5 days after the landlord receives the estimate, whichever is later. After the work is completed, the tenant pays the repairperson and deducts the cost from the rent payment. The landlord must be given an opportunity to inspect the work.

There are limits on the cost of repairs that can be deducted. If a tenant contracts the repair work out to a licensed or registered person or to a responsible person, if no other license is required, the total cost of repairs that may be deducted in this category is no more than 1 month's rent for each repair and no more than 2 month's rent in any 12-month period.

If a large repair that affects a number of tenants needs to be made, the tenants can join together, follow the proper procedure, and have the work done. Then each tenant can deduct a portion of the cost from his or her rent.

A tenant must be current in rent and utilities payments to use this procedure.

4. The tenant can make the repairs and deduct the cost from the rent if the work does not require a licensed or registered tradesperson. The tenant must give the landlord proper notice of the problem as outlined on page20. Then, if the landlord does not begin repairs within the required time, the tenant can make the repairs. The cost of materials and labor can be deducted from the rent.

   To use this procedure, the cost of the repairs cannot be more than half a month's rent. And, within any 12-month period, the tenant can deduct only a total of one month's rent.

   The landlord must be given a chance to inspect the repairs. Work must be done properly and meet local codes. The tenant could be held responsible for inadequate repair work.

5. Rent in escrow. After notice of defective conditions and after appropriate government certification of a defect, and when the waiting periods have passed, tenants may place their monthly rent payments in an escrow account. This procedure is very technical and cannot be described in full here. For copies of the law (RCW 59.18), write to the Code Revisor's Office or consult your attorney.

Illegal Actions by a Landlord

The law prohibits a landlord from taking certain actions against a tenant. These illegal actions include the following.

Lockouts.   The law prohibits landlords from changing locks, adding new locks, or otherwise making it impossible for a tenant to use the normal locks and keys. Even if a tenant is behind in rent, such lockouts are illegal.

A tenant who is locked out can file a lawsuit to regain entry. Some local governments also have laws against lockouts and can help a tenant who has been locked out of a rental. For more information, contact your city or county government.

Utility shutoffs.   The landlord may not shut off utilities because the tenant is behind in rent or to force a tenant to move out. Utilities may be shut off by the landlord only so that repairs may be made and only for a reasonable amount of time. If a landlord intentionally does not pay utility bills so that the service will be turned off, that can be considered an illegal shutoff.

If the utilities have been shut off by the landlord, the tenant should check with the utility company to see if it will restore service. If it appears the shutoff is illegal, the tenant can file a lawsuit. If the tenant wins in court, the judge can award the tenant up to $100 per day for the time without service, as well as attorney's fees.

Taking the tenant's property.   The law allows a landlord to take a tenant's property only in the case of abandonment. A clause in a rental agreement that allows the landlord to take a tenant's property in other situations is not valid.

If the landlord takes a tenant's property illegally, the tenant may want to contact the landlord first. If that is unsuccessful, the police can be notified. If the property is not returned after the landlord is given a written request, a court can order the landlord to pay the tenant up to $100 for each day the property is kept (to a total of $1,000).

Renting condemned property.   The landlord may not rent units that are condemned or unlawful to occupy due to existing uncorrected code violations. The landlord can be liable for three months' rent or treble damages, whichever is greater, as well as costs and attorney's fees for knowingly renting the property.

Retaliatory actions.   If a tenant exercises rights under the law, such as complaining to a government authority and deducting for repairs, the law prohibits the landlord from taking retaliatory action.

Examples of retaliatory actions are raising the rent, reducing the services provided to the tenant, and evicting the tenant. The law initially assumes that these steps are retaliatory if they occur within 90 days after the tenant's action unless the tenant was in some way violating the statute when notice of the change was received.

If the matter is taken to court, and the judge finds in favor of the tenant, the landlord can be ordered to reverse the retaliatory action as well as pay for any harm done to the tenant and pay the tenant's attorney's fees.

Moving Out

Proper notice to leave.   When a tenant wants to move out of a rental unit, it is important that the proper kind of notice be given to the landlord. The following sections discuss ways to end the two most common types of rental agreements. However, it is important that tenants check their own rental agreements to determine what kind of notice must be given before they move out.

Leases.   If the tenant moves out at the expiration of a lease, in most cases it is not necessary to give the landlord written notice. However, the lease should be consulted to be sure a formal notice is not required.

If a tenant stays beyond the expiration of the lease, and the landlord accepts the next month's rent, the tenant is assumed to be renting under a month-to-month agreement.

A tenant who leaves before a lease expires is responsible for paying the rent for the rest of the lease. However, the landlord must make an effort to rerent the unit at a reasonable price. If this is not done, the tenant may not be liable for rent beyond a reasonable period.

Month-to-month rental agreements.   When a tenant wants to end a month-to-month rental agreement, written notice must be given to the landlord. The notice must be received at least 20 days before the end of the rental period (the day before rent is due).

The day on which the notice is delivered does not count. A landlord cannot require a tenant to give more than 20 days' notice when moving out. What if a tenant moves out without giving proper notice? The law says the tenant is liable for rent for the lesser of 30 days from the day the next rent payment is due or 30 days from the day the landlord learns the tenant has moved out. However, the landlord has a duty to try to find a new renter. If the dwelling is rented before the end of the 30 days, the former tenant must pay only until the new tenant begins paying rent.

When a landlord wants a month-to-month renter to move out, a 20-day notice is required.

Return of Deposits

After a tenant moves out, a landlord has 14 days in which to either return deposits or give the tenant a written statement explaining why all or part of the money is being kept. It is advisable for the tenant to leave a forwarding address with the landlord when moving out. Under the law, the rental unit must be restored to the same condition it was in when the tenant moved in, except for normal wear and tear. Deposits cannot be used to cover normal "wear and tear" or damage that existed when the tenant moved in. (Under the law, a damage checklist should have been filled out when the tenant moved in.)

The landlord is in compliance with the law if the required payment, statement, or both are deposited in the U.S. mail with first-class postage paid within 14 days. If the tenant takes the landlord to court, and it is ruled that the landlord intentionally did not give the statement or return the money, the court can award the tenant up to twice the amount of the deposit.

Evictions

When a landlord wants a tenant to move out, certain procedures must be followed. This section discusses why landlords can evict tenants and what methods must be used. There are four types of evictions under the law, each requiring a certain type of notice

For not paying rent. If the tenant is even one day behind in rent, the landlord can issue a three-day notice to pay or move out. If the tenant pays all the rent due within three days, the landlord must accept it and cannot evict the tenant. A landlord is not required to accept a partial payment.

For not complying with the terms of the rental agreement. If a tenant is not complying with the rental agreement (for example, keeping a cat when the agreement specifies "no pets"), the landlord can give the tenant a 10-day notice to comply or move out. If the tenant remedies the situation within that time, the landlord cannot continue the eviction process.

For creating a "waste or nuisance." If a tenant destroys the landlord's property; uses the premises for unlawful activity, including drug-related activities; or damages the value of the property or interferes with another tenant's use of the property, the landlord can issue a three-day notice to move out. The tenant must move out after receiving this type of notice. There is no option to stay and correct the problem.

For no cause. Except in rent control areas, landlords can evict month-to-month tenants without having or stating a particular reason, as long as the eviction is not discriminatory or retaliatory.

If a landlord wants a tenant to move out and does not give a reason, the tenant must be given a 20-day notice to leave. The tenant must receive the notice at least 20 days before the next rent payment is due.

The tenant can be required to move out only at the end of a rental period (the day before a rental payment is due).

Usually, a 20-day notice cannot be used if the tenant has signed a lease. Check the specific rental document to determine if a lease can be ended this way.

If a rental is being converted to a condominium, the tenant must be given a 90-day notice under state law.

How must a landlord notify the tenant of eviction proceedings? For a landlord to take legal action against a tenant who does not move out, the landlord must first give written notice to the tenant in accordance with the law. The landlord's options include personal service, service by mail, and service by placing the notice in a prominent place on the premises. See the statute to ensure strict compliance.

What if a tenant continues to live in a rental unit after receiving notice? If the tenant continues to occupy the rental in violation of a notice to leave, the landlord must go to court to begin what is called an "unlawful detainer" action.

If the court rules in favor of the landlord, the sheriff will be instructed to move the tenant out of the rental if the tenant does not leave voluntarily. The only legal way for a landlord to move a tenant out physically is by going through the courts and the sheriff's office.

Abandonment

When is a tenant considered to have abandoned a dwelling? Under the law, abandonment occurs when a tenant has both fallen behind in rent *and* has clearly indicated by words or actions an intention not to continue living in the rental.

When a rental has been abandoned, the landlord may enter the unit and remove any abandoned property, which then must be stored in a reasonably secure place. A notice must be mailed to the tenant saying where the property is being stored and when it will be sold. If the landlord does not have a new address for the tenant, the notice should be mailed to the rental address so that it can be forwarded by the post office.

How long must the landlord wait before selling the abandoned property? That depends on the value of the goods. If the total value of the property is less than $50, the landlord must mail a notice of the sale to the tenant and then wait 7 days. Family pictures, keepsakes, and personal papers cannot be sold until 45 days after the landlord mails the notice of abandonment.

If the total value of the property is more than $50, the landlord must mail a notice of the sale to the tenant and then wait 45 days. Personal papers, family pictures and keepsakes can be sold at the same time as other property.

The money raised by the sale of the property goes to cover money owed to the landlord, such as back rent and the cost of storing and selling the goods. If there is any money left over, the landlord must keep it for the tenant for one year. If it is not claimed within that time, it belongs to the landlord.

If a landlord takes a tenant's property, and a court later determines there had not actually been an abandonment, the landlord can be ordered to compensate the tenant for loss of the property as well as paying court and attorney costs.

What happens to a tenant's deposit when the rental is abandoned? Within 14 days of learning of abandonment, the landlord is responsible for either returning a tenant's deposit or providing a statement explaining why the deposit is being kept.

2

Calculating
the Rent

This chapter provides landlords with methods and advice regarding how much rent to charge and the rules regarding rental deposits. Included is a worksheet for a landlord to use in determining how much rent to charge and how to set the required deposit.

Price

In most jurisdictions, the amount charged for rent is not controlled by law. In a few areas, mostly large cities, where there are rent control statutes and ordinances, local regulations may limit the amount a landlord may charge. In several states, such as Connecticut, a tenant may sue a landlord for charging excessive rent. If you are not in a jurisdiction that has rent control, the amount of rent you charge is completely up to you.

Some landlords follow a policy of charging just slightly below the market to encourage excellent tenants to stay longer in a unit. This policy is based on the concept that tenants who feel they are treated fairly are less likely to move and more responsive to a landlord's business needs.

Determining the Amount

Determining the amount of rent to charge is one of the most difficult questions for a landlord. If the price is too high, the property will not rent and the tenant turnover rate will be high. If the price is too low, not only will you lose money, but the property will be perceived by the tenants as being undesirable. The two most important factors are (1) the amount of rent you need to realize a profit and (2) the current price in the local housing market for similar units.

First, determine what you need to realize from the property to make a profit. For example, if the mortgage on the property is $1,200 a month and taxes and insurance are another $400 a month, you need at least $1,600 a month to break even on the cash flow. Then add to that amount a reasonable sum for maintenance and profit.

A determination of what similar units are renting for in your market area can be done by research. Check the weekend newspaper ads. Make a determination of what constitutes a similar unit. The determination should include consideration of the location of your property, the condition of the unit, and other amenities involved with the unit. A check of the local newspapers will give you an idea how competitive the rental market is for units similar to yours. Often the newspapers do not provide all the information you need, and you may need to visit similarly described units and see what they offer to compare them with your unit. Check with other landlords and leasing agents. I have found that most will share information. When checking with them, you want not only the current asking rental price but also the number of days the unit has been vacant. Remember that what the landlord is asking for rent and what the tenants are willing to pay may be two different things. The basic question is what tenants are willing to pay to live in the unit.

To determine what similar properties are renting for, often it is helpful to use a form similar to Form 2-1.

Each month a unit stays empty is a month you lose rent, and you are still obligated to pay the mortgage, taxes, and insurance. For example, it is better to collect $1,500 in rent for 12 months than $1,700 a month for 10 months.

Factors to consider in establishing the appropriate price for a unit include the following:

- The amount of rent you need to meet your expenses.
- The going market rate: The most important factor.
- Location: Is the property in a good neighborhood, near the beach, near bus lines, and so on?
- Packaging: Is the unit clean? This is very important. Are you presenting it in a professional manner?
- Marketing the property: Where are you listing the property for rent? What advertising are you doing to fill the vacancy?

Form 2-2 may be used to calculate the rent that should be asked for your rental unit. (This form, like all the other forms, is included on the enclosed CD and can

---

Property 1

Address _____

Rent amount _____ Deposit required _____

Number of bedrooms _____ Bathrooms _____

Appliances furnished: _____

Utilities paid? _____

Garage/storage _____ Extra cost _____

Pets allowed? _____ Pet deposit? _____

How long been available? _____

Area

Property 2

Address _____

Rent amount _____ Deposit required _____

Number of bedrooms _____ Bathrooms _____

Appliances furnished: _____

Utilities paid? _____

Garage/storage _____ Extra cost _____

Pets allowed? _____ Pet deposit? _____

How long been available? _____

Area

FORM 2-1 Rental market survey.

be printed out on your computer.) Using the cash flow method, the first step is to establish a fund for maintenance. The expected maintenance expenses are the most difficult items to forecast. They are determined by looking at the age of the property, the condition of the property, and the age of any furnishing or appliances. What will need to be replaced or repaired within the next year or so? You need to establish a maintenance reserve fund and each year adjust the fund as necessary.

Due Date for Rent

As a general rule, rental agreements call for rent to be paid monthly in advance and generally on the first day of the month. It is legal to agree with a tenant to pay the rent on any day of the month. Payment on the first day, however, is convenient and less likely to cause problems. If the due date falls on a weekend day

Cash Flow Worksheet

Expected maintenance expenses for the year: _____

Mortgage payments for the year: _____

Taxes, insurance, and other assessments
(unless included in your mortgage payment) _____

The total divided by 12 will get the amount of rent you need to meet your cash flow needs. In addition, you should include a reserve to take care of periods when the property is not rented.

[**Note:** If you own the property and do not have mortgage payments, in lieu of that expense, submit an expected rate of return if you invested a sum of money equal to the equity in the property.]

Market Rate Worksheet

Conduct a market survey using a rental market survey form. Determine what the average rental is for similar units. List the advantages and disadvantages your property has over the units surveyed. How much more or less would a tenant pay for your unit based on the advantages or disadvantages compared with the surveyed units?

Average rent for similar properties is $_____

Addition or deduction for advantages or disadvantages $ _____

Rent that should be expected: $_____

FORM 2-2   Calculating the rent.

or a legal holiday, the tenant has until the close of the next business day to pay the rent.

Many tenants operate under the belief that there is a 5- or 10-day grace period for paying the rent. This is not true. Unless a grace period is set forth in the lease, rent is delinquent the first day after the due date. You have a right to require that the rent be paid on the date it is due. In a few states, the law requires that the rent be past due for a few days before you may send a termination notice. To ensure timely payment, always stress to the tenants that rent must be paid on the due date.

A common problem a landlord can get caught in is in allowing tenants extra time to pay the rent. Be firm and demand that the rent be paid on the due date. If you do not allow exceptions, tenants will not use sob stories to extend the payment date.

Without an agreement in the lease about when the rent is due, it is due on the first day of the month, in advance, for rental units in Alaska, Arizona, Connecticut, Delaware, Florida, Hawaii, Iowa, Kansas, Kentucky, Louisiana, Montana, Nebraska, Nevada, New Mexico, Oklahoma, Rhode Island, South Carolina, Tennessee, and Virginia. It is due on the last day of the month in

California, Indiana, Michigan, New York, North Dakota, and South Dakota. *Always include in the lease agreement the day the rent is due.*

If you have tenants who have low-paying jobs or tend to move frequently, you may wish to require that the rent be paid twice a month or weekly. Individuals with low-paying jobs may have difficulty saving a portion of their weekly or bimonthly checks to pay the monthly amount.

Often, a tenant will take possession during a rental period, and the rent must be prorated. To determine the amount due for the partial rental period, use the following.

When a tenant starts the tenancy in the middle of a rental period, the tenant's rent must be prorated. The total rent for the rental period amount is divided by the number of days involved in the rental period and allocated on a daily basis.

Total rent divided by number of days in rental period equals average rental income per day.

Average rent per day is multiplied by the days the tenant occupies the property.

Example: Assume that a property rents for $475 per month. The tenant takes possession on the twenty-first day of a 31-day month. The proration would be as follows:

$475 ÷ 31 days = $15.32258 per day

$15.32258 × 11 days = $16854838, or

$168.55 due from tenant

Getting Help

Check the local telephone book for landlord associations that can provide you with help. Services available from an association generally include

- Information regarding local laws and regulations dealing with the rental of property
- Tenant screening and credit check services
- Practical advice
- A chance to meet other landlords

If there is no association listed in your local area, check with a national organization. The two most popular national associations are:

National Multi Housing Council
1850 M Street NW, Suite 540
Washington, DC 20036-5803
202-974-2300
www. nmhc.org

National Apartment Association
201 N. Union Street, Suite 200
Alexandria, VA 22314
703-518-6141
www.naahq.org

Duration of the Tenancy
Tenancy at Will

When there is no agreement and no written lease between the landlord and the tenant as to the length of the tenancy, the tenancy is an at-will tenancy. Most states provide that any such tenancy is deemed and held to be a tenancy at will unless it is in writing signed by the tenant. Such tenancy shall be from year to year, quarter to quarter, month to month, or week to week, to be determined by the periods at which the rent is payable. If the rent is payable weekly, the tenancy shall be from week to week; if payable monthly, from month to month; if payable quarterly, then from quarter to quarter; and if payable yearly, from year to year.

Written Lease without a Definition Period

Generally, where tenancy has been created by an instrument in writing from year to year, quarter to quarter, month to month, or week to week, to be determined by the periods at which the rent is payable, and the term of which tenancy is unlimited, the tenancy shall be a tenancy at will. If the rent is payable weekly, the tenancy shall be from week to week; if payable monthly, month to month; if payable quarterly, from quarter to quarter; and if payable yearly, from year to year.

Termination of Tenancy at Will

Generally, a tenancy at will may be terminated when either party gives notice as follows:

1. When the tenancy is from year to year, by giving not less than 3 months' notice prior to the end of any annual period
2. When the tenancy is from quarter to quarter, by giving not less than 45 days' notice prior to the end of any quarter
3. When the tenancy is from month to month, by giving not less than 15 days' notice prior to the end of any monthly period
4. When the tenancy is from week to week, by giving not less than 7 days' notice prior to the end of any weekly period

Holding Over after Term

Normally, when any tenancy created by an instrument in writing, the term of which is limited, has expired and the tenant holds over in the possession of said premises without renewing the lease by some further instrument in writing, such holding over is construed to be a tenancy at sufferance. The mere payment or acceptance of rent is not construed to be a renewal of the term, but if the holding over is continued with the written consent of the tenant, the tenancy becomes a tenancy at will under the provisions of the law.

Rent Control

Rent control exists only in certain communities in five states or jurisdictions; California, Maryland, New Jersey, New York, and the District of Columbia. In those states, only a few communities have rent control. The cities of Washington, DC; San Francisco; Los Angeles; Newark, NJ; and Takoma Park, MD, have some form of rent control. In those cities, a rent control board of 5 to 10 individuals controls the amount of rent a landlord may charge. If your property is in a city that has rent control, obtain a copy of the rent control regulations from the local rent control board. Often, in those cities local property owners' associations can give you guidance in dealing with rent control regulations.

Rent control boards, in addition to regulating rent, often regulate other landlord-tenant issues. For example, most have specific requirements that must be complied with before the landlord may terminate a tenancy and evict a tenant. Because local regulations change frequently and are often very complicated, check them out when dealing with tenants in an area that is under rent control.

Constitutional Status of Rent Control

Originally, rent control laws were enacted to remedy housing shortages during and after the first and second world wars. At the time, they were looked at as a temporary measure to resolve an emergency caused by an insufficient supply of dwellings and apartments so grave that it constituted a serious menace to the health, morality, and comfort of the people.

Today, the validity of rent control laws is not based on the existence of an emergency, but as an exercise of the state's police power. Any exercise of a state's police power needs a real and substantial relation to the public health, morals, safety, and welfare of the state's citizens; the courts have held such relationships are present when there is a shortage of rental housing that was likely to worsen, a swift increase in the population and number of households, and a lowering of the vacancy turnover rate because of the financial inability of tenants to purchase homes. For example, one court decision (*Westchester West No. 2 Ltd. Partnership v. Montgomery County*, 276 Md 448, 348 A2d 856) concluded that the implementation of rent control laws was a proper exercise of police power because the laws were reasonably calculated to eliminate excessive rent and at the same time provide landlords with a just and reasonable return on their property. Accordingly, rent control regulations, like any other form of regulation, are unconstitutional only if arbitrary, discriminatory, or demonstrably irrelevant to the policy the legislature is free to adopt and hence an unnecessary and unwarranted interference with individual liberties.

What is reasonable in the matter of rent for particular premises is a question of a kind that is constantly being submitted to and decided by juries. Therefore, a statute forbidding a landlord to exact more than a reasonable rent is not void for uncertainty.

Rent control laws have been upheld as constitutional against claims that

- The controls impair the obligation of a contract.
- They deprive landlords of equal protection under the law.
- They deprive landlords of due process.
- They are taking of property without just compensation.

Rent control laws that were found to be arbitrary, discriminatory, or not sufficiently relevant to the legislature's objective were held to be unconstitutional.

The enactment of rent control laws is now viewed as a legitimate exercise of a government's police power. However, some states have legislation that requires a finding of an emergency before a rent control program may be established.

According to one statute, the purpose of rent control provisions is to protect tenants from evictions prompted by rapid increases in rent and to foster the construction of housing, in that rent control allows landlords to increase rents sufficiently to profit from the operation of their properties.

Rent-Controlled Property

In most rent-controlled areas, not all rental properties are subject to rent control. Quite frequently, new buildings or owner-occupied properties are not covered. In some cities single-family rental units and luxury units that rent for more than a specified price are not subject to rent control. If you live in a rent control city, check to determine if your property is subject to rent control.

Rental Limits

Typically rent control ordinances set a base rent for each rental unit. This rent is determined by taking into account the rent that was charged before rent control took effect, the operation and upkeep expenses, the size of the unit, inflation, and housing supply and demand. The ordinances provide that the base rent may be increased under certain conditions. Most of the controls provide that existing rent may be increased when an increase in taxes, operational expenses, and the like, occurs. Many controls provide for annual increases or periodic increases. Some regulations allow the rent to be increased if the tenant agrees to it. In most cases, the landlord may increase the rent when a new tenant moves in. However, check the local regulations because, in a few areas, no rent increases are allowed even when a new tenant moves in.

Other Rent Control Restrictions

Most rent control regulations require landlords to register their units with the rent control board. This requirement permits the board to keep track of the rental units within the city. Generally, rent control regulations impose rules regarding security deposits or interest payments and the type of notice you may give tenants before you can raise the rent or terminate a tenancy. These requirements are in addition to those required by state law.

For rent control to work in cases in which the regulations allow an increase in rent, the regulations place restrictions on tenancy terminations. Most require a legal or just cause to terminate a tenancy unless the tenant moves on his or her own. This restriction is intended to prevent the landlord from evicting without cause and then raising the rent for a new tenant. Just cause normally is limited to significant violations of a lease: Tenant creates a nuisance, fails to pay rent, or is generally late on the rent. In some cases, a tenant may be evicted if the landlord intends to remodel the unit, and it is impossible to live in the unit during the remodeling. In most cases, the landlord may evict a tenant to move in a close relative such as a daughter or son into the unit or to move himself or herself into it.

Rent Control Information

If you are renting property that is subject to rent control, be careful to comply with all rent control regulations. Information regarding local rent control requirements may be obtained from:

- **Your city rent control board.** Rent control board offices have handouts and publications that pertain to the local rent control regulations.
- **Local property owners' association or apartment owners' association.** These organizations are familiar with the local requirements and are a good source of information.
- **Local attorneys who specialize in tenant-landlord issues.** Check with other landlords for a referral to a local attorney who specializes in this area. Even if you have only a single unit, the manager of a large apartment complex can provide you with the name of a local property attorney. The yellow pages in a phone book may be used, but I would try first for a referral from other landlords.

3

Selecting the
Right Tenants

This chapter contains a discussion on advertising for tenants and checking out and selecting prospective tenants. Sample advertisements, checklists for selecting the right tenants, and reference checking forms are included.

Finding Tenants

There are many creative methods for finding new tenants. Most landlords with whom I have discussed this issue consider that the best source of applicants is the local newspaper's ads, followed by "for rent" signs on the property, and then the use of referrals from current residents.

The biggest problem with using classified ads is that, if you run them for a significant length of time, they get expensive. To reduce the cost without reducing the effectiveness of your ad, keep the ad short with only the basic information, such as the rent, the amount of deposit required, number of bedrooms and baths, and whether pets are welcome. Many landlords place a teaser at the beginning of the ad. Examples of catchy teasers include brand-new home, luxury master suite, and nearly new house near a school with three bedrooms.

Do not put the address of the rental property in the ad. Make the applicants call your offices to get the address. This helps you keep track of the individuals who express interest in the property and does not advertise that the rental location is empty and thus a possible crime site.

As a general rule, rental property should be advertised approximately five weeks before its available date. If a tenant gives you a 30-day notice of termination of tenancy, immediately start advertising it. My experience is that some individuals want to secure a rental place before they move from the current unit and, others do not start the looking process until the week they need the property. As one landlord advised me, advertise four and five weeks before the unit will be available, and do not readvertise until about one week before it is available.

The Internet is also becoming a popular method to find new tenants. Advertising on the Internet is generally cheaper than using the local papers. Some newspapers post their ads on the Internet without an additional charge.

A "for rent" sign is an economical method to attract new applicants. Often individuals who call based on these signs are attempting to obtain a cheaper rental rate than is advertised in the local papers. An advantage of using a "for rent" sign occurs when a potential customer has seen your classified ad and has gotten the address from you; it is easier to find the right property. If you post a sign, make sure it is a professional-looking sign and is not hand-painted.

The use of referrals by current tenants is a good way to get good tenants. The use of a tenant referral program is recommended.

Establishing Minimum Rental Requirements

The first step in selecting tenants is to establish your minimum rental requirements. Failure to treat all applicants in a fair manner is an invitation to a civil or criminal lawsuit for discriminatory treatment.

Cliff's Rules on Establishing Minimum Rental Requirements

- It is easier to deny a rental to a deadbeat than to get rid of one.
- Put your rental requirements in writing.
- Treat everyone the same.
- Rent to the first applicant who meets your requirements.
- Establish minimum income requirements.
- Establish minimum credit score requirements.
- Require a lack of a criminal history.
- Establish maximum occupancy limits.
- Constantly review your forms and procedures to ensure compliance with fair housing and landlord–tenant laws and regulations.

Temporarily Allowing Possession of the Property

Often, tenants will approach you and explain that they are desperate to obtain living quarters, then request that they be allowed to move into the premises on a temporary basis. Never, never agree to such a request. Once a person has taken possession of your premises with your permission, he or she is a tenant, and you will need to legally evict that person. Unless you have approved a rental application, completed all the necessary forms with the tenant's required signatures, and received the necessary rent and deposits, do not under any circumstances give the keys to the unit to an applicant. I am surprised how often this rule is violated and how often a landlord is stuck with a problem tenant. Surrender the keys to an applicant only after everything has been completed. Giving the new tenant the keys is the last step, not an intermediate step, in establishing the tenancy.

If You Are Having Problems Renting Your Unit

Often, there is a tendency to loosen up on screening of tenants when you are having problems renting a residential unit. Remember, a problem tenant is far worse than an empty unit. Make an objective evaluation of why the unit is not renting. Is the rent too high? Is the unit unattractive? Does the unit need a new paint job or a new carpet? Consider all these things, and take the necessary action to remedy the problem. You also can try to attract new residents by using incentives; for example, the sixth month's rent is free if the tenant is current in his or her rent. Some landlords have used free cable TV or satellite TV to attract new residents. Also, evaluate your advertising program. Maybe you are not getting the information regarding the unit to sufficient potential renters.

Screening Tenants

The most common mistake made by landlords is failure to screen prospective tenants. *Screening is the most important part in selecting new tenants.* Many landlords look at applicants and think, "They look nice; I will rent to them," or "They are dressed nicely and have a nice car, so they must be good tenants." All prospective tenants should be screened as thoroughly as possible. Talk to them, make them complete the rental application, and check their credit and personal references. When a prospective tenant hands you a rental application that is missing critical information, that application should raise a red flag. People who pay their bills on time and are good renters generally have the records needed to complete a rental application. In my experience, the more precise a person is in completing an application, the more precise he or she will be in paying the rent on time.

There will be situations in which it is advisable to refuse an application without checking it out completely, but never approve one without a thorough check. In your first minutes talking with a prospective tenant, either in person or on the telephone, get a satisfactory answer to each of the three questions below or reject the individual without wasting any more time.

> ## No Sinners under My Roof
>
> Is it legal for landlords to refuse to rent to unmarried couples by claiming a religious freedom of exercise exemption from a statute that prohibits marital status discrimination? Probably not. In Michigan, a landlord who refused to rent apartments to unmarried couples because of their marital status was held liable for damages in a civil action. The court concluded that his actions were in violation of the State Civil Rights Act. (*McCready v. Hoffius*, 459 Mich. 131, 586 N.W. 2d 723.)

- Where are you living now?
- How long have you lived there?
- Why are you moving?

Often you will receive humorous answers to those questions. For example, one person informed me that he was moving because the landlord charged him a penalty every time he paid the rent two weeks late. Another person informed me that her present landlord objected to her late-night parties and loud music.

If the answers to those questions are not satisfactory, don't waste any more time with these individuals. If the answers are satisfactory, remember that some people are convincing liars. One person informed me that he had lived at his last out-of-state residence for six years. The only problem was that it was the state prison. Accordingly, satisfactory answers are not a good reason for approving applicants as tenants. When asking the questions, use a conversational tone; do not come across as if you were interrogating a witness.

If the prospective tenant provides satisfactory answers to the first three questions, move to the second group of questions:

- Where do you work?
- If the individual does not work, how will he or she pay the rent? **Note:** It is illegal to discriminate against a person who lives on disability, but it is not illegal to refuse to rent to a person who cannot establish the ability to pay the rent.
- Will you authorize a check of your credit and criminal background and that of each occupant of the unit?

Handling Rental Deposits

All states have imposed certain duties on landlords regarding the processing, holding, and returning of tenants' rental deposits. Make sure to check the regulations in your jurisdiction. Florida, which has adopted substantial portions of the

> ## Cliff's Rules for Selecting Tenants
>
> - Screen every applicant before you approve the rental application.
> - Run a credit check on every rental application before you approve it.
> - Do criminal-background checks on each individual who will be living in the unit.
> - It is better to have a vacancy than to have a unit occupied by a problem tenant or a tenant who does not pay the rent.
> - Do not disapprove rental applications on the basis of race, national origin, religion, age, gender, or disability.
> - Ask questions on the application that may help you recover money after the tenancy has ended, if necessary.

Model Landlord and Tenant's Act, is used in this section as an example of the responsibilities of the landlord in regards to rental deposits.

Florida Chapter 83.49 Deposit money or advance rent; duty of landlord and tenant:

(1) Whenever money is deposited or advanced by a tenant on a rental agreement as security for performance of the rental agreement or as advance rent for other than the next immediate rental period, the landlord or the landlord's agent shall either:

(a) Hold the total amount of such money in a separate non–interest-bearing account in a Florida banking institution for the benefit of the tenant or tenants. The landlord shall not commingle such moneys with any other funds of the landlord or hypothecate, pledge, or in any other way make use of such moneys until such moneys are actually due the landlord;

(b) Hold the total amount of such money in a separate interest-bearing account in a Florida banking institution for the benefit of the tenant or tenants, in which case the tenant shall receive and collect interest in an amount of at least 75 percent of the annualized average interest rate payable on such account or interest at the rate of 5 percent per year, simple interest, whichever the landlord elects. The landlord shall not commingle such moneys with any other funds of the landlord or hypothecate, pledge, or in any other way make use of such moneys until such moneys are actually due the landlord; or

(c) Post a surety bond, executed by the landlord as principal and a surety company authorized and licensed to do business in the state as surety, with the clerk of the circuit court in the county in which the dwelling unit is located in the total amount of the security deposits and advance rent he or she holds on behalf of the tenants or $50,000, whichever is less. The bond shall be conditioned upon the faithful compliance of the landlord with the provisions of this section and shall run to the Governor for the benefit of any tenant injured by the landlord's violation of the provisions of this section. In addition to posting the surety bond, the landlord shall pay to the tenant interest at the rate of 5 percent per year, simple interest. A landlord, or the landlord's agent, engaged in the renting of dwelling units in five or more counties, who holds deposit moneys or advance rent and who is otherwise subject to the provisions of this section, may, in lieu of posting a surety bond in each county, elect to post a surety bond in the form and manner provided in this paragraph with the office of the Secretary of State. The bond shall be in the total amount of the security deposit or advance rent held on behalf of tenants or in the amount of $250,000, whichever is less. The bond shall be conditioned upon the faithful compliance of the landlord with the provisions of this section and shall run to the Governor for the benefit of any tenant injured by the landlord's violation of this section. In addition to posting a surety bond, the landlord shall pay to the tenant interest on the security deposit or advance rent held on behalf of that tenant at the rate of 5 percent per year simple interest.

(2) The landlord shall, within 30 days of receipt of advance rent or a security deposit, notify the tenant in writing of the manner in which the landlord is holding the advance rent or security deposit and the rate of interest, if any, which the tenant is to receive and the time of interest payments to the tenant. Such written notice shall:

(a) Be given in person or by mail to the tenant.

(b) State the name and address of the depository where the advance rent or security deposit is being held, whether the advance rent or security deposit is being held in a separate account for the benefit of the tenant or is commingled with other funds of the landlord, and, if commingled, whether such funds are deposited in an interest-bearing account in a Florida banking institution.

(c) Include a copy of the provisions of subsection (3).

Subsequent to providing such notice, if the landlord changes the manner or location in which he or she is holding the advance rent or security deposit, he or she shall notify the tenant within 30 days of the change according to the provisions herein set forth. This subsection does not apply to any landlord who rents fewer than five individual dwelling units. Failure to provide this notice shall not be a defense to the payment of rent when due.

(3)(a) Upon the vacating of the premises for termination of the lease, if the landlord does not intend to impose a claim on the security deposit, the landlord shall have 15 days to return the security deposit together with interest if otherwise required, or the landlord shall have 30 days to give the tenant written notice by certified mail to the tenant's last known mailing address of his or her intention to impose a claim on the deposit and the reason for imposing the claim. The notice shall contain a statement in substantially the following form:

This is a notice of my intention to impose a claim for damages in the amount of _____ upon your security deposit, due to _____. It is sent to you as required by s. 83.49(3), Florida Statutes. You are hereby notified that you must object in writing to this deduction from your security deposit within 15 days from the time you receive this notice or I will be authorized to deduct my claim from your security deposit. Your objection must be sent to (landlord's address).

If the landlord fails to give the required notice within the 30-day period, he or she forfeits the right to impose a claim upon the security deposit.

(b) Unless the tenant objects to the imposition of the landlord's claim or the amount thereof within 15 days after receipt of the landlord's notice of intention to impose a claim, the landlord may then deduct the amount of his or her claim and shall remit the balance of the deposit to the tenant within 30 days after the date of the notice of intention to impose a claim for damages.

(c) If either party institutes an action in a court of competent jurisdiction to adjudicate the party's right to the security deposit, the prevailing party is entitled to receive his or her court costs plus a reasonable fee for his or her attorney. The court shall advance the cause on the calendar.

(d) Compliance with this section by an individual or business entity authorized to conduct business in this state, including Florida-licensed real estate brokers and sales associates, shall constitute compliance with all other relevant Florida statutes pertaining to security deposits held pursuant to a rental agreement or other landlord-tenant relationship. Enforcement personnel shall look solely to this section to determine compliance. This section prevails over any conflicting provisions in chapter 475 and in other sections of the Florida statutes, and shall operate to permit licensed real estate brokers to disburse security deposits and deposit money without having to comply with the notice and settlement procedures contained in s. 475.25(1)(d).

(4) The provisions of this section do not apply to transient rentals by hotels or motels as defined in chapter 509; nor do they apply in those instances in which the amount of rent or deposit, or both, is regulated by law or by rules or regulations of a public body, including public housing authorities and federally administered or regulated housing programs including s. 202, s. 221(d)(3) and (4), s. 236, or s. 8 of the National Housing Act, as amended, other than for rent stabilization. With the exception of subsections (3), (5), and (6), this section is not applicable to housing authorities or public housing agencies created pursuant to chapter 421 or other statutes.

(5) Except when otherwise provided by the terms of a written lease, any tenant who vacates or abandons the premises prior to the expiration of the term specified in the written lease, or any tenant who vacates or abandons premises which are the subject of a tenancy from week to week, month to month, quarter to quarter, or year to year, shall give at least 7 days' written notice by certified

mail or personal delivery to the landlord prior to vacating or abandoning the premises which notice shall include the address where the tenant may be reached. Failure to give such notice shall relieve the landlord of the notice requirement of paragraph (3)(a) but shall not waive any right the tenant may have to the security deposit or any part of it.

(6) For the purposes of this part, a renewal of an existing rental agreement shall be considered a new rental agreement, and any security deposit carried forward shall be considered a new security deposit.

(7) Upon the sale or transfer of title of the rental property from one owner to another, or upon a change in the designated rental agent, any and all security deposits or advance rents being held for the benefit of the tenants shall be transferred to the new owner or agent, together with any earned interest and with an accurate accounting showing the amounts to be credited to each tenant account. Upon the transfer of such funds and records as stated herein, and upon transmittal of a written receipt therefore, the transferor shall be free from the obligation imposed in subsection (1) to hold such moneys on behalf of the tenant. However, nothing herein shall excuse the landlord or agent for a violation of the provisions of this section while in possession of such deposits.

(8) Any person licensed under the provisions of s. 509.241, unless excluded by the provisions of this part, who fails to comply with the provisions of this part shall be subject to a fine or to the suspension or revocation of his or her license by the Division of Hotels and Restaurants of the Department of Business and Professional Regulation in the manner provided in s. 509.261.

(9) In those cases in which interest is required to be paid to the tenant, the landlord shall pay directly to the tenant, or credit against the current month's rent, the interest due to the tenant at least once annually. However, no interest shall be due a tenant who wrongfully terminates his or her tenancy prior to the end of the rental term.

The Application

A rental application (see Form 3-1) should be required from every person over age 18 years who will occupy the rental unit.

Checking Credit

Always conduct a credit check before approving a rental application. If your unit is a low-end rental, the applicants often will not have the best credit ratings, but check anyway. Pay special attention to any delinquent payments to property owners or rent management companies. Before checking an applicant's credit, get a signed written approval from the applicant and ask if he or she has any credit

Date: _____

Date occupancy desired: _____

Rental price range: _____

Type/size of rental home desired: _____

Personal Information of Applicant

Full name: _____

Birth date: _____

Driver's license/ID number/state: _____

Social Security Number:_____

Additional occupants (List every occupant's name and relationship, including children):
_____

Preferred Rental Due Date:

Monthly due on: _____

Payday plan due on: _____ and biweekly _____ weekly _____

How long do you plan on living in the rental home that meets your needs? _____

Do you have renter's insurance?_____

Do you have or plan to use any water-filled furniture? _____

Have you ever broken a lease? _____

Have you ever refused to pay rent for any reason? If so, why?_____
_____

Have you ever been evicted or asked to leave a rental unit? _____

Have you ever filed for bankruptcy? _____

Have you ever been convicted of a crime? _____

Do you give us permission to do a criminal background check?_____

Do you currently have any utilities in your name?_____

Do you currently have phone service in your name? _____

Is there anything to prevent you from placing utilities or a phone in your name?
_____

Do you know of anything or any reason that may interrupt your ability to pay rent?
_____

Residence History

Present street address: _____

City: _____ State:_____ Zip: _____

continued

FORM 3-1 Rental application.

Dates lived at this address:_____

Did you own _____ rent _____ occupy_____

Current phone: _____

How many pets do you have? _____ Type: _____

Name of present landlord/owner/mortgage company: _____

Address of present landlord/mortgage company: _____

Landlord's phone:_____ Monthly payment: _____

Reason for moving: _____

Is your rent or mortgage current? _____

Number of late payments in the last 12 months? _____

Security deposit amount currently held by landlord? _____

Previous residence address:

Previous landlord:_____

Previous landlord's phone: _____

Dates at this address: _____

Reason for moving:_____

Was your full security deposit returned? _____

Number of late payments: _____

Monthly payment: _____

Previous residence address:

Previous landlord:_____

Previous landlord's phone: _____

Dates at this address: _____

Reason for moving:_____

Was your full security deposit returned? _____

Number of late payments: _____

Monthly payment:_____

Income History

Current employment status:

Full-time:_____ Part-time (less than 32 hours.): _____ Student: _____

Retired: _____ Self-employed: _____ Unemployed:_____

Other: _____

FORM 3-1   Rental application (continued).

Primary source of employment

Applicant employed by: _____

Supervisor's name: _____

Average weekly hours: _____

How long at that place of employment? _____

Address: _____

City: _____ State: _____ Zip: _____

Phone:_____

Position: _____

Salary: _____

Weekly, biweekly, monthly, or annual average take-home pay: _____

Additional Employment

Employed by: _____

Supervisor's name: _____

Average weekly hours: _____

How long at that place of employment? _____

Address: _____

City: _____ State: _____ Zip: _____

Phone: _____

Position: _____

Salary: _____

Weekly, biweekly, monthly, or annual average take-home pay: _____

Additional Income/Payment Information

In the event of some emergency that would prevent you from paying rent when due, is there a relative, person, or agency that could assist you with rent payments?

_____

Emergency contact

_____ Relationship:_____

Address: _____

Phone _____ Additional phone: _____

Do you currently have a savings account, line of credit, or charge card sufficient to cover one month's rent?_____

continued

FORM 3-1   Rental application (continued).

Additional Income

(If there are additional, verifiable sources of income you would like considered, please list income source [e.g., self-employment, Social Security, benefit payments] and requested information regarding each source. Applicant may be required to produce additional documentation or provide and sign release statements. Child support, alimony, or separate maintenance need *not* be disclosed unless you want this additional income to be considered for qualification.)

Additional source:_____

Amount: $ _____ Per: _____

Contact person: _____

Phone:_____

How long have you been receiving income from this source?_____

How long do you expect this income to continue? _____

Is there any reason it would stop? _____

Other additional source: _____

Amount: $ _____ Per: _____

Contact person: _____

Phone:_____

How long have you been receiving income from this source?_____

How long do you expect this income to continue? _____

Is there any reason it would stop? _____

Assets, Credits, or Loans

Number of vehicles on property? _____

Valid registration and inspection? _____

Do you have any commercial vehicles, campers, boats, or motorcycles? _____

Vehicle (make/model/color/year):_____

Please note, only cars on application are authorized to be on premises.

Plate number: _____ State: _____

Financed/leased through: _____

Contact and phone number:_____

Acct. number: _____

Monthly payment: _____

Monthly payment: _____

FORM 3-1   Rental application (continued).

Credit Cards and Loans (including banks, department store, gas cards, student loans)

Creditor: _____

Address: _____

Phone: _____

Acct. Number: _____

Total amount owed: _____ Monthly payment: _____ Are your payments current? _____

Creditor: _____

Address: _____

Phone: _____

Acct. Number: _____

Total amount owed: Monthly payment: _____ Are your payments current? _____

List any other current monthly expenses

Hospital payment: _____ Health insurance: _____

Auto insurance: _____ Renter's insurance: _____

Child care: _____ Tuition: _____

Cable TV: _____ Other: _____

Total amount: _____

Bank Reference

Name of bank and branch: _____

Branch address: _____

Phone: _____

Checking acct. number: _____

Saving acct. number _____

Personal/Professional References

Character/personal reference:

Name: _____

Address: _____

City: _____ State: _____ Zip: _____

Relationship? _____

How long? _____ Phone: _____

continued

FORM 3-1   Rental application (continued).

Professional reference (e.g., attorney, accountant):

Name: _____

Address: _____

City: _____ State: _____ Zip: _____

Relationship? _____

How long? _____ Phone: _____

Name of nearest living relative:

Name: _____

Address: _____

City: _____ State: _____ Zip: _____

Relationship? _____

How long? _____ Phone: _____

Name of doctor or health-care provider:

Name: _____

Address: _____

City: _____ State: _____ Zip: _____

Phone: _____

Do you give owner or manager permission to contact the references listed above both now and in the future for rental consideration or for collection purposes should that be deemed necessary? _____

If management has a question regarding this application, what is the best contact phone number? _____

Day phone/contact person: _____

Night phone/contact person: _____

Thank you for completing the rental application. Please sign below.

A completed application requires submission of the following, which will be copied and attached to this application:

- Driver's license or government-issued picture ID
  [**Note:** Rentals will not be shown without picture ID]

- Copy of voided personal check (to verify bank)

- Two most current pay stubs of each income source listed

- If self-employed, most current Schedule C tax return and proof of current income

- A fee of $ _____ is charged on all rental applicants for the purpose of verifying the information furnished on this application. By signing below, applicant hereby represents that all information on this application is true and complete and hereby autho-

FORM 3-1   Rental application (continued).

rizes annual verification of information, references, and credit history for continual rental consideration or for collection purposes should that become necessary. This fee is refundable only if applicant meets our minimal criteria but is not selected because he or she was not the first qualified applicant.

Applicant acknowledges this application will become part of the lease agreement when approved. If any information is found to be incorrect, the application will be rejected and any subsequent rental agreement becomes void.

Applicant's signature: _____ Date: _____

FORM 3-1   Rental application (continued).

problems. If the applicant indicates that he or she has great credit, and the credit check reveals otherwise, then besides an applicant with poor credit, you have one who lies.

If the applicant indicates that he or she has had some credit problems, ask if he or she will explain why. If two applicants have equally marginal credit reports, and one admits it while the other denies any problems, I would favor the truthful applicant.

The credit report contains a lot of information that may be used in evaluating the application. It can tell you if the person has filed for bankruptcy in the last 15 years, has been late or delinquent in paying rent or bills in the last 7 years, has been evicted in the last 7 years, and has been involved in a court suit such as a personal injury claim.

There are local tenant screening businesses that will conduct the screening for you for a fee. Often, a local landlord association can help you or provide guidance with credit checking. You can also check directly with one of the three major credit reporting agencies:

Objective Criteria for Approving Rental Applications

Always establish objective criteria for approving rental applications. Your objective criteria could include the following:

- No bankruptcies within the last 10 years.
- No prior court evictions.
- Sufficient income to pay the rent, generally considered to be monthly income at least three times the monthly rent.
- At least two positive references from prior landlords unless the tenant has become a renter only recently. In that case, you need other positive references to overcome the lack of prior landlord references.

- **Equifax:** 800-997-2493 or www.equifax.com
- **Experian:** 888-397-3742 or www.experian.com
- **TransUnion:** 800-888-4213 or www.tue.com

The cost of obtaining a credit report depends on whether you want an oral report or a written report and how many times you will use the service. Use Form 3-2 to receive permission to do a credit check.

Showing the Property and Accepting Applications

Make it a rule to show the unit to any person who is interested. After you have shown the property, explain the minimal criteria for renting the property. If the individual insists on completing an application, take it and process it as you would any other application. Arbitrary denial often results in charges of discrimination. It is safer to accept the application and evaluate it on the basis of your previously established criteria. A polite refusal is less threatening than an obvious refusal to show the property or a refusal to accept a rental application.

Consent for Applicant Background and Reference Checks

The undersigned individuals authorize _____ property management agency (or leasing or screening company) to obtain information about us from any credit sources, current and previous landlords, employers, and personal references to enable the agency to evaluate the rental application for the premises located at _____[address]. We also authorize any credit source, credit bureau, current and previous landlord and employer, and personal reference to disclose to the agency information about us that is relevant to decisions regarding the application and tenancy. This permission will survive the expiration of the tenancy and may be accessed for any legitimate business purpose related to the tenancy.

Signed:

_____   _____
Signature   Signature

_____   _____
Typed or Printed Name   Typed or Printed Name

_____   _____
Social Security Number   Social Security Number

_____   _____
Address   Address

_____   _____
Phone Number   Phone Number

_____   _____
Date   Date

FORM 3-2   Written authorization to check credit, references, and other background information.

Proof of Identity and Residence Status

Ask applicants for a copy of a driver's license or other government-issued identification so that you can verify that they are using their real names. You also may ask applicants to provide evidence that they are legally in the United States. **Note:** You may not request such information selectively. If you decide to ask for this information, ask for it from all applicants, not just those you suspect may be in the country illegally. Also note that, if an individual is legally in the United States, you may not discriminate against that person on the basis of national origin. The federal Form 1-9 (Employment Eligibility Verification) can be used for this check. The form and instructions for completing it can be obtained at http://uscis.gov or 800-375-5283.

Checking Criminal History

Always ask the applicant if you can do a criminal-background check, and get the permission in writing. If an applicant admits before the background check that he or she has a criminal record, you may want to eliminate that applicant without doing a check. Otherwise, always check before making a decision on the application. **Note:** The requirement of a criminal-background check should also apply to any employees you hire who will have contact with tenants.

If an applicant has admitted having a criminal background, consider the individual facts before disqualifying the individual. For example, if the individual was convicted of failure to file an income tax return, I would not be too worried about this conviction. If, however, the individual has been convicted of a sex crime, a theft offense, or any violent crime, be wary of approving him or her. If the individual assures you that he or she has a clean record, and the check reveals otherwise, when acting on this application, remember you are dealing with a liar.

To verify the information you have received from an applicant, you will need the written authorization for every person who will be living in the unit who is over the age 18 years. Note that Form 3-2 contains written authorization for a criminal-background check and a credit check. Each adult must complete a separate law enforcement report waiver. If you rent the property to someone without doing a criminal-background check, you may become liable for civil damages, normally money damages, for any crimes committed by the person to your other renters. This issue is discussed in Chapter 10. Use Form 3-3 to get permission to do a law enforcement check. You may ask the applicant to take this form directly to the local police department. Each adult applicant should fill out a separate form. If the applicant lives outside an urban area, the form should go to the sheriff's department.

I declare that I have never been convicted of a felony. I hereby authorize the police department(s) of _____ and the sheriff's department(s) of _____ counties to give to the company _____ or its representative(s) any information that it might request to determine my fitness as a prospective client.

I also understand that any false information I may have given, written or oral, will be sufficient cause for rejection of services from the above-named company.

Name: _____ Date of birth: _____
       (first name)   (middle name)   (last name)

Other names used: _____
                           (maiden name or other married names)

Social Security number: _____

Address: _____

Signature: _____

FORM 3-3 Law enforcement report consent form.

Identity Theft

The newest crime of the twenty-first century is identity theft. Because of this, many applicants are reluctant to provide certain information, such as their Social Security numbers, credit card numbers, and checking account numbers. They are attempting to protect themselves from identity theft, yet they fail to realize that when they write checks, the checks contain their checking account numbers, and when they cash a check at a supermarket, many supermarkets require their Social Security numbers before the checks are accepted.

If an applicant is reluctant to provide this information, you should assure the applicant that it will be safeguarded. You may also inform the applicant that the law does not require anyone to provide you with a Social Security number, but that you have a right not to rent to individuals who fail to provide this information.

If you conduct yourself in a professional manner and create the perception that you are a professional, the applicant will be less inclined to object to providing

Keep It Confidential

When verifying income, criminal history, or any other confidential information on applicants, you are inquiring into their personal lives and have a duty to keep this information confidential. Do not discuss this information with anyone, except to assist you in making a decision on the application. This is not information you want to discuss over a friendly drink in a bar. *Keep it confidential.*

this information. You should be prepared to discuss with the person why you need this information and why you cannot approve any rental application without it.

Verifying Income and Employment

Make it a rule to verify an applicant's income and employment. Looking at a copy of a pay stub provided by the applicant is not sufficient. You should verify the applicant's employment for at least the last two years. If you find that the applicant has given you inaccurate information, verify every fact before considering the application.

If the individual is not working but is receiving disability income, consider it as equivalent to income. It is important not to discriminate against an individual because he or she is receiving disability income. If, however, the amount of disability income received each month is less than the minimum income previously set by your objective standards, you may disapprove the application on the basis of insufficient income. Note: If you have made exceptions for wage earners, you need to make the same exceptions for individuals on disability income.

Applications involving self-employed individuals are the most difficult to verify. If the individual has been in business for less than a year, be leery of basing a decision on expected income because most small businesses fail in the first year. A government publication indicated that 75 percent of start-up entrepreneurial businesses fail in the first year. In verifying self-employed income, you can request to see the individual's tax returns for the last two years and any Form 1099s that have been received. Self-employed income also can be verified by looking at bank. Use Form 3-4 to verify an applicant's employment, Form 3-5 for credit references, and Form 3-6 for bank verification.

Dear Sir or Madam:

_____ has applied to rent one of our rentals and has given your name as his or her employer. To verify the information he or she has given to us on the rental application, can you please supply us with the needed information below? Enclosed is a self-addressed envelope.

Thank you for your cooperation.

Sincerely,

_____

Rental Manager

Job title of applicant: _____

continued

FORM 3-4 Employment verification.

Full-time position (yes or no): _____ Permanent (yes or no): _____

Salary: $ _____ Weekly, Biweekly, Monthly: _____

How long has the applicant been employed? _____

Name of person providing this information: _____

Title: _____ Date: _____

FORM 3-4   Employment verification (continued).

Date: _____

From: _____, applicant

To: _____, credit reference

I have submitted a rental application to _____. I authorize you to give credit information regarding my account to my prospective landlord:

Signature: _____ Date: _____

Dear Sir or Madam:

To verify the information that _____ has given to us on the rental application, can you please supply us with the needed information below? I have enclosed a self-addressed envelope for your convenience.

Thank you for your cooperation.

Sincerely,

Manager

Requested Information:

Amount the applicant owes: _____

Monthly payments: _____ Since: Month: _____ Year: _____

Approximately how many more payments is the applicant responsible for? _____

Is payment currently up to date? _____

Has applicant ever been late? _____ Approximately how many times? _____

How many times has applicant been more than 30 days late? _____

Payment record: Excellent: _____ Fair: _____ Poor: _____

Name of person providing above information: _____

Title: _____ Date: _____

FORM 3-5   Credit reference verification.

From: _____

To (name of bank): _____ Branch: _____

Address: _____

City: _____ State: _____ Zip: _____

Re: Rental Application of _____:

I authorize the above-named financial institution to give the requested information below to: [rental management company].

Signature: _____ Date: _____

Account number: _____

Dear Sir or Madam:

Your immediate reply is requested. One of your customers, _____, has made an application with us for a rental unit and has given your bank as a reference.

To assist us in processing the person's rental application, would you supply us with the information requested below? As noted earlier, the applicant has given authorization so that this information may be released. I have enclosed a self-addressed stamped envelope for your convenience.

Your reply is appreciated and will be held in strict confidence. If you need to contact me by phone, my number is _____.

Thank you for your cooperation.

Manager

Requested information on rental applicant: _____

Social Security number: _____

Checking account number: _____ Date opened: _____

Average balance: _____

Would a check in the amount of $_____ clear at this time?

Yes _____ No _____ [amount of the rental deposit] _____

Savings account number: _____ Date opened: _____

Average balance: _____ Is this a joint account? _____

If so, other account owners? _____

Does applicant currently have a loan through your bank? _____

If so, date loan created: _____

Loan number: _____ Monthly payment amount: _____

Current loan balance: _____ Payments current? _____

If not, how late? _____

This information provided by:

Name: _____

Bank title: _____ Date completed: _____

FORM 3-6 Bank verification.

Previous Landlords

Make it a rule to check previous landlords or managers for references for applicants. Even if an applicant has a written letter of reference from a previous landlord, call the previous landlord to verify the contents of the letter. Have a written record of any telephone calls you make to previous landlords. Be careful, because a current landlord may be willing to give a good reference to get rid of a problem tenant. Use Form 3-7 or Form 3-8 to get a reference from an applicant' landlord.

If a previous landlord refuses to give you any information on the applicant, the refusal may be based on the fact that that landlord wants to have nothing to do with the former tenant or it may be based on an exaggerated fear of being sued by the former tenant. Ask some indirect questions such as, "I assume that your

---

Name of Applicant:_____

Address: _____

Previous Landlord

Contact (name, property owner or manager, address of rental unit):

_____

_____

Date: _____

Questions

When did tenant rent from you? _____

Monthly rent: _____ Did tenant pay rent on time?_____

Was tenant considerate of neighbors? _____

Did tenant have any pets? If so, were there any problems with the pets?

_____

Did tenant make any unreasonable demands or complaints? _____

Reason for tenant leaving:_____

Did tenant give timely notice before leaving? _____

Was the unit left in good condition? _____

Was the security deposit used to cover damages?_____

Any particular problems with tenant? _____

Would you rerent to this individual? _____

Other comments: _____

_____

_____

FORM 3-7   Reference from former landlord (Option 1).

reluctance to discuss the former tenant is based on a negative event while he or she was a tenant." If the landlord does not answer that question, it probably means that a negative event occurred. Ask the landlord if it is his or her policy to be silent on all reference checks. In response to that question, the landlord often will explain that his or her policy is to never comment on a prior tenant but that he or she had no problems with this particular tenant. Another good question to ask is whether, without explaining why, the landlord would rerent the premises to the tenant. If the landlord says no, consider that a negative response.

If the applicant has pets, make certain that previous landlords are questioned about whether the pet or pets caused any damage to the rental unit and were well behaved. **Caution:** If a pet is a "working animal" and is used to assist or help a

---

[Telephone check]

[Introduce yourself and then state:] _____ [applicant], a current or former resident, has applied to rent a property that I manage. The applicant has given me your name and permission to ask if you could please verify a few quick things regarding his or her rental history with you.

1. Can you tell me what his or her monthly rent was or is? [If the amount is different from the amount stated by the applicant on the rental application, ask for verification to determine whether you are dealing with a landlord who will be honest with you or one who is trying to get rid of a tenant. If the landlord does not correct you about the amount of rent paid, assume that you have a landlord willing to lie to you.]

2. How much notice did the resident given you that he or she is or was moving?

3. Was or is the applicant currently up to date with his or her rent payments?

4. How often in the last 12 months was the applicant late in paying the rent?

5. Has he or she ever paid the rent more than 30 days late?

6. How many months/years did the applicant reside in your property?

7. Did the applicant vacate before the end of the lease agreement?

8. Did you receive complaints of any kind from neighbors regarding the applicant?

9. How many pets did the resident have on the premises? Did the animal(s) live there with your permission?

10. Were there any complaints from the neighbors regarding the pets?

11. Was the resident asked to move because of nonpayment or for breaking the lease's terms?

12. Have you had to give a notice to the applicant for any reason during the last 12 months because of a rental agreement violation? If so, what was the notice for?

13. Did you have or will you have to withhold any deposit to cover any unpaid rent or damages?

14. Did you have or will you have to repaint or clean the carpets after the resident vacates?

Thank you. I appreciate your assistance.

FORM 3-8   Questions for previous landlord (Option 2).

mentally or physically handicapped person, you are required by state and federal law to accommodate the animal no matter how mangy it looks.

Using Tenant Screening Companies

It may be prudent to use a screening service for potential tenants. Several companies specialize in providing timely information, letting you know the background of your prospective tenants so that you can be right the first time around. A typical screening company offers the following services:

- **Credit reports:** Discloses the applicant's credit history for the last seven years. Shows applicant's debt load, payment history, and all public information (bankruptcies, liens, judgments, etc.). Reveals applicant's past and present employers and addresses. FICO score can be requested at an additional charge. (The FICO score is explained later in this chapter.)
- **Banking verification:** Verifies the existence, opening date, and average balance of the account.
- **County seven-year criminal record search:** Reveals any felony or misdemeanor records on the applicant for the last seven years in the county of residence or in former counties of residence.
- **Employment verification:** Verifies employment dates, positions held, performance, and eligibility for rehire as well as any additional information the previous employer is willing to reveal.
- **Personal reference verification:** Verifies personal references.
- **Rental history verification:** Provides an accurate picture of applicant's rental history and behavior. Reveals any late payments, property damage, skips, theft, or bad checks.
- **Statewide criminal search:** Reveals any felony or misdemeanor records on the applicant for the last seven years in the county of residence or former counties of residence.
- **Social Security number trace:** Verifies that the applicant has provided a valid Social Security number. Confirms cardholder's name, date and place issued, and date of birth.
- **Sex offenders verification:** Verification of applicants registered in the county on sex offenders list. By law, sex offenders must register in the county in which they reside.
- **Unlawful detainer search:** Searches for any evictions for nonpayment filed by landlords. This information is not recorded by the county until a judgment is awarded. Until that time, a record of eviction can be only obtained by going to the courthouse in the county where the applicant resides.

Three tenant screening companies are listed below:

- Fidelity Information Corporation, 17383 Sunset Blvd., Suite A-370, Pacific Palisades, CA 90272-4138, telephone 310-573-9944, e-mail info@gofic.com.
- VeriRes Inc., 14019 S.W. Fwy. Sts. 301-383, Sugar Land, TX 77478, e-mail verires@verires.com
- National Data Search, Inc., which offers tenant screening packages as well as individual services. Custom-designed packages are available by calling NDS customer service at 1-866-826-7336.

Other tenant screening companies may be located by conducting a web search of "tenant screening companies," checking the local yellow pages, or asking one of the local apartment rental associations.

Fair Housing Laws

Fair housing laws make it illegal to discriminate on the basis of race, religion, creed, color, ethnic origin, or disability. There are also laws that prohibit discrimination based on the age of applicants who are over 40 years old. Many housing agencies and HUD often test landlords. Their agents will call landlords to check how the landlords screen prospective tenants. Protect yourself by putting the minimum requirements in writing and complying with them.

An individual receiving disability income has the same right to rent property as an employed individual. It is also illegal to discriminate against an applicant with a handicap. A landlord is expected to make reasonable accommodations to meet the needs of disabled tenants. Those accommodations include the following:

- Provide closed-in parking that is reserved for handicapped individuals. The parking should be spacious to allow use by a wheelchair-bound tenant.
- Guide dogs or other service animals should be allowed without the payment of a pet deposit.
- If an individual's finances are managed by a government agency, the landlord may need to adjust the date the rent is due to accommodate the payment schedule of the disabled person.
- For rental properties first occupied after March 1991, which have four or more rental units, the building must be designed so that it is accessible and so that the primary entrance of each rental unit is accessible by a wheelchair-bound person. In addition, the public and common areas need to be readily accessible.
- If your unit is not included in the above requirement, and an individual in a wheelchair wants to rent your unit and volunteers to pay to make the unit

accessible, you must rent to that person if he or she meets your minimum requirements.

Some states, such as New York, make it illegal to deny an application because of an individual's occupation. For more information about the Fair Housing Act, free copies of federal fair housing posters, and technical assistance on accessibility requirements, call HUD's Housing Discrimination Hotline at 800-669-9777 or contact one of HUD's regional offices (see accompanying CD). State consumer protection agencies can provide more specific information on state fair housing laws and free information on landlord–tenant laws. A list of state agencies can be obtained by visiting the website maintained by the Federal Citizen Information Center: www.consumeraction.gov.

Reasons for Denying an Application

You need to establish a system to ensure that all applicants are approved or rejected on the basis of your preestablished criteria. A point system is recommended. Form 3-9 shows one point system that may be used.

Give a score of one point (or more when applicable) for each of the following criteria. You may designate any criterion to be worth more than one point in value as long as you are consistent in giving the same value to select criteria for all applicants. [Put an asterisk by those worth double points]. Add up the total points to see if the applicant reaches your minimum acceptable score. [**Note:** If the applicant has poor credit, that is sufficient to deny the application.]

_____ Minimum score on credit report of _____.

(Over _____ credit score = 2 points. Also use negative points if credit is bad.)*

_____ Sufficient income—Monthly income is three times the rental amount. (add + 1)

_____ Sufficient income—Monthly income is four times the rental amount. (add + 1)

_____ Verifiable source of income or employment.

_____ Same source of income for a minimum of 1 year. (2 years = 2 points, 3 years = 3 points)*

_____ Able to pay deposit and rent requested.

_____ Currently paying comparable amount of rent.

_____ No negative remarks on credit history.

_____ No excessive financial obligations more than _____percent of income.

FORM 3-9   Objective point system for resident selection.

_____ Has a checking account.

_____ Has a savings account.

_____ Able to provide credit references.

_____ No late notices from current landlord.

_____ No prior evictions.

_____ Able to provide a cosigner. (2 points if cosigner owns real estate)*

_____ Produced items requested (e.g., identification, application fee, deposit, references).

_____ Filled out application completely and truthfully.

_____ Resided at current address minimum of 1 year. (2 years = 2 points, 3 years = 3 points)* [Residents receive points only if they were responsible for rent payment.]

_____ No security deposit to be withheld because of proper upkeep of current residence.

_____ No notices of any kind from current landlord regarding a rental agreement violation.

_____ No neighbor complaints of residents or pets or police reports for disturbing the peace.

_____ Applicant has current phone in his or her name by a primary local telephone service provider.

_____ Petless or owns pet and able to provide proof of license, tags, shots, references, insurance, neutered, declawed.

_____ Good report from the landlord before to the current landlord.

_____ No criminal history.

_____ Able to verify all above criteria.

_____ Move-in date within an acceptable time period.

Applicant's Total Score: _____ [total score of _____ points is acceptable; set your minimum score based on the type of property and the market demands]

If score is between ____and _____points, resident may still qualify if he or she meets the following conditions: _____

[Additional conditions may include additional security deposit or cosigner.]

Date of application: _____

Above information verified by: _____ Date verified:_____

Action taken: _____ Applicant notified of acceptance or denial by _____

Date applicant notified: _____

Method of notification: _____

Any follow-up actions taken: _____

FORM 3-9 Objective point system for resident selection (continued).

Denial Letters

Care should be taken in notifying an applicant of the denial of his or her rental application. If necessary, explain to the applicant that the denial was based on his or her objective score. If the applicant is informed by telephone or orally, always follow up in writing, using a form similar to the ones included in this chapter.

Denial Because of Credit History

The preferred method of eliminating deadbeat tenants is to deny their rental applications. The golden rule is that if in doubt about a tenant's willingness and ability to pay rent, do not approve the rental application. Err on the side of caution.

The most important fact on a person's credit report is the payment history followed by the amount of outstanding debt compared with the individual's income. If an individual has a history of late payments, do not assume that that individual will treat you any differently.

An objective method of making a decision about the creditworthiness of an applicant is to establish a minimum credit score requirement. Most credit reporting companies will calculate the credit score and provide it to you. Although many different types of credit scores are used, the most frequently used is the Fair, Isaac & Company's (FICO) score developed for use in real estate transactions. The Federal Fair Credit Reporting Act (FCRA) governs credits reports and contains numerous regulations to protect the privacy rights of individuals. Note: The reporting agency will provide the credit history of the applicant but will not make a decision regarding the application. You alone will make that decision. A good credit report should discuss certain aspects of a person's credit history to help you make the decision.

If you deny a person a lease because of a poor credit history, you are in most cases required to give that person in writing the name, address, and telephone number of the agency that provided the report on which you based your decision. Form 3-10 may be used to inform the applicant.

Form 3-11 may be used when the reason for denial of an application includes factors other than credit information.

Requiring a Cosigner

There is always a risk to renting property. The tenant may not pay the rent and/or may damage the property. Although your lease gives you a right to take the ex-tenant to court, and you may get a judgment for unpaid rent and/or damages, if the defendant has no money or nonexempt property, your judgment may not be

To: [Applicant] _____

[Street Address] _____

[City, State, and Zip Code] _____

THIS NOTICE is to inform you that your rental application to rent the property at _____ [rental property address] has been denied because of: (check one or more below reasons)

[ ] Insufficient information in the credit report provided by _____
_____ [name, address, and telephone number of consumer credit reporting agency providing credit report; include toll-free telephone number if this is a national credit reporting agency]

[ ] Negative information in the credit report provided by _____
_____ [name, address, and telephone number of consumer credit reporting agency providing credit report; include toll-free telephone number if this is a national credit reporting agency]

The consumer credit reporting agency noted above did not make the decision not to rent to you and did not explain why your application was rejected. It only provided our office with information about your credit history.

Provided that this notice meets the requirements of the federal Fair Credit Reporting Act as amended by the Fair and Accurate Credit Transactions (FACT) Act of 2003 (15 U.S.C. § 1681), you have the right under the act to obtain a free copy of your credit report from the consumer credit reporting agency named above if your request is made within 60 days of this notice or if you have not requested a free copy within the past year (15 U.S.C. § 1681j). You also have the right to dispute the accuracy or completeness of your credit report and add your own "consumer statement" (up to 100 words) to the report (15 U.S.C. § 1681i). For more information, contact the above-named credit reporting agency.

Manager _____ Date _____

FORM 3-10   Denial of rental application based on credit report information.

satisfied (paid). If the prospective tenant's credit is marginal or there are other negative indicators regarding the tenant's creditworthiness, consider requiring a cosigner.

Generally, any promise to pay the debt of another person must be in writing to be enforceable. Accordingly, get it in writing. Do not accept a cosigner until you have checked his or her creditworthiness just as you do for prospective tenants. If you determine that a cosigner is necessary, have that person sign the cosigner agreement before you accept the tenant application and allow the tenant to move into the property.

With a properly written and signed cosigner agreement, the cosigner becomes liable for all past-due rent, property damages, other expenses, and legal fees to the same extent as the tenant. Generally, a cosigner agreement has a clause regarding the requirement for notice to the cosigner. Play it safe: Any time you

Date: _____

Dear _____:

Your request for tenancy has been denied for the reason(s) indicated below [check all that apply]:

_____ Application incomplete

_____ Unable to verify employment

_____ Insufficient credit references

_____ Temporary or irregular employment

_____ Unable to verify credit references

_____ Unable to verify income

_____ Length of employment

_____ No credit file

_____ Insufficient income

_____ Bankruptcy

_____ Delinquent credit obligation

_____ Previous eviction(s)

_____ Excessive obligations

_____ Garnishment, foreclosure, or repossession

_____ Low applicant score [based on a point system]

_____ Unacceptable rentals terms

_____ Length of lease requested too short

_____ Negative information received from: _____

If you were turned down because of information provided by a third party, that party or agency is listed.

Notice

Under the Fair Credit Reporting Act, you have the right to make a written request, within 60 days of receipt of this notice, for disclosure of the nature of the adverse information. The Federal Equal Credit Opportunity Act prohibits creditors from discriminating against credit applicants on the basis of race, color, religion, national origin, sex, marital status, age (provided the applicant has the capacity to enter into a binding contract), because all or part of the applicant's income derives from any public assistance program, or because the applicant has in good faith exercised any right under the Consumer Credit Protection Act. The federal agency that administers compliance with this law concerning creditors is the Federal Trade Commission, Equal Credit Opportunity, Washington DC 20580.

The credit information considered was received from the consumer credit reporting agency below:

_____

FORM 3-11   Reason for nonacceptance.

send a notice to the tenant regarding past due rent, a notice to pay or quit, and the like, send a copy to the cosigner. In many cases, a cosigner will work with a tenant to remedy the problem, because the cosigner does not want to be held liable (see Form 3-12).

Using a Finder's Fee

Generally, you may discount other tenants' rent for recommending a new tenant. Many landlords allow a $25 or $50 credit to any current residents who recommend a new tenant, if the recommended individual is accepted as a tenant and moves into one of the rental units. It may not be legal to charge the new tenant for the amount paid or credited to the recommending resident. Even if it is legal, I recommend that the landlord not pass on the cost of the discount to the new tenant. It makes this appear to be a method of squeezing additional money out of a tenant.

Addendum _____ to Rental Agreement

This agreement shall serve as an addendum to the rental agreement dated _____ between _____ (Manager) and _____ (Applicant/Tenant).

I/We, the cosigner(s):_____ residing at _____ have completed an Application for Residency for the express purpose of enabling the Manager to check my/our credit and verify the stated information. I/We have read the rental agreement and hereby guarantee the Tenants' compliance with the financial obligations of the contract.

Cosigner(s) agrees to be jointly and severally liable with Tenant for Tenant's obligations arising out of the lease or rental agreement, including but not limited to unpaid rent, property damage, and cleaning and repair costs that exceed Tenant's security deposit.

Cosigner(s) further agrees that Manager will have no obligation to report to Cosigner(s) should Tenant fail to abide by the terms of the lease or rental agreement. Manager has no duty to warn or inform Cosigner and may demand that Cosigner(s) pay for these obligations immediately.

I/We understand that this Cosigner agreement will remain in full force and effect throughout the term of the lease period regardless of any extensions and/or changes in terms unless specified otherwise in writing by the Manager.

Cosigner _____ Date _____

Cosigner _____ Date _____

Accepted by Manager_____ Date _____

FORM 3-12 Cosigner agreement.

Deposit with Application

When a prospective tenant submits an application, the landlord normally requires that the applicant submit a deposit. The receipt for the deposit should indicate clearly that the deposit does not bind the landlord to rent the property to the applicant. There should be an understanding that the deposit will be returned, minus the actual cost of verifying the applicant's information. A rental application will inform the applicant of these conditions.

Approval

Form 3-13 can be used for approval of a rental application.

Form 3-14 may be used to return the application deposit when no suitable rental unit is available or the application has been denied.

Form 3-15 may be used when an individual has indicated an interest in your rental but has taken no other steps. I recommend sending some type of follow-up letter to each individual who visits your rental.

Dear _____

Your rental application has been approved for _____,
with occupancy to begin on _____ [date].

Please set up an appointment within _____ hours to sign the lease and pay the balance of the required deposits and/or rent as noted below. Failure to pay the balance due and sign the lease will cause forfeiture of rent/deposit paid to date.

Sincerely,

_____
Manager

Balance due is as follows:

First month's rent: $_____

Additional rent: $_____

Deposit: $_____

Additional deposit: $ _____

Fee(s) or other: $ _____

                                    Total $_____

Paid to date: $_____

Balance due: $_____

FORM 3-13   Approval of rental application.

Date: _____

Dear _____ :

Enclosed is a check in the amount of $ _____, which constitutes the return of your rental application/rental reserve deposit. The nonrefundable application processing fee of $ _____ was deducted from the amount refunded to you.

Thank you for your interest in our rental property, and I wish you the best of luck in locating the best residence for you and your family.

Sincerely,

_____

Manager

FORM 3-14   Return of application deposit.

Date: _____

Dear _____ :

It was a pleasure meeting you at our rental home and showing the property to you. I am pleased that you are considering making it your new home. We have sent you some information about the home, which we discussed, as well as additional information to help you make your decision about whether this would be the right place for you and your family.

As a reminder, our home can offer you all of the following features:

_____

We are in a convenient location near the following:

_____

I trust that this information is helpful to you. I look forward to discussing our home with you if you have any additional questions.

If you would like us to hold property for you, we will need you to complete a rental application and submit it with the necessary fees. Best of luck in your search for a new home.

Thank you again for your interest in our home. Please call us at: _____.
I look forward to hearing from you soon.

Sincerely,

_____

Manager

FORM 3-15   Follow-up inquiry.

Establishing Occupancy Limits

The placing of restrictions on the number of persons who may occupy a unit is one of the most controversial issues in the rental housing industry. Most state laws and federal law allow you to establish an occupancy limit that is reasonably tied to health and safety standards. Also, limits may be valid if they are based on the capacities of the plumbing or electrical systems. At one time, HUD had a rule of two people per bedroom. Recently, that was replaced by a rule limiting the number of people per square foot. State laws also regulate the placing of occupancy limits. Before establishing a limit, check with a local real estate attorney or landlord association.

Allowing a Tenant to Run a Home Business in a Rental Unit

It is not unusual for an applicant to ask that the rental agreement be modified to allow him or her to run a home business. Before you say yes or no, check out the law in that regard. For example, in California and New York, a landlord may not be permitted to prevent a renter from operating a home-based child-care business. In some states, regulations or court cases limit the right of the landlord to deny permission to a tenant to operate a home-based child care business under the concept that there is a strong public need for home-based child care. If in doubt regarding restrictions on your right to deny permission for a home-based business, check with your local or state consumer protection office (California Health & Safety Code § 1597.40 and New York City Civil Court in *Haberman v. Gotbaum*, 698 NYS 2nd 406).

Before agreeing to the business, check with your insurance company to determine if you need a modification to your liability and property insurance. You may want to require the tenant to have liability insurance. You do not want to wind up paying when someone is hurt on the rental property, such as a business visitor who trips on the steps to the unit. In addition, you should check to determine if the business will violate any local zoning regulations. Your local zoning office can provide that information.

Another issue is that, if your property is used for a commercial business, you may need to meet the accessibility requirements for handicapped persons under the Americans with Disabilities Act (ADA). For information, check the ADA website at www.ada.gov or call the Disability Rights Section of the Department of Justice at 800-514-0301.

Optional Forms Involving the Tenant Selection Process

Several other forms may be useful to a manager or landlord in the process of selecting the right tenant. Forms, like all others, are 3-16 through 3-18 on the CD accompanying this book.

Homes/Apartments for Rent by: _____

Phone:_____

1. Address:_____

   Directions:_____

   Size/optional features: _____

   Number of bedrooms: _____ Date available: _____

   Maximum occupancy number for this home: _____

   Garage: _____ Basement: _____ Fenced yard:_____

   Schools: _____ Off-street parking: _____

   Washer/dryer hookup: _____ Pets allowed:_____

   Rent per month: _____ Biweekly:_____ Per week:_____

   Deposit: _____ Lease term: _____

   Other information: _____

2. Address:_____

   Directions:_____

   Size/optional features: _____

   Number of bedrooms: _____ Date available: _____

   Maximum occupancy number for this home: _____

   Garage: _____ Basement: _____ Fenced yard:_____

   Schools: _____ Off-street parking: _____

   Washer/dryer hookup: _____ Pets allowed:_____

   Rent per month: _____ Biweekly:_____ Per week:_____

   Deposit: _____ Lease term: _____

   Other information: _____

Additional Notes:

All homes are clean and well kept and include: _____
_____

We do not normally include appliances as part of the rental package. Let us know if they are needed.

All utilities and yard upkeep are the resident's responsibility unless otherwise indicated.

No pets are allowed, of any size or age, unless otherwise indicated.

We do check references before move-in, which usually takes _____ working day(s).

If you have had the same source of income for less than one year, you will need a cosigner.

Please drive by any home that interests you and then give us a call at
_____ and we can make arrangements to show you a home.
Please do not knock on the door of any home listed.

We will be glad to show the home to you.

FORM 3-16 Rental availability summary sheet for prospective residents (a handout for prospective applicants).

Move-in date: _____

Applicant's name: _____   Phone: _____

Current address: _____

The applicant agrees to rent housing accommodations located at:

_____ on a _____ month-to-month basis or _____ for a period of _____ months.

The applicant also posts a holding deposit for the accommodations in the amount of $ _____. This holding deposit shall be applied toward the tenant's _____ security deposit or _____ rent when the rental agreement is signed.

In the event the application for residency is not approved or accepted or if the residence is not ready for occupancy, the deposit will be returned to the applicant. If the applicant fails to sign the rental agreement or fails to provide additional funds required for occupancy, or does not take occupancy on the scheduled move-in date, $ _____ of this holding deposit will not be refunded to the applicant and will be retained by the owner/manager.

By signing below, applicant acknowledges receipt of a copy of this notice.

Date_____   Monies received $_____

By cash _____   By check_____

FORM 3-17   Receipt for deposit.

---

1. The Manager is required to investigate the information that you have set forth on your application. This may include obtaining a credit report or another report from a credit bureau or a tenant screening service confirming information that you have set forth in your application. The manager may also contact prior landlords, employers, financial institutions, and personal references.

2. Before we start a review of your application, you must pay a tenant screening fee of $_____. The manager acknowledges receipt of this fee. This fee represents payment for costs incurred by the manager to screen your application. The costs may include costs incurred for a credit report or another screening report, long-distance phone calls, and time spent calling landlords, employers, financial institutions, and personal references.

3. You have a right to dispute the accuracy of the information provided by the tenant screening service, credit bureau, or the entities listed on your application who will be contacted for information about you. However, the manager is forbidden by law from giving you certain information about your credit report, and this may be obtained from the credit bureau or tenant screening agency named below.

4. Tenant Screening Service. The tenant screening service or credit bureau used by owner, if any, is: _____

FORM 3-18   Screening disclosure.

Name: _____

Address: _____

City: _____ State: _____ Zip: _____

5. By signing below, applicant acknowledges receipt of a copy of this notice.

Applicant _____ Date _____

Applicant _____ Date _____

Manager _____ Date _____

FORM 3-18   Screening disclosure (continued).

4

The Lease

This chapter contains a discussion of the necessary and recommended items to include in the lease. Sample leases and other forms and agreements are included in the chapter. Note: Electronic copies of the forms, agreements, and letters are included on the CD that accompanies the text. Updates, if any, are posted on the website at www.rentforprofit.com.

Lease Provisions

The terms of a lease are governed by the provisions of the agreement, and in cases where specific terms are not provided for by the agreement, the lease is to contain what is termed the usual, and only the usual, provisions. For example, in the absence of an express stipulation in the lease, the landlord cannot restrict a tenant's right to assign or sublet the property.

Prohibited Provisions in Rental Agreements

In most states, any provision in a rental agreement is void and unenforceable to the extent that it:

1. Purports to waive or preclude the rights, remedies, or requirements set forth in the landlord-tenant act.
2. Purports to limit or preclude any liability of the landlord to the tenant or of the tenant to the landlord arising under law.

If such a void and unenforceable provision is included in a rental agreement entered into, extended, or renewed, and either party suffers actual damages as a result of the inclusion, the aggrieved party may recover the damages sustained.

Unwritten Leases and Agreements to Make a Lease

An oral agreement to lease contemplates a later writing and is legally enforceable only if the parties agree on the terms to be incorporated in the later writing. However, in some jurisdictions, an oral agreement to create a lease is never enforceable. The validity of an agreement to make a lease is governed by the contract provisions of the state's statute of frauds. In most cases, an agreement for a lease must be certain as to the terms of the future lease; if it shows on its face that other details are to be agreed on later between the parties, it is not a binding agreement. For example, a letter containing the terms of a proposed lease was not sufficient to constitute a binding agreement to execute a lease where it failed to provide for the time and manner of payment of rent despite the fact that the letter contained a statement that the monthly rent would be $400 (*Smith v. House of Kenton Corp.*, 23 NC App 439).

Standard Leases

Forms 4-1 through 4-3 show sample leases.

This residential lease is entered into between _____ (Landlord) and _____ and _____, (Tenant(s)). The Landlord hereby leases the residential property to the tenant(s). The Tenant(s) hereby accepts the lease. The terms of the lease are as follows:

1. The lease pertains to the property located at:_____

2. The lease shall be for a period of _____, commencing on _____ day of _____, _____, and ending on _____ day of _____, _____.

3. The monthly rent for the property is $_____, payable on the first day of every month. There will be a late fee of $_____ if the rent is not paid by the 5th of the month. Tenant agrees to pay to Landlord the sum of $_____ as a security deposit, to be promptly returned upon the termination of the lease and compliance with all provisions of this lease.

4. The Tenant shall be responsible for providing all utilities except as noted below:

   _____

5. The Tenant agrees to return possession of the premises at the conclusion of the lease in its present condition, except for normal wear and tear.

6. Only the following persons will reside on the premises: _____

FORM 4-1   Fixed-term residential lease (Option 1).

7. The Tenant shall not assign or sublease the premises without written permission of the landlord.

8. No material or structural alterations of the premises will be made without the prior written permission of the landlord.

9. The Tenant will comply with all zoning, health, and use ordinances.

10. Pets are not allowed on the premises without prior written permission of the Landlord.

11. This lease shall be subordinate to all present and future mortgages against the premises.

12. In the event that legal action is necessary to enforce any provisions of the lease, attorney fees may be recovered by the prevailing party.

13. Additional lease terms:

14. The following listed addendums are hereby incorporated into this lease:

Signed this _____ day of _____, _____.

_____   _____   _____
Landlord   Tenant   Tenant

FORM 4-1   Fixed-term residential lease (Option 1).

This Agreement is entered into between _____ ('Tenant[s]) and _____(Landlord). Each Tenant is jointly and severally liable for the payment of rent and performance of all other terms of this Agreement.

1. Premises located at _____ (the premises) is the subject of this lease. Subject to the terms and conditions in this Agreement, Landlord rents to Tenant(s), and Tenant(s) rent from Landlord, for residential purposes only, the premises, together with the following furnishings and appliances:

   _____.

   Rental of the premises also includes _____.

2. The premises are to be used only as a private residence for Tenant(s) listed in Clause 1 of this Agreement and the following minor children: _____.

   Occupancy by guests for more than seven days is prohibited without Landlord's written consent and will be considered a breach of this agreement.

3. The term of the rental will start on _____, ____, and end on _____. If Tenant(s) vacate before the term ends, Tenant(s) will be liable for the balance of the rent for the remainder of the term.

4. Tenant will pay to Landlord a monthly rent of $_____, payable in advance on the first day of each month, except when that day falls on a weekend or legal holiday, in which case rent is due on the next business day. Rent will be paid to _____ at _____ or at such other place as the Landlord may designate.

continued

FORM 4-2   Fixed-term residential lease (Option 2).

5. Rent may be paid:

   [   ] by mail, to _____

   [   ] in person, at _____

6. Form of payment.

   Landlord will accept payment in these forms:

   [   ] personal check made payable to _____

   [   ] cashier's check made payable to _____

   [   ] credit card

   [   ] money order

   [   ] cash

7. For the period from Tenants(s)'s move-in date on _____, ____, through the end of the month, Tenant(s) will pay to Landlord the prorated monthly rent of $_____. This amount will be paid on or before the date the Tenant(s) takes possession of the property.

8. If Tenant(s) fail to pay the rent in full before the end of the _____ day after it is due, Tenant(s) will pay Landlord a late charge of $_____, plus $_____ for each additional day that the rent remains unpaid. The total late charge for any one month will not exceed $_____. Landlord does not waive the right to insist on payment of the rent in full on the date it is due. If any check offered by Tenant(s) to Landlord in payment of rent or any other amount due under this Agreement is returned for lack of sufficient funds, a "stop payment," or any other reason, Tenant(s) will pay Landlord a returned check charge of $_____.

9. On signing this Agreement, Tenant(s) will pay to Landlord the sum of $_____ as a security deposit. Tenant(s) may not, without Landlord's prior written consent, apply this security deposit to the last month's rent or to any other sum due under this agreement. Within __ days after all Tenant(s) have vacated the premises, returned keys, and provided Landlord with a forwarding address, Landlord will give Tenant(s) an itemized written statement of the reasons for, and the dollar amount of, any of the security deposit retained by the Landlord, along with a check for any deposit balance.

10. Tenant(s) will pay all utility charges, except for the following, which will be paid by Landlord: _____.

11. Tenant(s) will not sublet any part of the premises or assign this Agreement without the prior written consent of Landlord.

12. Except as provided by law or as authorized by the prior written consent of Landlord, Tenant(s) will not make any repairs or alterations to the premises.

13. Tenant(s) will not, without Landlord's prior written consent, alter, rekey, or install any locks to the premises or install or alter any burglar alarm system. Tenant(s) will provide Landlord with a key or keys capable of unlocking all such rekeyed or new locks as well as instructions on how to disarm any altered or new burglar alarm system.

FORM 4-2   Fixed-term residential lease (Option 2) (continued).

14. Tenant(s) are entitled to quiet enjoyment of the premises. Tenant(s) and guests or invitees will not use the premises or adjacent areas in such a way as to:

    a. violate any law or ordinance, including laws prohibiting the use, possession, or sale of illegal drugs;
    b. commit waste (severe property damage); or
    c. create a nuisance by annoying, disturbing, inconveniencing, or interfering with the quiet enjoyment and peace and quiet of any other tenant or nearby resident.

15. No animal, bird, or other pet will be kept on the premises, except service animals needed by blind, deaf, or disabled persons and _____ under the following conditions: _____.

16. Tenant(s) will keep the premises clean, sanitary, and in good condition and, upon termination of the tenancy, return the premises to Landlord in a condition identical to that which existed when Tenant(s) took occupancy, except for ordinary wear and tear.

    a. Tenant(s) will immediately notify Landlord of any defects or dangerous conditions in and about the premises of which Tenant(s) becomes aware.
    b. Tenant(s) will reimburse Landlord, on demand by Landlord, for the cost of any repairs to the premises damaged by Tenant(s) or Tenant(s)'s guests or business invitees through misuse or neglect.
    c. Tenant(s) have examined the premises, including appliances, fixtures, carpets, drapes, and paint, and has found them to be in good, safe, and clean condition and repair, except as noted in the checklist.

17. Landlord or Landlord's agents may enter the premises in the event of an emergency, to make repairs or improvements, or to show the premises to prospective buyers or tenants. Landlord also may enter the premises to conduct an annual inspection to check for safety or maintenance problems. Except in cases of emergency, Tenant(s)'s abandonment of the premises, court order, or where it is impracticable to do so, Landlord shall give Tenant(s) two days' notice before entering.

18. Tenant(s) will notify Landlord in advance if Tenant(s) will be away from the premises for _____ or more consecutive days. During such absence, Landlord may enter the premises at times reasonably necessary to maintain the property and inspect for needed repairs.

19. Tenants acknowledge receipt of, and have read a copy of, tenant rules and regulations, which are incorporated into this agreement by this reference.

20. If, after signing this Agreement, Tenant(s) fails to take possession of the premises, Tenant(s) will still be responsible for paying rent and complying with all other terms of this agreement.

21. Tenant(s) acknowledges that Landlord has made the following disclosures regarding the premises:

    [ ] Disclosure of Information on Lead-Based-Paint and/or Lead-Based Paint Hazards

    [ ] Other disclosures: _____.

22. In any action or legal proceeding to enforce any part of this Agreement, the prevailing party shall recover reasonable attorney fees and court costs.

continued

FORM 4-2   Fixed-term residential lease (Option 2) (continued).

23. The failure of Tenant(s) or Tenant(s)'s guests or invitees to comply with any term of this Agreement, or the misrepresentation of any material fact on Tenant(s)'s Rental Application, will be grounds for termination of the tenancy.

24. This document constitutes the entire agreement between the parties, and no promises or representations, other than those contained here and those implied by law, have been made by Landlord or Tenant(s). Any modifications to this agreement must be in writing signed by Landlord and Tenant.

25. Additional Provisions

    Additional provisions that are incorporated into this agreement are as follows:

    _____

26. Validity of Each Part

    If any portion of this Agreement is held to be invalid, its invalidity will not affect the validity or enforceability of any other provision of this Agreement.

Signed on_____[date]:

_____

Manager

_____   _____

Tenant   Tenant

Contact number and Address for Tenant(s) _____

_____

FORM 4-2   Fixed-term residential lease (Option 2) (continued).

This Agreement is entered into between _____ "Tenant(s)" and _____"Landlord." Each Tenant is jointly and severally liable for the payment of rent and performance of all other terms of this agreement.

1. The Landlord rents to Tenant(s), and Tenant(s) rent from Landlord, for residential purposes only, the premises located at _____,"the premises," together with the following furnishings and appliances: _____.

Rental of the premises also includes_____.

2. The premises are to be used only as a private residence for Tenant(s) listed in Clause 1 of this agreement and the following minor children: _____.

Occupancy by guests for more than seven days is prohibited without Landlord's written consent and will be considered a breach of this agreement.

3. The rental will begin on _____, _____, and continue on a month-to-month basis. Landlord may terminate the tenancy or modify the terms of this agreement by giving the Tenant(s) _____ days' written notice. Tenant(s) may terminate the tenancy by giving the Landlord _____ days' written notice.

FORM 4-3   Month-to-month residential rental agreement.

4. Tenant will pay to Landlord a monthly rent of $_____, payable in advance on the first day of each month, except when that day falls on a weekend or legal holiday, in which case rent is due on the next business day. Rent will be paid to _____ at _____ or at such other place as the Landlord may designate.

5. Rent may be paid:

   [   ] by mail, to _____

   [   ] in person, at _____

6. Landlord will accept payment in these forms:

   [   ] personal check made payable to _____

   [   ] cashier's check made payable to _____

   [   ] credit card

   [   ] money order

   [   ] cash

7. For the period from Tenant(s)' move-in date _____, ____, through the end of the month, Tenant(s) will pay to Landlord the prorated monthly rent of $_____. This amount will be paid on or before the date the Tenant(s) moves in.

8. If Tenant(s) fail to pay the rent in full before the end of the _____ day after it is due, Tenant(s) will pay Landlord a late charge of $_____, plus $_____ for each additional day the rent remains unpaid. The total late charge for any one month will not exceed $_____. Landlord does not waive the right to insist on payment of the rent in full on the date it is due. If any check offered by Tenant(s) to Landlord in payment of rent or any other amount due under this agreement is returned for lack of sufficient funds, a "stop payment," or any other reason, Tenant(s) will pay Landlord a returned check charge of $_____.

9. On signing this agreement, Tenant(s) will pay to Landlord the sum of $_____ as a security deposit. Tenant(s) may not, without Landlord's prior written consent, apply this security deposit to the last month's rent or to any other sum due under this agreement. Within _____ days after all Tenant(s) have vacated the premises, returned keys, and provided Landlord with a forwarding address, Landlord will give Tenant(s) an itemized written statement of the reasons for, and the dollar amount of, any of the security deposit retained by the Landlord, along with a check for any deposit balance.

10. Tenant(s) will pay all utility charges, except for the following, which will be paid by Landlord: _____.

11. Tenant(s) will not sublet any part of the premises or assign this agreement without the prior written consent of Landlord.

12. Except as provided by law, or as authorized by the prior written consent of Landlord, Tenant(s)

    a. Will not make any repairs or alterations to the premises.

continued

FORM 4-3   Month-to-month residential rental agreement (continued).

b. Tenant(s) will not, without Landlord's prior written consent, alter, rekey, or install any locks to the premises or install or alter any burglar alarm system. Tenant(s) will provide Landlord with a key or keys capable of unlocking all such rekeyed or new locks as well as instructions on how to disarm any altered or new burglar alarm system.

13. Tenant(s) are entitled to quiet enjoyment of the premises. Tenant(s) and guests or invitees will not use the premises or adjacent areas in such a way as to:

a. violate any law or ordinance, including laws prohibiting the use, possession, or sale of illegal drugs;

b. commit waste (severe property damage); or

c. create a nuisance by annoying, disturbing, inconveniencing, or interfering with the quiet enjoyment and peace and quiet of any other tenant or nearby resident.

14. No animal, bird, or other pet will be kept on the premises except service animals needed by blind, deaf, or disabled persons and _____ under the following conditions: _____.

15. Tenant(s) will keep the premises clean, sanitary, and in good condition and, upon termination of the tenancy, return the premises to Landlord in a condition identical to that which existed when Tenant(s) took occupancy, except for ordinary wear and tear.

a. Tenant(s) will immediately notify Landlord of any defects or dangerous conditions in and about the premises of which Tenant(s) becomes aware.

b. Tenant(s) will reimburse Landlord, on demand by Landlord, for the cost of any repairs to the premises damaged by Tenant(s) or Tenant(s)'s guests or business invitees through misuse or neglect.

c. Tenant(s) has examined the premises, including appliances, fixtures, carpets, drapes, and paint, and has found them to be in good, safe, and clean condition and repair, except as noted in the checklist.

16. Landlord or Landlord's agents may enter the premises in the event of an emergency, to make repairs or improvements, or to show the premises to prospective buyers or tenants. Landlord also may enter the premises to conduct an annual inspection to check for safety or maintenance problems. Except in cases of emergency, Tenant(s)' abandonment of the premises, court order, or where it is impracticable to do so, Landlord shall give Tenant(s) two days' notice before entering.

17. Tenant(s) will notify Landlord in advance if Tenant(s) will be away from the premises for _____ or more consecutive days. During such absence, Landlord may enter the premises at times reasonably necessary to maintain the property and inspect for needed repairs.

18. Tenants acknowledge receipt of, and have read a copy of, tenant rules and regulations, which are incorporated into this agreement by this reference.

19. If, after signing this agreement, Tenant(s) fails to take possession of the premises, Tenant(s) will still be responsible for paying rent and complying with all other terms of this agreement.

FORM 4-3   Month-to-month residential rental agreement (continued).

20. Tenant(s) acknowledges that Landlord has made the following disclosures regarding the premises:

    [ ] Disclosure of Information on Lead-Based-Paint and/or Lead-Based Paint Hazards

    [ ] Other disclosures: _____.

21. In any action or legal proceeding to enforce any part of this lease, the prevailing party shall recover reasonable attorney fees and court costs.

22. The failure of Tenant(s) or Tenant(s)' guests or invitees to comply with any term of this agreement, or the misrepresentation of any material fact on Tenant(s)'s Rental Application, will be grounds for termination of the tenancy.

23. This document constitutes the entire agreement between the parties, and no promises or representations, other than those contained here and those implied by law, have been made by Landlord or Tenant(s). Any modifications to this agreement must be in writing, signed by Landlord and Tenant.

24. Additional provisions which are incorporated into this agreement are as follows:

    _____

25. If any portion of this agreement is held to be invalid, its invalidity will not affect the validity or enforceability of any other provision of this agreement.

Signed on_____[date]:

_____

Manager

_____   _____

Tenant   Tenant

Contact number and Address for Tenant(s) _____

_____

FORM 4-3 Month-to-month residential rental agreement (continued).

Although there is a provision in these leases agreeing that no unlawful activity will be conducted on the premises, many landlord's feel that a separate "crime-free lease" addendum provides additional needed emphasis on this issue. Form 4-4 is commonly used for this purposes.

If the tenants are in the military or military reserve, a military addendum should be added to the lease. Form 4-5 may be used for that purpose.

ADDENDUM _____ TO LEASE

In consideration of the execution or renewal of a lease of the premises located at
_____, Manager and Tenant(s) agree as follows:

1. Tenant(s) and any other member of the tenant's household or guest, or other person under tenant's control, shall not engage in criminal activity, including drug-related criminal activity, on or near the said premises. "Drug-related criminal activity" means the illegal manufacture, sale, distribution, use, or possession with the intent to manufacture, sell, distribute, or use a controlled substance.

2. Tenant(s) and any other member of the tenant's household or guest, or other person under tenant's control, shall not engage in any act intended to facilitate criminal activity, including drug-related criminal activity on or near the premises.

3. Tenant(s) or members of the household will not permit the dwelling unit to be used for or facilitate criminal activity, including drug-related criminal activity, regardless of whether the individual engaging in such activity is a member of the household or a guest.

4. Tenant and no other member of the tenant's household or guest, or other person under tenant's control, shall not engage in the unlawful manufacturing selling, using, storing, keeping, or giving of a controlled substance at any location, whether on or near the dwelling unit, premises, or otherwise.

5. Tenant and any other member of the tenant's household or guest, or other person under tenant's control, shall not engage in any illegal activity, including prostitution, criminal street gang activity, threatening or intimidating, battery, including but not limited to the unlawful discharge of firearms on or near the dwelling unit premises, or any breach of the lease agreement that jeopardizes the health, safety, and welfare of the landlord, his agent, or other tenants, or involving imminent or actual serious property damage.

6. Violation of the above provisions shall be considered as material and an irreparable violation of the lease and constitutes good cause for termination of the tenancy. A single violation of any provision of the addendum shall be deemed a serious violation and a material and irreparable noncompliance. It is understood that a single violation shall be good cause for immediate termination of the lease. Unless otherwise provided by law, proof of violation shall not require a criminal conviction.

7. In case of conflict between provisions of this addendum and other provisions of the lease, the provisions of the addendum shall govern.

8. This LEASE ADDENDUM is incorporated into the lease executed or renewed this day between Landlord and Tenant(s).

Signed on_____[date]: _____

_____   _____
Tenant(s)   Signature(s)

                                              [signed by each tenant]

Manager's Signature: _____ Date: _____

FORM 4-4   Crime-free lease addendum.

Under the provisions of the Soldiers and Sailor's Civil Right Act of 1940, residents who are currently active in military service or who enter military service after signing a rental agreement or lease have a right to terminate their rental agreement provided that certain conditions are met. Management requires that steps be taken as outlined below and that the tenant(s) agree to the following terms:

1. Tenant(s) must notify by mail or written notice of their intent to terminate their tenancy for verifiable military reasons to the manager.

2. The termination notice must include the exact date of when tenant(s) plan to vacate the property.

3. Once a notice of intent to move is mailed or delivered, the tenancy will terminate 30 days after the next rent due date. For example, if the next rent due date is May 1 and the tenant mails a notice on April 26, the tenancy will terminate on May 30.

4. Mail any notice or communication to the manager at the following address:

5. The manager may show the premises to any prospective resident any time during the following hours: _____. If the tenant(s) can't be reached after the manager has made a good faith effort to do so, the manager or manager's agent may enter and show the rental.

6. If this military option is exercised, tenant(s) agrees to:

   a. Promptly return the keys to the manager and completely move and vacate the premises on or before the date stated in the termination notice.

   b. Leave the rental in a clean condition and free of any and all damages.

   c. Provide a forwarding address to the manager prior to vacating the rental.

7. The security deposit will be returned provided that the tenant(s) has complied with the above terms, there are no unpaid outstanding charges of any kind due from the tenant, and there are no damages to the property other than normal wear and tear.

Tenant's Signature: _____ Date: _____

Manager's Signature:_____ Date: _____

FORM 4-5 Military addendum to residential lease.

If the rental property has limited parking, or there are other reasons to control the parking, Form 4-6 may be used for that purpose. It also can be used when you want to rent parking spaces. For example, the rental unit may have outside unrestricted parking and also have carports. Form 4-6 could be used to cover rental of the carports.

If you have garages on your rental property, and the garages do not come automatically with a rental unit and are rented separately, you will need to use a garage rental agreement similar to Form 4-7.

Date:

Tenant: _____

Car description:_____

Make: _____ Model:_____

Year: _____ Color: _____

Tag number: _____ State issued: _____

Parking address: _____

Rental period from: _____ To: _____

Rate per Month: _____ Biweekly:_____

A month's rent in the amount of _____, a security deposit in the amount of _____, and the last month's rent in the amount of _____ have been received. A penalty of _____ per month will apply for each payment received after the 5th of each month. Rent is due on the first day of the preceding month. If the tenant breaks the lease at any time before the lease expires, the security deposit and the last month's rent will be forfeited. The tenant must notify the manager in writing 30 days before the lease expires of the intention to vacate or renew the lease. Failure to do so will be considered a breach of contract and result in forfeiture of all security deposits.

Tenant's Signature: _____ Date: _____

Manager's Signature: _____ Date: _____

FORM 4-6   Parking agreement.

_____ (Renter(s)) agrees to rent garage located at
_____.

The term of this agreement is month-to-month with a minimum term of _____ months starting and continuing until terminated by either party as provided in this agreement

If renter vacates before the minimum term, renter agrees to be responsible for payment of a rerental fee of $ _____ that will be due to cover the cost of obtaining a new renter.

The discount rental rate is $ _____ per month when paid by the _____ of the month, which is the rent due date. The normal rent if paid after the _____ day of the month is $ _____ . In the event the rent is received more than _____ days after the rent due date, there is an additional late fee. The late fee is a per-day late fee assessed at $ _____ per day.

A security deposit of $ _____ is required. This deposit is refundable to the renter at the end of the rental agreement as long as possession of the garage is returned in the same condition it was given and the renter is not in default. Either party must give the other a written notice at least 30 days before the end of any rental month if either desires to end the agreement.

Renter agrees to the following terms:

FORM 4-7   Garage rental agreement.

1. In the event a check is not paid by a bank and is returned to the manager, a fee of $ _____ shall be due immediately.

2. Renter agrees to provide his or her own lock or security measures. The manager and the owner are not responsible for any security.

3. Renter agrees to carry insurance on belongings in the garage. Manager and owner are not liable for any loss or damage to items stored in the garage or storage facility.

4. Renter shall not store any hazardous, explosive, inflammable, illegal, or combustible materials in the facility.

5. Renter shall not keep any pets or animals in the facility.

6. Renter is responsible for keeping the facility and the surrounding area clean and free from oil and grease.

7. The manager has the right to enter the storage space for periodic inspections.

8. Renter shall make no alterations to the storage space without written consent of the owner.

9. Manager is not responsible for snow removal.

10. Renter agrees not to disturb or create conflict with renters or neighbors who may be living on or near the premises adjacent to the facility. Loud noises are not permitted in and around the premises.

11. No doorways or walkways are to be blocked at any time, and no unmovable items may be left outside the facility or on the common driveway or parking areas. No car parts are to be stored outside of the garage.

12. Any items left outside, including a nonoperative vehicle, will be removed at the Renter's expense if left unattended for more than three days, No car repair or painting is permitted on the premises.

13. No business of any kind is to be operated on the premises without written permission of the owner. Renter shall not assign or sublet the storage space.

14. Unless otherwise agreed in writing, renter is responsible for upkeep and minor repairs of the facility.

15. In the event the premises are damaged by fire or other casualty and rendered unusable, either party may cancel this agreement.

16. In the event the renter fails to pay rent due under this agreement, or in any other way breaches this agreement, this agreement is terminated, and if state law permits, the landlord may deny the renter access to the facility and remove any property (at the renter's expense) belonging to the renter. For any unpaid rent or damages, the manager shall have the right to sell the property at public or private sale to recoup any losses.

I acknowledge that I have read and understand this agreement and have been given a copy on this date.

Renter's Signature:_____ Date: _____

Manager's Signature: _____ Date: _____

FORM 4-7   Garage rental agreement (continued).

Pets can be a big problem for a landlord. Tenants may be unreasonable regarding the care and handling of their pets. In addition, pets often damage the rental unit, especially the carpets. If you allow pets, restrictions need to be placed on them. In addition, to protect your property you need to require additional security. Form 4-8 and 4-9 may be used as an addendum to the lease. **Note:** If the pet is a certified service animal used by a handicapped person to help that person overcome his or her handicap, you should not require a deposit or extra rent.

Form 4-10 may be used when a tenant requests permission to have a waterbed in the rental unit. A leaking waterbed can do a lot of damage to a rental unit. Accordingly, it is important to protect management from liability when other tenants' property is damaged and also to protect the building.

Note: A number of states provide that a landlord may not prohibit a tenant from using a flotation bedding system in a dwelling unit, provided that the flotation bedding system does not violate applicable building codes. The tenant shall be required to carry in the tenant's name flotation insurance as is standard in the industry, in an amount deemed reasonable to protect the tenant and owner against personal injury and property damage to the dwelling units. In any case, the policy shall carry a loss-payable clause to the owner of the building.

The agreement becomes a part of the lease signed between _____ (Tenant) and _____ (Management).

By this agreement Tenant agrees that only the pet described and named below will occupy premises.

By signing this document, the tenant states that the pet is not a service animal needed for a handicapped individual.

No additional or different pet is authorized under this agreement.

Tenant agrees that the pet shall be kept under the direct control of Tenant at all times.

If pet becomes annoying, bothersome, or in any way a nuisance to other tenants or to the community, Tenant shall immediately upon notice from Manager remove the pet from the premises.

An additional pet deposit in the sum of $ _____ will be paid by the tenant. This amount is NONREFUNDABLE and does not prohibit Landlord from recovery of any and all damages to the subject premises caused by said pet.

Type of Pet: _____ Breed: _____

Name of Pet: _____ Age: _____ Weight: _____

Color of Pet: _____ License tag number: _____

All Tenants over 18 years of age residing in the unit must sign this pet agreement.

Date signed: _____

_____   _____   _____
Tenant   Tenant   Tenant

FORM 4-8   Pet agreement (Option 1).

Description of pet:_____(picture of pet must accompany this addendum)

Pet type: _____ Weight: _____ Color: _____

Pet owner: _____ Pet's name: _____

Other than the above-listed pet, no other animals of any kind are permitted on the rental premises (even on a short-term or temporary basis), including dogs, cats, birds, fish, reptiles, and any other animals. The manager grants to tenant permission to keep the above-described pet in the premises subject to the following terms and conditions, and this becomes part of the rental agreement

Additional Security Deposit $_____

Additional Monthly Rent $_____

Other Fee $_____

1. It is agreed between the parties that Tenant may keep the pet described above.

2. The additional deposit listed above may be used only after Tenant has vacated to apply, if necessary, toward carpet replacement, cleaning, spraying of the rental, repair of damages, or delinquent rent. The deposit or portion thereof will be returned within _____ days once any damages are assessed and it is proved that the pet has vacated the premises

3. Tenant agrees to purchase special liability insurance, with a minimal amount of $ ____ liability coverage that would cover injuries or damage that may be caused by the pet. Tenant also agrees to list landlord as an "additional insured" on the policy.

4. Tenant agrees that this agreement is only for the specific pet described above and agrees to not harbor, substitute, or "pet sit" any other pet and remove any of the pet's offspring within 30 days of birth. Any animal found on the premises other than the pet specified above will be considered a stray and removed at the tenant's expense.

5. Tenant agrees to have an identification tag on pets whenever they are outside the tenant's unit.

6. The pet shall be on a leash or otherwise under the tenant's control, and not left unattended, when it is outside tenant's unit.

7. Pet(s) are not permitted in the following restricted areas:

    [List areas such as clubhouse and weight room.]

8. Tenant agrees to immediately clean up after the pet, both inside and outside the premises, and to dispose of any pet waste promptly and properly.

9. Tenant agrees not to leave food or water for the pet outside the tenant's unit, where it may attract other animals.

10. Tenant agrees to abide by all local, city, or state ordinances, licensing, and health requirements regarding pets, including vaccinations.

11. Tenant agrees to do whatever is necessary to keep the pet from making noise that would cause an annoyance to others and take steps immediately to remedy complaints by neighbors or other residents made to the Manager.

continued

FORM 4-9 Pet agreement (Option 2).

12. Tenant agrees to pay immediately for any damage, loss, or expense caused by the pet. Any payment not made for such damage or expense will be considered additional rent due.

13. Failure to comply with the terms of this addendum shall give the manager the right to revoke permission to keep the pet and is also grounds for immediate termination of the rental agreement.

14. Tenant shall be liable for any damages caused by the pet, and the deposit shall be applied to said damages.

_____ _____ _____
Date signed   Tenant   Tenant

[All tenants over the age of 18 years must sign.]

Manger: _____

FORM 4-9 Pet agreement (Option 2) (continued).

Date: _____

Tenant(s), _____, have requested permission to have a waterbed at the following address: _____.

This addendum is hereby incorporated into the Rental Agreement dated _____ between Tenant(s) and _____ Owner. Tenant(s) agree to the following terms and conditions in exchange for permission to have waterbed on premises:

In consideration of the additional risks involved in waterbed installation, Tenant(s) agrees to pay additional deposit of $ _____.

At the end of the rental term, Manager will inspect the property for any damages that were caused by the waterbed and deduct from said deposit any monies needed for repairing and/or cleaning of floors or floor covering and any other related waterbed damages.

Tenant(s) agrees to pay promptly for any damages exceeding the amount of the waterbed deposit.

Tenant(s) agrees to keep only the waterbed approved by the manager. The waterbed shall consist of a mattress with specifications which meet the Waterbed Manufacturers' Association standards.

Tenant(s) agrees to allow Manager to inspect the waterbed installation at any reasonable times, and Tenant(s) agrees to remedy any problems or potential problems immediately.

Any money due related to waterbed damages or problems will be immediately considered additional rent due and grounds for termination of the rental agreement if not paid.

Tenant(s) agrees to consult with the Manager about the location of the waterbed. Tenant(s) agrees to hire qualified professionals to install and dismantle the bed according to the manufacturer's specifications and further agree not to relocate it without the Manager's consent.

FORM 4-10 Waterbed agreement.

Tenant(s) will furnish Manager with a copy of valid certificate of waterbed liability insurance policy for at least $100,000 covering the waterbed installation.

Tenant(s) also agrees to keep the insurance policy in force at all times and to renew the policy as necessary for continuous coverage and provide a copy of the renewal policy to Owner.

Tenant(s) agrees not to damage the waterbed or allow a guest to do the same and agrees to become personally liable for any and all damages should damage occur.

Tenant(s) agrees to pay immediately for any damage caused by the waterbed and will add $ _____ to the security deposit, any of which may be used for cleaning, repairs, or delinquent rent when Tenant(s) vacates. This deposit, or what remains of it when waterbed damages have been assessed, will be returned to Tenant(s) within _____ days after Tenant(s) vacates the property.

Failure to comply with any of the terms of this agreement allows Manager to exercise the right to revoke this permission to keep a waterbed should Tenant(s) violate this agreement.

The manager may revoke this permission for good cause.

Tenant(s): _____ Date: _____

Tenant(s): _____ Date: _____

Manager: _____ Date: _____

FORM 4-10 Waterbed agreement (continued).

The use of satellite dishes and antennas needs to be regulated. In addition, the installation or removal of the dishes and antennas may cause damage to your property. In some parts of the country, an improperly installed dish or antenna may draw lightning. Before getting permission for the installation of a dish or antenna, the tenant should be required to establish that he or she has insurance covering the dish or antenna and will comply with the manager's directions regarding their installation (see Form 4-11).

1. The tenant may install only one satellite dish or antenna within the premises that are leased to you, for your exclusive use. A satellite dish may not exceed 40 inches in diameter. An antenna or dish may receive but not transmit signals.

2. The location of the satellite dish or antenna is limited to inside your dwelling or in an area outside your dwelling such as a balcony, patio, or yard of which you have exclusive use under your lease. The location must be approved by the manager before it is installed. Installation is not permitted on any parking area, roof exterior wall, window, windowsill, fence, or common area or in an area that other residents are allowed to use. A satellite dish or antenna may not protrude beyond the vertical and horizontal space that is leased to you for your exclusive use.

continued

FORM 4-11 Satellite dish and antenna addendum to residential lease.

3. The installation must comply with reasonable safety standards; may not interfere with the cable, telephone, or electrical systems, or those of neighboring properties; may not be connected to the telecommunication systems; and may not be connected to our electrical system except by plugging into a 110-volt duplex receptacle. If the satellite dish or antenna is placed in a permitted outside area, it must be safely secured by one of three methods: securely attaching it to a portable, heavy object such as a small slab of concrete, clamping it to a part of the building's exterior that lies within your leased premises (such as a balcony or patio railing), or any other method approved by us. No other methods are allowed. The manager may require reasonable screening of the satellite dish or antenna by plants, etc.

4. Signal transmission from exterior dish or antenna to interior of dwelling. Tenant may not damage or alter the leased premises or drill holes through outside walls, door jams, windowsills, etc. The manager must approve the manner in which the signal is transmitted to the interior of the dwelling.

5. For safety purposes, tenant must obtain approval of (1) the strength and type of materials to be used for installation and (2) the person or company who will perform the installation. Installation must be done by a qualified person or company that has worker's compensation insurance and adequate public liability insurance.

6. Tenant must obtain any permits required by the city or county for the installation and comply with any applicable city or county ordinances.

7. The tenant has the sole responsibility for maintaining the dish or antenna and all related equipment. Management may temporarily remove the dish or antenna if necessary to make building repairs.

8. Tenant must remove the satellite dish or antenna and all related equipment when vacating the dwelling. Tenant must pay for any damages and for the cost of repairs or repainting that may be reasonably necessary to restore the leased premises to its condition prior to the installation of the satellite dish or antenna and related equipment.

9. Liability insurance coverage must be no less than $ _____ and must remain in force while the satellite dish or antenna remains installed. Tenant agrees to defend, indemnity, and hold management harmless from claims by others because of the equipment.

9. An additional security deposit in the amount of $ _____ is required to help protect management against possible repair costs, damages, or any failure to remove the satellite dish or antenna and related equipment at the time of move-out. Acceptance of a security deposit increase does not imply a right to drill into or alter the leased premises.

10. Tenant may start installation of a satellite dish or antenna only after signing this addendum, providing the manager with written evidence of liability insurance referred to in this addendum, paying the additional security deposit, and receiving the manager's written approval of the installation materials and the person or company who will do the installation.

Tenant:_____ Date: _____

Manager: _____ Date: _____

FORM 4-11   Satellite dish and antenna addendum to residential lease (continued).

Frequently, a landlord will be requested by a tenant to allow the tenant to relet the rental unit. Form 4-12 may be used to ensure that the terms by which the landlord granted permission are in writing to prevent any misunderstanding.

Form 4-13 may be used to allow the tenant to sublease the rental unit.

Address of the property: _____
Apt number:_____

City_____ , State _____ , Zip _____

Current Tenant(s): _____

Lease Expiration Date:_____

The Current Tenant(s) has requested permission to relet that rental residence. The Tenant(s) understands that in order for the manager to consider granting permission for reletting the premises, the Current Tenant(s) agrees to and complies with the following terms:

1. The Tenant(s) is responsible for any advertising costs incurred.

2. The Tenant(s) is responsible to show the premises and find the new Tenant(s).

    However, the new prospective Tenant(s) must complete a rental application and be approved by the manager. The manager has the sole right to accept or reject the new prospective Tenant(s) per his/her current credit and selection criteria.

3. Until new Tenant(s) has been accepted, signed a rental agreement, paid the first month's rent for the premises plus a deposit, and accepted the keys, the current Tenant(s) is not released from obligations according to the rental agreement.

4. Should a new resident be found but for whatever reason cancel or not be able to fulfill the initial obligations required to move in, the current Tenant(s) is still obligated to fulfill all responsibilities under his/her rental agreement.

5. If new Tenant(s) is accepted, the current Tenant(s) agrees to have deducted from his/her deposit monies that may be necessary to clean or repair the premises and move out at least _____ days prior to the new Tenant(s)'s move-in date.

5. The current Tenant(s) understands that he/she will be charged a reletting fee of $ _____.

6. The current Tenant(s) will turn in his/her keys and provide a forwarding address to the owner and under no circumstances give a copy of any key to the new Tenant(s).

7. The current Tenant(s) agrees to pay rent according to the terms of the agreement until the new Tenant(s)'s move-in date.

8. The current Tenant(s) understands that the security deposit is refundable provided that the Tenant(s) has complied with the terms herein, has no unpaid charges of any kind, and is not in violation of the rental agreement.

THE NEW TENANT(S), if accepted, must agree to pay a full month's rent in advance and a security deposit and sign a rental agreement.

continued

FORM 4-12 Relet agreement.

The above terms are accepted by the following parties:

Current Tenant(s):_____ Date: _____

New Tenant(s):_____ Date: _____

Manager: _____ Date: _____

FORM 4-12 Relet agreement (continued).

This residential sublease is entered into between _____ (Tenant), _____ (Subtenant), and _____, (Tenant(s)). The Tenant hereby subleases the residential unit located at:

to the Subtenant(s). The Subtenant(s) accepts the lease, and the Landlord by signing this sublease agrees to the sublease. The terms of the sublease are:

The sublease shall be for a period of _____, commencing on _____ day of _____, 20_____, and ending on _____ day of _____, 20_____.

The Subtenant shall pay Tenant the monthly rent of $_____ payable on the first day of every month. There will be a late fee of $_____ if the rent is not paid by the 5th of the month. The Subtenant agrees to pay to Tenant the sum of $_____ as a security deposit, to be promptly returned upon the termination of the sublease and compliance with all provisions of this sublease.

The Subtenant shall be responsible for providing all utilities except as noted below.

The Subtenant agrees to return possession of the premises at the conclusion of the lease in its present condition, except for normal wear and tear.

Only the following persons will reside on the premises:

The subtenant shall not further assign or sublease the premises without written permission of the Landlord and the Tenant.

No material or structural alterations of the premises will be made without the prior written permission of the Landlord and Tenant.

The Subtenant will comply with all zoning, health, and use ordinances.

Pets are not allowed on the premises without prior written permission of the Landlord and Tenant.

This sublease shall be subordinate to all present and future mortgages against the premises.

In the event that legal action is necessary to enforce any provisions of this contract, attorney fees may be recovered by the prevailing party.

Additional sublease terms: _____

Date signed _____

Landlord _____ Tenant_____

Subtenant _____

FORM 4-13 Sublease.

Often a tenant wants to share a rental unit with a roommate. Form 4-14 may be used to allow a roommate.

When there is a roommate, the landlord may request an additional security deposit from the roommate. Form 4-15 may be used for that purpose.

If a change to an executed lease is necessary, and both parties agree to it, the change may be made by adding an amendment to the lease. Forms 4-16 and 4-17 may be used for that purpose. Care should be taken to ensure that the amendment contains all the changed terms agreed to by the parties. Once signed by

---

_____ and _____, intending to share a dwelling unit located at
_____, in consideration of
the mutual promises contained in this agreement, agree as follows:

They shall share the unit as follows: _____

Rent shall be paid as follows: _____

Each party shall be responsible for his/her own long-distance and toll charges on the telephone bill(s) regardless of whose name the bill is in.

The other utilities and fees shall be paid as follows: _____

No party is obligated to pay another party's share of the rent or other bills, but in the event one party finds it necessary to pay a bill for another party to stop eviction or termination of service, the party paying shall have the right to reimbursement in full. In the event the nonpaying party fails to reimburse such amounts, the paying party shall be entitled to interest at the highest legal rate, attorneys' fees, and court costs if legal action is necessary.

The parties also agree:

  Smoking_____

  Overnight guests_____

The parties also agree

  to respect each other's privacy to keep the shared areas reasonably clean

  not to make unreasonable noise during normal sleeping hours

  not to leave food where it would invite infestation and to be courteous and considerate of the other's needs

  that if their guests do not follow these rules, such guests shall not be permitted in the unit

  not to do anything that violates the lease and could cause eviction

The parties further agree as follows:

Date signed _____

_____(roommate) _____(roommate)

Approved by: _____Manager

FORM 4-14 Roommate agreement.

The agreement is an addendum to the security deposit regarding the rental unit located at_____.

The following terms are agreed to by the following Tenant(s)s (roommates):

The security deposit stays with the manager of the rental unit until the last roommate or tenant vacates the rental. All roommates/tenants agree to give a forwarding address to the manager before vacating the premises. If one or more roommates move out prior to the others, it has been agreed among all parties that the balance of the security deposit (after the final accounting of any debts or charges owed) will be refunded and/or divided according to the instructions below after the last roommate vacates.

If additional roommates are added to the rental agreement, and they contribute to the security deposit, it is understood that all parties (both old and new) must agree to the original instructions below regarding disbursement of any deposit due at the termination of the tenancy. However, any disbursement of deposits will not apply to any roommate who did not contribute monies to the deposit.

The final accounting and itemization of the security deposit, including any refund due, will be equally divided among all roommates, whether or not they were the last ones residing at the premises at the conclusion of the tenancy.

The final accounting and itemization of the security deposit, including any refund due, will be given to the last roommate still residing in the premises at the termination of this tenancy. In the event there is more than one roommate residing at the termination of tenancy, then any refund due shall be equally divided among those remaining individuals.

A copy of the final accounting and itemization of security deposit, including any refund due, will be sent the individual(s) who paid the deposit (and based on the proportions paid) regardless of who is residing in the premises at the time the termination of this tenancy. Therefore, if two people each contributed 50 percent of the total deposit paid, then only those two people will receive 50 percent of the deposit due, even if one is no longer living in the premises and others later moved in and stayed until the tenancy ended.

The undersigned Tenant(s)/(roommates) acknowledge that they have read and understood this Roommate Security Deposit Addendum. And they further agree that the security deposit stays with the owner until the tenancy is terminated and all rents, debts, charges, and damages have been paid.

Date Signed: _____

Tenant _____

Tenant: _____

Tenant: _____

Tenant: _____

Manager: _____

FORM 4-15   Roommate security deposit addendum.

both parties, the original lease is modified as set forth in the amendment. Note that the standard leases recommended in this chapter all contain the clause that amendments to the lease must be in writing.

Form 4-18 may be used to extend an original lease.

Date: _____

To: _____ (current tenant)

Both Landlord and Tenant(s) agree to the below change(s) to the lease entered into between the parties on _____ [date original lease signed] regarding the property located at _____.

Effective the following date _____, the lease will be changed as follows:

The changes or amendments are based in part on the following reasons:

Date signed: _____ Manager:_____

Date signed: _____ Tenant(s): _____

FORM 4-16   Notice of change—amendment to rental agreement (Option 1).

This is an Amendment to the lease or rental agreement dated _____ ("the Agreement") between _____ ("Manager") and _____ ("Tenant(s)") regarding property located at _____ .

Manager and Tenant agree to the following changes and/or additions to the Agreement:

_____

_____

_____

_____

_____

_____

_____

_____

_____

Date _____ Manager _____

Date _____ Tenant_____

Date _____ Tenant_____

FORM 4-17   Amendment to lease or rental agreement (Option 2).

This amendment extends the lease between the parties below that was entered into on _____ [date of original lease] between _____, (Landlord), and _____ and _____, (Tenant(s)).

The Landlord and Tenant for good and valuable consideration hereby extend the said lease for a period of _____ (months) (years) commencing on _____ and terminating on _____, 20_____.

All other terms of the original lease as hereby extended shall remain in force.

Signed this _____ day of _____, 20_____.

_____   _____   _____
Landlord   Tenant   Tenant

FORM 4-18   Extension of lease.

When the landlord has an option to extend the lease, Form 4-19 may be used. It should be delivered to the tenant by certified mail or another type of delivery that gives the landlord proof that the tenant received the notice.

Frequently, prospective tenants want some assurance regarding future rent increases. In long-term leases, be careful about agreeing to limit increases in rent, especially during periods of rising inflation. Form 4-20 may be used to limit rent increases.

Form 4-21 may be used to notify a tenant of possible lead-based paint. **Note:** Property constructed before 1978 may have lead-based paint.

Date: _____

_____[name and address]

Re: Notice to exercise option to extend lease

To: _____[lessee]

This is to officially notify you that we are exercising our option to extend the lease on the property located at [address of property].

Under the terms of the present lease, we have the option to extend or renew the said lease for a _____ term. Pursuant to the lease options, you are advised that it is our election to exercise the option to renew or extend the lease on the terms of the present lease.

Sincerely,

Lessor

FORM 4-19   Notice to exercise option to extend lease.

This agreement is between _____, Tenant(s), and Landlord, regarding rental premises located at _____ and is incorporated into the residential lease between the parties regarding the rental premises that was executed on _____ date (date original lease was signed).

The tenant requests an option to renew the rental agreement, upon its expiration, with a cap or limit to the amount of future rent increase the landlord can place on the renewal of the lease. In return for this agreement, the tenant agrees to pay to the landlord a non-refundable option fee of $ _____ or agrees to _____.

By virtue of this agreement, the tenant has the right to renew or extend his or her rental agreement at the stated location for an additional period once the initial rental/lease agreement expires. The initial rental/lease agreement between the two parties begins _____ and ends _____.

This option also limits any future rent increases to no more than _____ percent or to no more than the dollar amount of $ _____. This option to renew and limit the rent increase is guaranteed as long as the terms of the lease are fully complied with and the tenant(s) are not in default on rental payments or other conditions set forth in the lease between the parties dated _____.

Landlord gives the tenant(s) the option to renew/extend the rental lease for another term of _____ beginning on expiration of original term for period stated above and to limit any future rent increase to no more than _____ percent or no more than the dollar amount $ _____.

Tenant(s) understands and agrees to notify the manager at least _____ days/months before expiration of the original term if tenant(s) plans to exercise the option to extend the lease. This notification must be in writing, signed by all tenants, and delivered to the manager at the following address:

Failure to properly exercise this option will cause the lease to expire and the option consideration to be forfeited.

Should tenant violate any of the terms stated in the rental/lease agreement, such violation may be immediate cause for termination and forfeiture of option consideration.

The tenant(s) acknowledges that he or she has read and understands this agreement and has been given a copy of this agreement.

Date signed: _____

Tenants(s): _____ Manager:_____

FORM 4-20 Option to limit future rent increases.

NOTICE: Lead-Based Paint Warning

Housing built prior to 1978 may contain lead-based paint. Lead from paint, paint chips, and dust can pose health hazards if not taken care of properly. Lead exposure is especially harmful to young children and pregnant women. Before renting pre-1978 housing, land-lords must disclose the presence of known lead-based paint and lead-based-paint hazards in the dwelling. Tenants must receive a federally approved pamphlet on lead poisoning prevention.

Presence of lead-based paint or lead-based-paint hazards (check one below):

_____ Known lead-based paint or lead-based-paint hazards are present in the housing (explain):

_____ Lessor has no knowledge of lead-based paint and/or lead-based-paint hazards in the housing.

Records and reports available to the lessor (check one below):

_____ Lessor has provided the lessee with all available records and reports pertaining to lead-based paint and/or lead-based-paint hazards in the housing (list documents below).

_____ Lessor has no reports or records pertaining to lead-based paint and/or lead-based-paint hazards in the housing.

Acknowledgment (initial)

_____ Lessee has received copies of all information listed above.

_____ Lessee has received the pamphlet "Protect Your Family from Lead in Your Home."

Agency's Acknowledgment (initial)

_____ The Agency has informed the lessor of the lessor's obligations under 42 U.S.C. 4582(d) and is aware of his/her responsibility to ensure compliance.

Certification of Accuracy

The following parties have reviewed this notice and, certify that to the best of their knowledge, the information above is true and accurate.

Lessor_____ Date_____

Lessee_____ Date_____

FORM 4-21   Disclosure of information on lead-based paint and lead-based paint hazards.

Rarely will Form 4-22 need to be used. However, if there are certain items about which you need to advise an applicant before the signing of a lease, this form can be used for that purpose and for any other type of disclosure.

The landlord needs a checklist to ensure that all new tenants have received the required information and documents. A copy of this checklist (see Form 4-23) should be retained in the tenant's file during the tenancy.

Re: Residential property located at: _____

Dear _____

This notice is to inform you that the property you are applying for at the above address has a unique set of conditions related to it that are not readily apparent. These conditions in no way take away from the safety of the building, but at times could require either adjustments on your part or a reduction in the enjoyment of the dwelling.

The following conditions may exist during your tenancy: _____

Though this may seem minor, it is our responsibility to notify you of everything related to the rental dwelling, so that you will be fully informed in making a decision about your next residence.

Sincerely,

Manager

FORM 4-22   Nonapparent disclosure regarding rental property.

Tenant: _____

Address: _____

Tenant has received or completed the following:

(Initial by tenant)

_____ Copy of signed rental agreement and addenda

_____ New Resident Manual

_____ Inspection of rental unit with manager

_____ Completed Property Condition Checklist

_____ Inspection of additional areas and parking/storage space(s) with manager

_____ Tenant has read and signed the Lead Disclosure form (if applicable)

_____ Tenant has received a copy of the Resident Rules and Regulations

_____ Introduction to special customer programs (introductory letters with benefits)

_____ Pet and/or parking policies (if applicable)

       Date_____ Account number_____

_____ Connect utilities _____

       _____

_____ Connect utilities _____

       _____

_____ Other items _____

Note: Keys will not be issued until everything on this list is completed.

FORM 4-23   Rental checklist.

A move-in payment schedule (see Form 4-24) often is used by landlords to ensure that there is no disagreement about what payments are due before the keys are surrendered to the tenant(s).

Often tenants will agree to perform maintenance on the property in return for reduced rent. If this is the case, Form 4-25 may be added to the lease.

Date: _____

The following payments are due to cover initial move-in charges and rent at the following address: _____. Upon the payment of the below-listed monies and the signing of the appropriate documents, the keys to the residential home will be given to the tenant(s).

First Month's Rent:_____

Security Deposit:_____

Application Fee: _____

Key Deposit: _____

Other Deposits:_____

Tenant agrees to pay the total amount due in the following manner: _____

Tenant understands that if payment is not made as agreed, the rental/ lease agreement becomes void and any money given becomes nonrefundable and is applied to rent for the number of days the premises is held or occupied as well as to rerenting expenses.

Date:_____

Signed: _____Applicant _____Applicant

Date:_____

Signed_____Manager

FORM 4-24   Move-in payment schedule.

It is agreed that the rental required in this lease is a reduced rate because of the Tenant's agreement to accept the responsibilities outlined in the following paragraph. Tenant agrees that he or she has inspected the subject premises, furnishings, and equipment and that the same now are in good order and condition except as herein noted.

Tenant agrees to be responsible for all plumbing repairs, including but not limited to leaks, stoppage, frozen pipes and water damage, appliances, furnishings, equipment, and the entire premises, including but not limited to glass, screens, and doors.

 Tenant will keep the grounds clean and neat and free of trash and debris, including mowing the lawn and trimming trees and shrubs.

FORM 4-25   No-fault maintenance plan.

The parties agree that this paragraph amends and modifies other language in the Lease Agreement form, the Rules and Regulations that are a part of that, and Landlord's duty to maintain the subject premise.

Date:_____ Tenant_____

Date:_____ Manager _____

FORM 4-25 No-fault maintenance plan (continued).

For tenants who are paid every two weeks or weekly, it may be to your advantage and their advantage to make the rent payable on a payday plan, rather than on the first of every month. Form 4-26 may be used to establish a payday payment plan.

Date: _____

Resident:_____

Address: _____

Dear_____(Resident)

This letter provides you with the opportunity to pay your rent in biweekly payments rather than in the larger monthly sum. It appears that you may want to benefit from our new payday rent payment plan.

Many residents are paid every two weeks, and some residents like the convenience of paying rent biweekly at the same time they receive their paychecks. In this way, you can budget your money better by making smaller rent payments every two weeks instead of one big monthly payment on the first day of each month.

If you select this payday payment plan option, your rent payment will be due the same day every other week, in your case every other _____ (day of week due).

By having payments due on _____, you have time to receive your paycheck on _____ and mail, deliver, or deposit the required rent to us by the _____ due date, before any additional late charges would be due. Your rent would be in equal payment amounts.

For the convenience and privilege of paying biweekly instead of once a month, the amount of each biweekly payday payment would be $ _____.

If at any time you wish to switch back your payment plan, simply give us a 30-day advance notice.

If you wish to take advantage of this offer, please contact us within the next three days if you prefer to pay biweekly using the Payday Payment Plan. The manager is available between the hours of _____ and _____daily to discuss this program with you.

Sincerely,

Manager

FORM 4-26 Payday payment plan.

Form 4-27 may be used to ensure that a new tenant has transferred the utilities into his or her name.

To Applicant(s):

Your rental application has been accepted. However, before you can take possession of the home or apartment, this form must be completed within _____ days and signed by representatives of each utility company that will provide utility service to you. These are services that according to the rental agreement, as Tenant(s), you are responsible for. You must apply in person at each utility company and make the necessary arrangements. Your signature gives permission for the manager to verify the following information provided by the utility company.

Tenant(s)'s signature:_____

To Utility Companies:_____

We have accepted the following applicant(s):

_____residency at:

_____

Property is managed by:_____

It is important that the utility be put into the Tenant(s)'s name as soon as possible to provide correct billing and payments. The above applicant/Tenant(s) gives permission for the information below to be provided to the manager to complete the rental application process. Thank you for your assistance.

Gas company: _____

Gas service to be turned on/transferred to applicant/Tenant(s) on the following date:

_____

Name on account:_____

Amount of deposit required: $ _____ Account number:_____

Signed by gas company representative_____ Date _____

Electric power company: _____

Utility to be turned on/transferred to applicant/Tenant(s) on following date:_____

Name on account:_____

Amount of deposit required: $ _____ Account number: _____

Signed by power company representative: _____ Date _____

Water department: _____

Utility to be turned on/transferred to applicant/Tenant(s) on following date:_____

Name on account:_____

Amount of deposit required: $ _____ Account number:_____

Signed by water dept. representative _____ Date _____

FORM 4-27   Utilities transfer form.

It is important that management keep track of all keys to a rental unit. Failure to do so may subject the landlord/owner to civil liability when someone enters the rental unit using a key. One method is to require that each time a key is issued to a tenant, the tenant must sign a receipt and the receipts are retained for the life of the tenancy (see Form 4-28). When a tenancy ends, management is under a duty to change the locks in the apartment. When one of my sons was attending university, a former tenant went into his college apartment and stole his computer. The apartment complex was required to replace the computer because it had failed to change the locks on the apartment when the prior tenant moved out.

Form 4-29 should be provided to the tenant(s) at both move-in and move-out to inform the tenant(s) what is necessary for them to get the full deposit back.

Rules and regulations (see Form 4-30) are a necessary requirement to help ensure that a tenancy is problem-free. They also provide the tenants with information about what is expected of them. A copy should be given to each new tenant, and the tenant should be required to acknowledge receipt of a copy of them.

Form 4-31 should be used to record the condition of the premises when the new tenant takes possession. It should be retained in the tenant files, so that the condition of the property may be compared at move-out to determine the extent, if any, of damages to the property during the tenancy.

Tenant(s):_____

Address: _____

Tenant(s) have received the following number of keys: _____

Entrance door keys: _____

Other keys: _____ for the following: _____

Tenant(s) acknowledges receipt of the keys referred to above.

Loss of any keys must be reported immediately to the manager.

It is agreed that the tenant will not add any additional locks or make any lock changes or additional keys without the manager's written permission. It is further understood that if the Tenant(s) is permitted to rekey or add/change the locks, a set of new keys will be given immediately to the manager.

At the end of the rental relationship all keys are required to be returned by the tenants.

The Tenant(s) acknowledges receipt of the copy of this statement.

Signed/Tenant(s): _____ Date: _____

Signed Manager: _____ Date: _____

FORM 4-28 Receipt for keys.

Date: _____

Dear_____(Resident)

This list is provided at move-in and move-out so that you can take the necessary steps to avoid these expenses and do what is necessary to get all of your deposit back.

Cleaning (if not cleaned by you)

Refrigerator	$40
Stove top or oven	$25–$50
Kitchen cabinet or countertop	$20
Kitchen or bathroom floor	$25
Bathtub/shower	$25
Toilet	$25
Carpet cleaning or deodorizing	$100–$150
Extensive cleaning	$75 per hour

Damages

Remove crayon or other marks	$25
Small/large nail hole repair	$10–$25
Replace interior/exterior door	$100–$250
Replace sliding glass door	$200
Replace faucets	$50
Replace bathroom mirror or cabinet	$50–$75
Replace shower heads	$15
Replace toilet	$155
Replace garbage disposal	$100
Replace countertop	$250–$450
Repair windowpane	$50–$150
Replace blinds	$75
Replace tile/linoleum	$200–$450

Missing Items

Replace light bulb	$2
Light fixture globe	$15
Light fixture	$50
Electrical outlet/switch	$5
Electrical cover plate	$2
Replace key	$2

FORM 4-29   To receive your full deposit back when you move.

Replace shower curtain	$10
Replace refrigerator shelves	$25
Replace oven knob	$8
Replace window screen	$25
Additional Charges	
Replace door lock	$25
Replace curtain rod or towel bars	$20
Replace smoke detector	$40
Remove junk and debris	$75
Fumigate for fleas	$150
Replace fire extinguisher	$40
Replace thermostat	$75
Remove wallpaper	$150
Repaint wall	$25
Vacuum entire unit	$50
Clear drain stoppage	$75
Fence replacement	$25 per foot

Tenant(s) agrees that subject to the conditions above, the deposit will be refunded in full within _____ days after vacating premises. It is understood that the above amounts are minimum charges.

Signed:

Tenant(s): _____ Date: _____

FORM 4-29 To receive your full deposit back when you move (continued).

1. No signs, notices, or advertisements shall be attached to or displayed by tenant on or about said premises. Additionally, no antenna or satellite dish shall be attached to or displayed on or about the premises without manager's written consent.

2. Profane, obscene, loud, or boisterous language or unseemly behavior and conduct is prohibited, and Tenant obligates himself or herself, and those under him or her, not to do or permit to be done anything that will annoy, harass, embarrass, or inconvenience any of the other tenants or occupants in the subject or adjoining premises.

3. No motor vehicles shall be kept on the property that are unlicensed, inoperable, or in damaged condition. Damaged condition includes, but is not limited to, flat tires. Any such vehicle that remains on the property for more than five days after a notice to

continued

FORM 4-30 Residents' rules and regulations.

remove it has been placed on the vehicle will be towed and stored at the tenant's and/or the vehicle owner's expense.

4. In keeping with Fire Safety Standards, all motorized vehicles including motorcycles, must be parked outside. No motorized vehicles shall be parked in any building structure on the property except authorized garage spaces.

5. In accordance with Fire Safety Standards and other safety regulations, no tenant shall maintain, or allow to be maintained, any auxiliary heating units, air-conditioning units, or air-filtering units without prior inspection and written approval of the manager.

6. The sound of musical instruments, radios, televisions, phonographs, and singing shall at all times be limited in volume to a point that is not objectionable to other tenants or occupants in the subject or adjoining premises.

7. Tenant shall not alter, replace, or add locks or bolts or install any other attachments, such as doorknockers, on any door, except when prior approval is given by the manager.

8. Only persons employed by manager or his agent shall adjust or have anything to do with the heating or air-conditioning plants or with the repair or adjustment of any plumbing, stove, refrigerator, dishwasher, or any other equipment that is furnished by Landlord or is part of the subject premises.

9. No defacement of the interior or exterior of the buildings or the surrounding grounds will be tolerated.

10. No awning, Venetian blinds, or window guards shall be installed, except when prior approval is given by the manager.

11. No spikes, hooks, or nails shall be driven into the walls, ceiling, or woodwork of the leased premises without consent of Landlord. No crating of or boxing of furniture or other articles will be allowed within the leased premises.

12. If furnished by Landlord, garbage disposal shall be only used in accordance with the disposal guidelines. All refuse shall be, in a timely manner, removed from the premises and placed outside in receptacles.

13. It is specifically understood that Landlord reserves solely to itself the right to alter, amend, modify, and add rules and regulations.

14. It is understood and agreed that Landlord shall not be responsible for items stored in storage areas.

15. Manager has the right immediately to remove combustible material from the premises or any storage area.

16. Manager will furnish two keys for each outside door of the premises. All keys must be returned to manager upon termination of the occupancy.

17. Lavatories, sinks, toilets, and all water and plumbing apparatus shall be used only for the purpose for which they were constructed. Sweepings, rubbish, rags, ashes, or other foreign substances shall not be thrown therein. Any damage to such apparatus, and the cost of clearing plumbing resulting from misuse, shall be the sole responsibility of, and will be borne by, Tenant.

FORM 4-30   Residents' rules and regulations (continued).

I have received a copy of the above rules and regulations and acknowledge that they are considered a part of the lease agreement.

Date signed: _____

Tenant _____   Tenant_____

FORM 4-30   Residents' rules and regulations (continued).

Address of property: _____

	Condition on Move-In	Condition on Move-Out	Estimated Cost of Damage Repair or Replacement
Living Room			
Door and Locks			
Drapes and Window			
Fireplace			
Floors and Floor			
Light Fixtures			
Smoke Detector			
Walls and Ceilings			
Windows, Screens, and Doors			
Other			
Kitchen			
Cabinets			
Counters			
Floors and Floor Coverings			
Light Fixtures			
Walls and Ceilings			
Stove/Oven			
Refrigerator			
Dishwasher			
Garbage Disposal			
Sink and Plumbing			
Windows, Screens, and Doors			

continued

FORM 4-31   General condition of rental premises checklist.

	Condition on Move-In	Condition on Move-Out	Estimated Cost of Damage Repair or Replacement
Smoke Detector			
Other			
Dining Room			
Floors and Floor Covering			
Walls and Ceilings			
Light Fixtures			
Windows, Screens, and Doors			
Smoke Detector			
Other			
Bathroom	1st Bath 2nd Bath	1st Bath 2nd Bath	
Floors and Floor Coverings			
Walls and Ceilings			
Windows, Screens, and Doors			
Light Fixtures			
Bathtub/Shower			
Sink and Counters			
Toilet			
Other			
Bedroom	1st 2nd 3rd Bedroom	1st 2nd 3rd Bedroom	
Floors and Floor Coverings			
Windows, Screens, and Doors			
Walls & Ceilings			
Light Fixtures			
Smoke Detector			
Other			
Other Areas			
Heating System			
Air-Conditioning			
Lawn/Garden			

FORM 4-31   General condition of rental premises checklist (continued).

	Condition on Move-In	Condition on Move-Out	Estimated Cost of Damage Repair or Replacement
Stairs and Hallway			
Patio, Terrace, Deck, etc.			
Basement			
Parking Area			
Other			

FORM 4-31 General condition of rental premises checklist (continued).

Form 4-32 should be used when the rental unit is a furnished rental.

	Condition on Move-In	Condition on Move-Out	Estimated Cost of Damage Repair or Replacement
Living Room			
Coffee Table			
End Tables			
Lamps			
Chairs			
Sofa			
Other			
Kitchen			
Broiler Pan			
Ice Trays			
Other			
Dining Room			
Chairs			
Stools			
Table			
Other			

continued

FORM 4-32 General condition of furnished property.

	Condition on Move-In	Condition on Move-Out	Estimated Cost of Damage Repair or Replacement
Bathroom	1st Bath 2nd Bath	1st Bath 2nd Bath	
Mirrors			
Shower Curtain			
Hamper			
Other			
Bedroom	1st 2nd 3rd Bedroom	1st 2nd 3rd Bedroom	
Beds			
Ceiling fans			
Chests			
Chairs			
Dressing Tables			
Lamps			
Mirrors			
Night Tables			
Other			
Other Areas			
Bookcases			
Desks			
Pictures			
Other			

Comments _____

_____

_____

Tenant Checklist completed on moving in on _____ and approved by:

_____   _____
Manager   Tenant

_____   _____
Tenant   Tenant

FORM 4-32   General condition of furnished property (continued).

Checklist completed on moving out on _____ and approved by:

_____   _____
Manager   Tenant

_____   _____
Tenant   Tenant

[   ] Tenants acknowledge that all smoke detectors and fire extinguishers were tested in their presence and found to be in working order, and that the testing procedure was explained to them. Tenants agree to test all detectors at least once a quarter and to report any problems to Manager in writing. Tenants agree that they are responsible for replacing all smoke detector batteries as necessary.

FORM 4-32   General condition of furnished property (continued).

5
Managing the Property

This chapter includes a discussion of and the forms used for the day-to-day management of rental property.

Place and Method of Payment of Rent

The lease should specify where the tenant should pay the rent and how it should be paid. It is common practice to require no cash transactions and require instead that a tenant pay only by check or money order. If a tenant's checks do not clear the bank, you may require payment by money order. If you allow tenants to pay by mail, although it is convenient, the payment is not considered late if the envelope is postmarked on the due date. Issues can be raised about whether the check was lost in the mail.

Many landlords send someone to each unit every month to collect the rent. This is an old-fashioned method, and often the tenant is not home. In some cases, however, it is useful to have face-to-face contact with the tenant to collect the rent. If you have an on-site office, you should have the tenant pay at that office. This works only when you have an office on-site and a convenient drop box. It probably will not be feasible to require the tenant to drive across town to make a payment, because some tenants won't get around to delivering the check.

If the rental agreement does not specify where the rent is to be paid, state law applies. For example unless there is a different agreement in the lease, you must pick up the rent at the rental unit in Alaska, Arizona, Connecticut, Iowa, Kansas, Kentucky, Louisiana, Nebraska, New Mexico, New York, Oklahoma, Rhode

Island, South Carolina, and Tennessee. *Always put a clause in the lease specifying the location where the rent is to be paid.*

Accountability

Frequently, landlords provide a notice of accountability to new residents to let them know the importance of establishing a good credit record. A letter similar to the one in Form 5-1 may be used for this purpose.

Date: _____

Dear _____[new tenant]:

Welcome to our community. As a new resident, it is important you know that our company works with one or more nationwide credit reporting agencies. The functions of these agencies are to track and maintain credit records on residents, including information about your credit history and pay performance as a resident. This information is then made available to future landlords, property managers, lenders, creditors, and employers as they request it.

The management of this property is our business. We promise to treat you in a professional, businesslike manner, and we expect to be treated the same way in return. It is our policy to hold all our residents accountable for their actions—whether favorable or unfavorable. Your reputation as a resident and as a creditworthy individual is on the line. The payment reputation you establish here will remain on your records for many years to come.

Any business, company, or person who reviews your record in the future will have access to the payment records you establish with us. To keep you advised about the status of your record, the manager will do a semiannual review of your payment record and give you a copy of all satisfactory reviews of that record. A good payment record should prove helpful to you. You can retain and use any satisfactory payment reviews to future landlords, banks, loan agencies, etc.

If you give us cause to report unfavorable information about you to credit reporting agencies, that will also be available to employers, banks, home mortgage companies, insurance companies, and other creditors with whom you wish to do business and who request a report. In most cases, the manager will advise you before submitting an adverse report. An adverse credit and rental history report can make it very difficult for you in the future to get the job you want, rent another apartment, purchase a car, or get a loan, including student and medical emergency loans.

Accordingly, a favorable record is vital to your future. You can use your time as a rental resident to build a good payment history and build your credit. If there is ever a dispute over the accuracy of information reported by a credit reporting agency, there are certain procedures that you may follow, including the right to be given the name and phone number of the agency reporting any information you dispute.

We reserve the right to furnish information regularly and routinely to credit reporting agencies about the performance of lease obligations by residents. Such information may

---

FORM 5-1   Notice of accountability.

be reported at any time and may include both favorable and unfavorable information regarding the resident's compliance with the lease, rules, and financial obligations. Generally, we will give a resident a 72-hour warning notice to correct or remedy a payment or lease violation before any information is reported to a credit reporting agency.

Sincerely,

_____

Manager

Date notice was delivered:_____ Delivered by: _____

Method of delivery (check appropriate):

Hand delivered to resident: _____ Sent by certified mail:_____

FORM 5-1 Notice of accountability (continued).

Resident Survey

Some landlords use a year-end resident survey (see Form 5-2) to find out information regarding any problems or concerns a tenant may have.

Date: _____

Dear: _____[tenant]

Each year management conducts a year-end survey so that we may better serve you. Please complete each question and return the survey in the enclosed or attached self-addressed stamped envelope.

1. How long have you resided in the home? _____
2. How did you first find out about the residence you are now renting? _____
3. What things do you most like about your present residence or the area? _____
4. What do you like the least about the residence?_____
5. How have your concerns or requests been taken care of? Satisfactorily or not satisfactorily? If not satisfactorily, please explain_____
6. Have you reported any concerns that were not taken care of? If so, what were they?

   _____

7. Name three stores in the local area where you prefer to shop: _____
8. Which school does your child or children attend?_____
9. How do you rate the local school? _____
10. Name two places you go for recreation (health spa, club, restaurant, country club, theater, library, bookstore, church socials, bowling alley, etc.):

    1. _____ 2. _____

continued

FORM 5-2 Year-end resident survey.

11. Of the following rental extras or upgrades, check the items or services you would like us to offer next year and would be willing to pay extra rent or a service fee for each month.

Computer _____   Renter's insurance _____

Ceiling fan _____   Internet access _____

Mini-satellite dish _____   Garage/extra storage _____

Water filter system_____   Monthly cable TV service_____

Extra phone jack_____   Weekly house cleaning_____

FORM 5-2   Year-end resident survey (continued).

Changes in Rent

Form 5-3 may be used to notify a tenant of a change in rent. **Note:** Make sure that the lease permits such a change.

Notice of Additional Charges

Form 5-4 may be used to notify the tenant that he or she is required under the terms of the lease to pay additional charges. **Note:** If the additional charges are because of failure to pay rent in a timely manner, use the appropriate form in Chapter 6.

Tenant Moving-Out Notice

If you find out that a tenant is considering moving, Form 5-5 may be sent to inform the tenant of the expenses involved in a move. **Note:** This letter should be sent only to a tenant you wish to keep.

Date: _____

Dear _____[tenant(s)]

Pursuant to the terms of the lease, you are notified that starting on the 1st day of _____, 20_____, the monthly rent on your leased property will be increased to the monthly total of $_____.

This is a change from your present rate of $_____.

Sincerely,

Manager

FORM 5-3   Notice of change in rent.

Date: _____

Dear _____[tenant(s)]

Pursuant to the terms of your lease, you are hereby notified that an additional sum of $_____ is due on or before [date].

The additional sum is due to the below factors:

[list reasons for additional charges]

Payment of the additional sum should be made directly to the manager.

Sincerely,

Manager

FORM 5-4   Notice of additional charges.

Date: _____

Dear_____[tenant]

I understand that you're thinking of moving. You are considered a valuable resident, and management would like for you to remain. List below is a checklist of the costs you'll have to pay if you do move out. This information is provided so that you will know up-front what the expenses are going to be before you make the decision to move.

If you do decide to stay, I would certainly appreciate it if you would let us know before I rent the space to someone else. I really would feel terrible if that happened, because I've always valued you as a tenant. Anyway, here is the moving checklist that I use. I hope it helps you know in advance the money you will have to come up with:

1. A security deposit

2. Income lost (time off from work)

3. First (and possibly the second) month's rent in advance

4. The actual moving cost and packing and unpacking cost

5. Deposit on utilities

6. New telephone installation

7. Any items broken and replaced during the move

8. Any other items you may need in the new location

I hope this checklist has been helpful. If I can help out in any other way, please let me know. Please let me know in the next 10 days what you decide, so that I don't lease your unit to someone else without your knowing about it in advance. But you really ought to stay, because otherwise somebody else is going to take it, and we don't want to lose you.

Sincerely,

Manager

FORM 5-5   Tenant planning to move letter.

Early Renewal Program

Form 5-6 may be used to encourage tenants to renew their leases earlier. Generally, it is to your advantage to lock up good tenants for a lengthy period.

Property Address: _____

Date: _____

Dear: _____[tenant]

Your current lease will expire within the next 90 to 120 days, on _____.
Each year your rent is adjusted to account for increased expenses and inflation; however, we let residents help determine how much the rent increase will be. For the upcoming year, your rent increase will be between $20.00 and $100.00. This increase is necessary because of increasing operational expenses, taxes, and utilities. Because you are a valuable resident, we want to keep your increase to a minimum, and so we encourage you to respond to this letter as soon as possible. The rent increase will be only $20 if you renew your agreement before the following date: _____, after which your rent is subject to an additional increase of $40.00 per month if you renew after the above date and before _____.

If you do not renew prior to the _____ date, the maximum rent increase will be $100. As you can see, the earlier you renew your agreement, the more you save and the lower your rent increase will be.

The reason we offer the early renewal savings is that the sooner we know if you will be staying in the property, the less we have to prepare to advertise and rerent the premises. The sooner we know, the easier you make our job, and so we offer greater savings for letting us know early.

Please sign below and return this letter as soon as possible to the following address: _____ no later than _____ to take advantage of the biggest rent savings and discount. The date we actually receive this letter is the date we use to calculate your savings. We value your tenancy and hope you plan to stay and save as much as possible. After this letter is returned to us, we'll send back a copy for your records and an addendum to your rental agreement with the new rental rate. If you have any questions regarding your renewal savings, please call me at _____. Thank you for your cooperation.

RESPONSE

Yes, I wish to renew/extend my lease an additional year. I also wish to save as much money as possible on the rent increase. Please prepare a new lease for my signature.

Resident's signature: _____

Owner's signature: _____

Date received: _____

FORM 5-6   Renew early—save money.

Resident's Checklist

Form 5-7 may be used as a summer checklist for residents.

Date: _____

Dear: _____[tenant]

Before you travel out of town during the summer months, we would like to recommend the following steps to help prevent any problems from occurring in regard to your residence. If you are going to be away for an extended period, please advise us so that we can make occasional checks on your property.

____ Notify management of your absence. Call and inform us of any dates when you will be away from your rental for an extended period (beyond three days).

____ Leave an emergency number where you can be reached.

____ Prepay your rent. Before leaving, prepay the rent, especially if you are traveling near the rental due date. This way, you can avoid late fees and preserve your excellent payment and credit history. Reminder: We offer special automatic draft or electronic transfer payment plans that allow you to focus on your trip and not worry about mailing payments and possible late fees.

____ Use automatic timers for your lights. Lighted windows give the impression that someone is home. Your automatic timer can turn on your lights in the evenings and off in the morning.

____ Yard maintenance: If your rental agreement states that residents are responsible for yard maintenance (regular lawn cutting), be sure to make arrangements for someone to cut the grass during your absence. Management reserves the right to hire someone to cut the grass if it is left unattended for two weeks and bill the resident for the charges.

____ Stop newspaper and mail delivery. Stop all routine deliveries so that there is no evidence that you are away. Items accumulated at your front door, on your yard, or in your mailbox are signals that you are not home.

____ Inform your immediate neighbors. Designate and ask at least one neighbor to keep an eye on your property during your absence. Give that neighbor our telephone number in case a problem should arise. Please provide management with the name and phone number of the designated neighbor.

____ Secure all doors and windows. Weather changes can damage carpet, drapes, and furniture. Close and lock all doors and windows. Be sure we have duplicate keys to all locks.

____ Avoid leaving any appliances plugged in, including your television, computer, microwave, iron, toaster, and other small appliances. Check all cords for fraying to ensure that a fire will not occur while you are away.

continued

FORM 5-7 Summer checklist for residents.

_____ Check your gas stove's burners and oven. Before leaving your premises, always make a final check of the stove to ensure the burners are off to eliminate the possibility of a gas explosion.

_____ Eliminate the possibility of returning to an insect-infested home. Empty all trash containers and garbage bags and remove them from the home. Secure open food containers and put them in the refrigerator.

_____ Before an extended absence, water all houseplants and place them in the kitchen sink. Make arrangements for a friend to water your plants.

_____ Do not leave messages on your voice mail system or answering machine that reveal you are on a vacation or away for an extended period.

_____ Do not leave any animals unattended. If your lease permits a pet, do not leave pets in the residence unattended while you are gone.

Sincerely

Manager

FORM 5-7   Summer checklist for residents (continued).

Renter's Insurance

Encourage your tenants to have renter's insurance. Generally, when there are thefts, fires, and the like, and the tenant is insured, it is less likely that the tenant will try to get reimbursement from the landlord. Form 5-8 also advises the tenant that the landlord's insurance does not cover the tenant's property.

From: _____

Date: _____

To:_____

Dear:_____

Management wants to make sure your family's belongings are protected against fire or theft during the time you are residing on the property. The insurance management has on the building covers only the building itself against fire. Our insurance does not cover your property in the event of fire or burglary. If your child breaks a neighbor's window or your guest is accidentally injured because of a hazard you allowed to be left on your property, there is a lot you can lose by not having renter's insurance.

You need to protect your personal belongings against such calamities. To protect yourself, it is recommended that you obtain a renter's insurance policy, which most insurance companies provide. Most likely, your loss would come from theft, vandalism, or fire. In considering whether you need such insurance, consider how much your entertainment system is worth. What about your jewelry and other valuable possessions? In the event of a fire, do

FORM 5-8   Renter's insurance.

you know that all your furniture, clothing, and other possessions probably add up to tens of thousands of dollars? Many rental residents have learned through a tragedy that they lost everything because they did not buy renter's insurance.

If you are already carrying auto insurance, adding renter's insurance through the same company may cost you very little more. Most insurance companies offer a multipolicy discount if you add renter's insurance to your current policy. This will save you some money.

If you have no current policy, we can recommend a company that provides renter's insurance at a reasonable rate. Whatever you do, don't put your family's personal property at risk. Renter's insurance is something you do not want to be without. It's well worth it.

If you are not currently working with an insurance agent, below is the name and phone number of an insurance agent who should be able to assist you.

Be sure to tell him or her that you were referred by: _____

During the year, we may have representatives from the insurance company that has coverage on the building you are living in visit the dwelling to do an inspection and take pictures of the property's condition.

We always ask the insurance company to give us advance notice so that we may inform you ahead of time. We would appreciate your cooperation when we call on you.

Sincerely,

Manager

FORM 5-8   Renter's insurance (continued).

Resident's Release for Use of Recreational Items

If a tenant wants to use or install certain recreational items, a form similar to Form 5-9 should be used to obtain a release of liability from the tenant. This form can be used for a swimming pool, swing set, jungle gym set, and so on. **Note:** If there are defects to the item that management knows or should have known about, there is a duty to warn the other tenants of the defect.

Date: _____

To: Management, rental property located at _____

From: _____[tenant]

I, _____, resident of the above address, wish to use the recreational items located on the premises.

Those items include: [list items]

continued

FORM 5-9   Resident release for use of recreational items.

I, _____ (tenant) understand that the use of these items is NOT part of the rental agreement between myself and the owner. I hereby agree to bear sole responsibility for the setup, structure, maintenance, and ongoing upkeep of those items listed above.

I agree to bear sole liability and responsibility for any and all direct and indirect costs, damages, and expenses incurred as a result of any physical or other injury sustained or caused to myself, members of my family, or guests resulting from the use of the above recreational item(s).

I further agree not to hold the owner or managers responsible in any way for any injury or damages that may occur.

I have also purchased liability insurance that provides up to $_____ in coverage for possible injury or damages and have named the landlord as a coinsured under the policy.

Resident's signature:_____ Date:_____

Owner's signature: _____ Date:_____

FORM 5-9   Resident release for use of recreational items (continued).

Preparing for Cold Weather

Form 5-10 may be used to alert tenants about cold weather and advise them of the steps they need to take to prevent damage to the property.

Date: _____

Dear Residents:

Cold weather will soon be here. Please use the attached checklist to keep your heating bills down this winter and make your home warmer and safer for you and your family. Planning ahead can save you money and prevent frustration. Under the lease agreement, any preventable damage (such as freezing pipes) is your responsibility, so we want you to take all necessary precautions to avoid unnecessary costs.

Outside Preparation

- Check and close all the vents/windows to the basement/crawl space.
- Unhook your garden hoses.
- Prevent water lines from freezing by wrapping exterior pipes. Newspapers covered with a waterproof material may prevent freezing of the pipes.
- When the weather forecast is for extremely cold weather, leave outside faucets dripping but don't allow outside faucets to flow into the street, sidewalks, and other areas where people may walk.
- Check to ensure that the caulking around the outside windows and any weather-stripping around frames are still in place to stop cold air.

FORM 5-10   Preparation checklist for colder weather.

- Don't forget to close storm windows. Make sure storm chains, if present, are attached on any storm doors. This prevents strong winds from blowing the door off or damaging the door.

- Keep the gutters cleaned out. If they are clogged with leaves, the water will overflow and cause the house to rot or will back up under the roof and into the house.

Inside Preparation

- Keep the heat set so that it never goes below 50 degrees, even when you are not at home. If the temperature is forecast to drop below freezing, leave at least one inside faucet dripping lukewarm water so that both hot and cold pipes are protected.

- Leave cupboard doors open in the kitchen and bathrooms, so that the pipes inside will be exposed to heat.

If you will be away for more than two consecutive days this winter, please let us know at least one week in advance, so that we can check on your property if a sudden freeze occurs. We also want to be able to reach you in case of an emergency

If you have central heat/air, changing or cleaning the filters monthly can make a big difference in your energy bills. Make sure the attic access door is in place. If you have a fireplace, the chimneys need to be cleaned yearly or a chimney fire may occur. Call a professional to do a complete job and check the safety of the chimney.

Test your smoke alarm(s). There are more fires in the winter, and a smoke alarm is one of the best safety features. If you don't have one, or if it doesn't work, let us know. Make sure your smoke alarms have a battery and are working. You also might want to consider buying a small fire extinguisher for your kitchen and garage.

Again, the above-noted precautions are important for your safety and your family's. Should pipes freeze, don't use open flames to thaw out lines. This may catch the house on fire or, worse, create an explosion caused by expanding steam between two plugs of ice. Pipes don't always burst the first time they freeze. However, should a pipe burst, locate your water shutoff valve and quickly turn it off. If you don't know where the shutoff valve is, let us know now, before any problems occur. If the pipe that breaks is a hot water line, close the valve on the top of the water heater. If you think a plumber needs to be called, please use the plumber approved by us.

We greatly appreciate your efforts in helping to make sure your residence is kept warm and as safe as possible during the upcoming winter months.

Thank you.

Manager

FORM 5-10   Preparation checklist for colder weather (continued).

Lockout Assistance

Most tenants at one time or another will lock themselves out of their homes. Form 5-11 may be used to record the assistance and provide the necessary information to the tenant regarding the assistance.

Date: _____

The following resident, _____, requested assistance in getting into his/her residence because he/she was locked out of the premises located at
_____.

Date of request: _____

Time of request:_____

The resident was locked out because of the following reason: _____.

The resident understands that the owner or manager must check identification, review files, and verify that the individual requesting lock-out assistance is indeed a valid resident and current lease holder. Nonresidents are not permitted entry. The following identification was shown/given as proof that the individual was a current resident:_____

The resident understands and agrees to the following fees in regard to lockout assistance:

_____ Charge for lockout assistance during business hours: $15 from 9 a.m. to 5 p.m.

_____ Charge for lockout assistance outside business hours: $30 from 5 p.m. to 9 a.m.

An additional charge of $ _____ will be assessed if the resident's key is lost and the lock has to be replaced completely. All fees are due and payable at time assistance is provided.

Payment received from: _____

Amount received: $ _____

If payment is not received, resident agrees that the following amount of $ _____ is owed and that this amount will be immediately considered as additional rent due and paid by the following date _____ or the resident is subject to eviction for nonpayment.

It should also be noted that this is the _____ time the resident has needed lockout assistance. If assistance is requested more than three times, an additional fee of $ _____ will be assessed.

Resident's Signature: _____ Manager's Signature: _____

FORM 5-11   Lockout assistance receipt.

Holiday Season

Form 5-12 may be distributed to your tenant before the holiday season to help them prepare for the holidays. It also gives you a chance to communicate with the tenants. You also can use the letter to advise tenants of any changes or improvements planned for the coming year.

Lease Renewal

Several months before a tenant's lease is due to expire, you should send a letter to the tenant reminding him or her of the expiration and offering him or her an opportunity to renew the lease. Form 5-13 may be used for that purpose.

Date: _____

Dear _____[tenant]

I hope that you and your family have a very happy holiday and have a happy and healthy new year. Thank you to all tenants who have paid their rent on time and to those who have kept their homes nice.

There are a few changes for the new year. [list of changes]

We are trying to improve our maintenance and response to your service calls. Remember to call us at _____ should you need something. If no one is in, please leave your name, phone number, address, and what you need. Please be specific.

We hope that you stay with us for a long time. Thank you for all your help in keeping your home nice.

BEST WISHES for the NEW YEAR!

Sincerely,

Manager

FORM 5-12 Happy Holidays!

Date: _____

Dear _____

This letter is to remind you that your lease will expire on _____. Please advise us no later than _____ (date) whether you intend to renew your lease.

If so, we will prepare a new lease for your signature(s). If you do not intend to renew your lease, the keys should be delivered to us at the address below on or before the end of the lease along with your forwarding address. We will inspect the premises for damages, deduct any amounts necessary for repairs, and refund any remaining balance as required by law.

If we have not heard from you as specified above, we will assume that you will be vacating the premises and will arrange for a new tenant to move in at the end of your term.

Sincerely,

Manager

FORM 5-13 Reminder letter: continuation of tenancy.

Additional Tenant

Form 5-14 may be used to give permission for an additional resident in the rental home.

Date: _____

Dear _____

You have requested permission to add another resident and/or roommate to your rental agreement. Your request has been accepted and approved for an additional resident/and or roommate by the name of _____.

Before this new resident can move in, both you and him/her must sign a new updated rental agreement. In addition, below is a breakdown of any additional monies that must be collected:

$ _____ Rent for the following period

$ _____ Additional security deposit required.

$ _____ Additional fees or charges for _____

$ _____ Total due BEFORE move-in of additional resident/roommate

Please understand that you, as the current resident, will become jointly and severally liable for all current and future payments required of the new resident and for his or her performance of all other terms of the rental agreement. Please contact us as soon as possible, so that we can arrange to meet with both you and the new resident to sign the new rental agreement, collect all monies due, and give keys and all items and documents needed for move-in. We can be reached at _____ during our regular business hours: _____

Thank you for your continued cooperation.

Sincerely

Manager

FORM 5-14   Approval of additional resident.

Assignment of Lease

Frequently, a tenant will want to assign his or her lease. Form 5-15 may be used to take this action.

_____ ("Manager") and _____ ("Tenant(s)") and _____ ("Assignee") agree as follows:

Tenant(s) leased the premises at _____ from Manager.

The lease was signed on _____, and expires on _____.

Tenant(s) is to assigning the balance of Tenant(s)' lease to Assignee, beginning on _____, and ending on _____.

Tenant(s) understands that their financial responsibilities under the terms of the lease are not ended by virtue of this assignment. Tenant(s) understands that:

FORM 5-15   Manager's consent to assignment of lease by tenant(s).

> If Assignee defaults and fails to pay the rent as provided in the lease, namely, on _____, Tenant(s) will be obligated to do so within _____ days of being notified by Manager, and
>
> If Assignee damages the property beyond normal wear and tear and fails or refuses to pay for repairs or replacement, Tenant(s) will be obligated to do so.

As of the effective date of the assignment, Tenant(s) permanently gives up the right to occupy these premises.

Assignee is bound by every term and condition in the lease that is the subject of this assignment.

_____   _____
Date   Manager

_____   _____
Date   Tenant

_____   _____
Date   Tenant

_____   _____
Date   Assignee

_____   _____
Date   Assignee

FORM 5-15   Manager's consent to assignment of lease by tenant(s) (continued).

Tenant Alterations

Often a tenant requests permission to alter a rental unit. Form 5-16 may be used to approve the request and explain the details of the agreement.

Date: _____

_____ ("Manager") and _____ ("Tenant") agree as follows:

The tenant has request permission to may make the following alterations to the rental unit at _____.

Tenant will accomplish the work described by using the following materials and procedures: _____.

Tenant will do only the work outlined above by using only the materials and procedures outlined in this agreement.

continued

FORM 5-16   Tenant alterations agreement.

The alterations carried out by Tenant [select one]:

[   ] will become the owner's property and are not to be removed by Tenant during or at the end of the tenancy.

[   ] will be considered Tenant's personal property and, as such, may be removed by Tenant at any time up to the end of the tenancy. Tenant promises to return the premises to their original condition upon removing the improvement.

Manager will reimburse Tenant only for the costs checked below:

[   ] the cost of the following materials:

[   ] labor costs at the rate of $_____ per hour for work done in a workmanlike manner acceptable to Manager, up to _____ hours.

After receiving appropriate documentation of the cost of materials and labor, Manager shall make any payment by:

[   ] lump sum payment within _____ days of receiving documentation of costs, or

[   ] by reducing Tenant's rent by $_____ per month for the number of months necessary to cover the total amounts under the terms of this agreement.

If the alterations are Tenant's personal property, Tenant must return the premises to their original condition upon removing the alterations. If Tenant fails to do this, Manager will deduct the cost to restore the premises to their original condition from Tenant's security deposit. If the security deposit is insufficient to cover the costs of restoration, Manager may take legal action, if necessary, to collect the balance.

If Tenant fails to remove an improvement that is his or her personal property on or before the end of the tenancy, it will be considered the property of Manager, who may choose to keep the improvement (with no financial liability to Tenant) or remove it and charge Tenant for the costs of removal and restoration.

Manager may deduct any costs of removal and restoration from Tenant's security deposit. If the security deposit is insufficient to cover the costs of removal and restoration, Manager may take legal action, if necessary, to collect the balance.

If Tenant removes an item that is Manager's property, Tenant will owe Manager the fair market value of the item removed plus any costs incurred by Manager to restore the premises to their original condition.

If Manager and Tenant are involved in any legal proceeding arising out of this agreement, the prevailing party shall recover reasonable attorney fees, court costs, and any costs reasonably necessary to collect a judgment.

_____   _____

Date   Manager

_____   _____

Date   Tenant

FORM 5-16   Tenant alterations agreement (continued).

Safety and Maintenance Update

Form 5-17 may be used to notify a tenant of a safety and maintenance update.

Date: _____

Dear _____[tenant]

It is time to perform a safety and maintenance update. Accordingly, please complete the following checklist and note any safety or maintenance problems in your residential home or on the premises.

Please describe the specific problems and the rooms or areas involved. For example, please inform us of any garage roof leaks, excessive mildew in the rear bedroom closet, fuses blow out frequently, door lock sticks, water comes out too hot in shower, exhaust fan above stove doesn't work, smoke alarm malfunctions, peeling paint, and mice in basement.

You are also requested to note any potential safety and security problems in the neighborhood and anything else you consider a serious nuisance. Indicate the approximate date when you first noticed the problem and list any other recommendations or suggestions for improvement.

Please return this form with this month's rent check.

Thank you.

_____

Manager

Update

Name: _____

Address: _____

Please indicate and explain any problems or concerns with the following items:

[   ] Windows, screens, and doors _____

[   ] Window coverings (drapes, miniblinds, etc.) _____

[   ] Walls and ceilings _____

[   ] Electrical system and light fixtures _____

[   ] Plumbing (sinks, bathtub, shower, or toilet) _____

[   ] Heating or air-conditioning system _____

[   ] Cupboards, cabinets, and closets _____

[   ] Furnishings (table, bed, mirrors, chairs) _____

[   ] Laundry facilities _____

[   ] Major appliances (stove, oven, dishwasher, refrigerator) _____

continued

FORM 5-17   Safety and maintenance update.

[ ] Floors and floor coverings_____

[ ] Basement or attic _____

[ ] Locks or security system_____

[ ] Smoke detector _____

[ ] Fireplace_____

[ ] Elevator _____

[ ] Stairs and handrails _____

[ ] Hallway, lobby, and common areas _____

[ ] Garage _____

[ ] Patio, terrace, or deck _____

[ ] Lawn, fences, and grounds _____

[ ] Pool and recreational facilities _____

[ ] Roof, exterior walls, and other structural elements _____

[ ] Driveway and sidewalks _____

[ ] Neighborhood_____

[ ] Nuisances_____

[ ] Other _____

Specifics of problems:_____

_____

_____

_____

Other comments: _____

_____

_____

_____

Date _____ Tenant _____

FOR MANAGEMENT USE

Action/Response:

_____

_____

_____

_____

Date _____ Manager _____

FORM 5-17   Safety and maintenance update (continued)

State and local regulations require that most residential properties have smoke detectors. It is not sufficient to install them and forget them. You need to establish a system by which smoke detectors are checked and batteries are replaced at regular intervals. Form 5-18 may be used for that purposes.

Date: _____

Dear _____ [tenant]

We are concerned as to whether the smoke detectors are correctly functioning in your residential unit. Please take a few minutes of your time to double-check the condition and safe operation of the smoke detectors. According to the records, smoke detectors should be located at all the locations shown below.

Smoke Detector 1

Location: _____

Date battery changed: _____

Smoke detector tested: OK _____ Didn't operate _____

Smoke Detector 2

Location: _____

Date battery changed: _____

Smoke detector tested: OK _____ Didn't operate _____

Please take a minute to complete this survey and return it to us. Here are some facts you should know regarding smoke detectors:

1. The battery (or batteries) in each of your smoke detectors should be replaced at least once a year. If they are older than that (or if you are unsure), they MUST be replaced. It's important to replace them with batteries of the same type.

2. The smoke detectors should be tested by pushing the test button. They should be retested once each month.

3. If smoking is permitted in your rental agreement, an additional smoke detector should be installed in the bedroom—even if no one smokes in bed, This is extremely important, and if there is not one in your bedroom, we will be happy to install one without charge. Does anyone in the household smoke?   Yes   No

4. If you are having trouble with smoke detectors going off from kitchen odors or from someone smoking, let us know. Do not remove the batteries; a detector with a silencer can be installed.

REMINDER, IN CASE OF FIRE, your personal belongings and furniture are not covered under the company's fire insurance. Be sure you have renter's insurance.

Do you have renter's insurance?   Yes   No

Would you like us to send you an application for renter's insurance?   Yes   No

Sincerely,

Manager

FORM 5-18 Smoke detector check.

Security Notices

Form 5-19 may be used to alert the tenant about a security violation.
Form 5-20 may be used to notify a tenant of a safety inspection.

Date: _____

Dear _____[tenant]

To assist you in preventing a crime on your property, the information contained in this notice is forwarded to you. A drive-by inspection of your residence found:

Door left open/unlocked (front, back, patio) _____

Windows left open/unlocked/broken_____

Window screens off/damaged_____

Items left on porch, patio, or balcony _____

Other: _____

We did not know if you were aware of the above conditions, and we know your safety and the safety of your property are important.

Thank you for your cooperation.

Manager

FORM 5-19   Security notice.

Date: _____

Dear _____[tenant]

As part of our management program, regular inspections of your residence are made so that it remains safe for you and your family. Please allow one of our employees or agents to view the interior of your home during the next safety check, scheduled for the week of _____ 20_____.

Your assistance is needed to help to keep your home safe. Please inform us of anything you see in or around your home that may be a hazard or dangerous to you, a family member, or guests. We will then inspect your residence and do all we can to make your home safer. After your home is inspected for safety, the managers will have a copy of this letter for you to sign. If, right now, everything appears safe to the best of your knowledge, please sign below and mail this letter back to us with your next payment. If there are any unsafe conditions, let us know that as well.

Thank you for your cooperation,

Sincerely,

Manager

FORM 5-20   Saftey letter.

CHECKLIST

The following to be checked by the resident and returned to the manager.

____ As of this date there are NO unsafe conditions in or around my home.

____ There is a condition that I believe is unsafe. That condition is described as follows:

_____

Date: _____

Name: _____

Address: _____

FORM 5-20　Saftey letter (continued).

Notice of Entry

Form 5-21 may be used to notify the tenant that an agent of management intends to enter his or her rental unit.

Date: _____

Dear _____[tenant]

Address: _____

According to the rental agreement, the manager or a designated agent may enter the property you are renting to perform part of the management duties. Except in the case of an emergency, this will done only after giving a reasonable notice of at least 24 hours in advance.

This letter is to notify you at least 24 hours in advance that the _____ intends to enter the premises you are renting at the address noted above for the purpose of:

_____

Approximate time of entrance:_____

Estimated duration of stay: _____

If you will be available at the above time, please let the manager know. However, it is not necessary that you be on the premises at the time of entry. The manager, after knocking to determine if anyone is home, will use a passkey to gain entrance.

If the manager or designee is unable to enter because the locks have been changed or rekeyed, the manager will use a locksmith to open the door and locks will be rekeyed.

A new key will be given to resident, who will be charged for the service.

You are always welcome to be present at the time of entry. If you have any questions, or if the date or time listed above is inconvenient, please notify us by the following date

continued

FORM 5-21　Notice of intent to enter.

_____, so that we can attempt to schedule an alternative time that would be better for you. You may call us between _____ and _____ on the following days: _____. Our phone number is _____.

We will need to enter the dwelling no later than_____

Thanks for your cooperation.

Sincerely,

Manager

Delivered in person by: _____

Signed: _____

Date:_____ Time:_____

FORM 5-21 Notice of intent to enter (continued).

Inspections

Form 5-22 can be used to announce an inspection.

Form 5-23 may be used when the inspection of a rental property indicates that corrective action needs to be taken by a tenant.

Date: _____

Dear_____[tenant]

It is time for one of the regular inspections of the dwelling in which you reside. We will be sending one of our staff over during the next week. Please contact our office to set up an inspection date and time that is convenient for you. If we do not hear from you, someone will be by for inspection at either of the following times: _____

Thank you for your cooperation.

Sincerely,

Manager

FORM 5-22 Inspection due.

Date: _____

Dear_____[tenant]

During a recent inspection of your residence, the following conditions were found to be below the standards required in your Lease Agreement and listed on your Inspection Due letter. Corrective action must be taken within three days of receipt of this letter.

Failure to correct the problems will leave us no alternative but to take the actions allowed us in your Lease Agreement to terminate the tenancy. We hope that will not be necessary.

FORM 5-23 Inspection failure report.

____ Health, safety, or fire hazard found in: _____

____ Pickup and remove trash from:_____

____ Cleaning needed for the following area(s): _____

____ Replace furnace filters or air-conditioner pads and/or smoke detector batteries

____ Remove mildew buildup in bathroom and cleaning needed for: _____

____ Remove excessive materials stored on premises: _____

____ Replace or replace broken light bulbs, fixtures, or outlets and switch plates

____ Tighten all loose hardware on _____ and replace lost or damaged items

____ Remove the inoperative automobile you have stored on the premises

____ Repair or replace windows, screens, or doors.

____ Clean up after animals; municipal ordinances prohibit these unsanitary conditions

____ Lawn needs care; water, fertilize, trim edges, and mow lawn to prevent damage

____ Other: _____

Thank you for your cooperation.

Manager

FORM 5-23   Inspection failure report (continued).

Notice of Repair

You may use Form 5-24 and 5-25 to notify a tenant that repair work will be done on his or her rental unit and provide the tenant with an estimate of the time required to complete the repair.

Date _____   Tenant_____

Street Address_____   [City and State]_____

Dear _____[tenant],

Thank you for promptly notifying us of the following problem with your unit: _____. [Use this sentence if tenant called the problem to the management's attention. If the tenant did not alert management to the problem, delete it.]

The following problem, _____, is expected to be corrected on _____, due to the following:

_____

Management regrets any inconvenience this delay may cause. Please do not hesitate to inform management if there are any other problems with your rental home.

Sincerely,

Manager

FORM 5-24   Time estimate for repair (Option 1).

Date: _____

Dear _____[tenant]

Address _____

Thank you for your written notification on _____ [date] of the following situation with your rental home: _____

We expect to respond to that situation by the following date:_____

The following reasons affect when and how the situation will be responded to: _____
_____

If there is an unwarranted delay in responding to your notification, we will grant you a rental credit (prorated) on a daily basis. The guarantee goes into effect if there is a delay beyond ____days after your initial notification date. Rent rebate begins from that point and will be sent after the next on-time rental payment is received.

We need you to provide us, or any contractors working with us, access to your property. If there is any problem getting access to the property, our maintenance guarantee is voided.

We appreciate your cooperation with this matter.

Sincerely,

Manager

FORM 5-25   Time estimate for repair (Option 2).

Tenants should be given a notice that describes the general nature and locations of the planned renovation activities and the expected starting and ending dates. If the property was constructed before 1978, there is a requirement to notify tenants within 60 days of a renovation that is likely to generate lead-paint dust. Renovation is generally defined as any activity that results in the disturbance of more than 2 square feet of paint per building component, including the removal of large structures such as walls and ceilings, replastering, and window replacement and surface preparation activities such as sanding, scraping, or other activities that generate lead-paint dust. The notice in Form 5-26 complies with the regulations regarding lead-paint-dust notification.

Date:

Dear _____

Attached to this notice is a copy of the pamphlet "Protect Your Family from Lead in Your Home," informing you of the potential risk of lead exposure from renovation activity to be performed in your residential unit.

Sincerely,

Manager

FORM 5-26   Notice of renovation.

ACKNOWLEDGMENT OF RECEIPT

I received this pamphlet on _____ before the work began.

Property address: _____

Printed name of resident: _____

Signature of resident: _____

[Note: If an occupant refuses to sign the acknowledgment of receipt of the pamphlet, the manager can certify delivery.]

_____ I certify that I have made a good faith effort to deliver the pamphlet "Protect Your Family from Lead in Your Home" to the unit listed below at the dates and times indicated and that the occupant refused to sign the acknowledgment. I further certify that I have left a copy of the pamphlet at the unit with the occupant.

Property address:_____

Attempted delivery dates and times: _____

Printed name of manager:_____

Signature of manager: _____

Date: _____

[If resident is unavailable for signature, the manager can use the following section.]

_____ I certify that I have made a good faith effort to deliver the pamphlet "Protect Your Family from Lead in Your Home" to the unit listed below and that the occupant was unavailable to sign the acknowledgment. I further certify that I have left a copy of the pamphlet at the unit by sliding it under the door.

Property address:_____

Attempted delivery dates and times: _____

Printed name of person leaving pamphlet:_____

Signature of manager: _____

Date: _____

FORM 5-26   Notice of renovation (continued).

Problem Tenants

When there are problems with a tenant, sometimes the tenant will be upset. Often a personal letter is sufficient to correct the situation. Form 5-27 may be used for this purpose.

Form 5-28 may be used to notify a tenant of a rental upkeep violation.

Form 5-29 may be used to notify tenants of a violation of the terms of the lease.

Date: _____

Dear _____[tenant]

You're a tenant I really value and enjoy talking to from time to time. I haven't seen you around for some time, and I can't understand why. I wish I knew the reason. It must be the incident that took place the other evening. Of course, I heard the other side and have yet to hear your side.

Anyway, I hope we can get together and discuss the situation, if only because I value you as a tenant and want you to be happy. I'm willing to do whatever it takes to get back in your good graces because I care about you and value our relationship. Please call me to set up a meeting.

Sincerely,

Manager

FORM 5-27   Personal letter to a tenant.

Date: _____

Dear _____[tenant]

We do regular inspections of the rental properties we manage. Your rental/lease agreement provides that you are responsible for the general upkeep of your residence, both in the interior and on the exterior of the property. On our last inspection of your rental property, it was noticed that you are in violation of the terms of the lease by not keeping up with the upkeep of your property. Specifically: _____

To meet the standards necessary to avoid eviction, you must:

_____

Please correct this problem immediately. If you fail to correct the problem in a timely fashion, we will contract with someone to correct the problem and you will be billed for the services. Remember that this is your obligation.

Thank you for you prompt cooperation. If you have any questions or problems, please do not hesitate to call.

Sincerely,

Manager

FORM 5-28   Rental upkeep violation notice.

Date _____

Tenant_____

Street Address _____

City and State_____

Dear _____[tenant],

Your lease prohibits _____ [violation]. It has come to my attention that you have violated this condition of your tenancy by _____.

It is our desire that you and all other tenants enjoy living in your rental units. To make sure this occurs, we enforce all terms and conditions of our leases. So please immediately _____.

If you fail to remedy this violation, management may exercise its legal right to terminate your lease and begin eviction proceedings.

Please contact me if you would like to discuss this matter further and clear up any possible misunderstandings.

Yours truly,

Manager

FORM 5-29   Notice of lease violation (Option 1).

Date _____

Tenant_____

Street Address _____

City and State_____

Dear _____[tenant],

This letter is to remind you that the lease prohibits _____ [violation]. It is noted that, starting on _____ [date of violation] and continuing to the present, you have violated this condition of your tenancy by _____.

It is our desire that you and all other tenants enjoy living in your rental units. To make sure this occurs, we enforce all terms and conditions of our leases. So please immediately _____.

Failure to resolve this matter promptly will be grounds to exercise the legal right to terminate the lease and begin eviction proceedings.

Please contact me if you would like to discuss this matter further and clear up any possible misunderstandings.

Sincerely

Manager

FORM 5-30   Warning letter for lease or rental agreement violation (Option 2).

Form 5-31 may be used when it is discovered that a tenant has a pet or pets on the premises without permission. Form 5-32 covers noise violations.

Date: _____

Dear _____ [tenant]

Your rental agreement clearly states that pets (unless specifically included in the lease) are not permitted on the rental premises, inside or out, even on a temporary basis. This includes _____.

During the last inspection of the premises, it was noticed or brought to our attention that you have broken your rental agreement by allowing a pet/animal to occupy or remain on the premises.

To comply with your rental agreement and remedy this violation, you are notified that one of the following actions must be done within 72 hours or this violation will lead to a notice to terminate the rental agreement.

The pet must be removed by _____ (date).

You may request an application to have the pet added to the rental agreement, subject to approval and additional monthly rent and deposit.

Please contact the manage at the following number, _____, within 72 hours to inform us of your actions regarding this matter.

Animals on the property that are not listed on the rental agreement are considered strays and are subject to removal by appropriate authorities, with any costs billed to the resident.

Thank you for your cooperation,

Manager

FORM 5-31   Pet rule violation.

Date: _____

Dear _____ [tenant]

I have received several reports regarding loud music and noise coming from your residential home. While it is not management's wish to restrict your enjoyment of your home, management must consider the rights and privileges of the other residents in the complex.

Excessive noise or high levels during the wrong time of the day are a violation of your standard rental agreement, which states: _____

We trust management will not receive any additional complaints from neighbors or have to notify you about any more violations. If disturbances continue and you fail to comply with the noise rules and regulations, you will place yourself in further default of your rental agreement and the agreement may be terminated and/or not renewed.

FORM 5-32   Noise violation notice.

If you have any questions call _____ between _____ and _____.

Your cooperation in this matter will be greatly appreciated.

Sincerely,

Manager

FORM 5-32   Noise violation notice (continued).

When a tenant's handling of trash is a problem, a letter similar to Form 5-33 may be sent to the tenant to correct the problem.

An essential factor in making a profit as a landlord is reducing your expenses. One method is to make sure you are not paying for wasted water. Form 5-34 may be used to request a tenant to check his or her faucets. **Note:** If the tenant fails to respond, notify the tenant of an intention to enter the unit to inspect the faucets.

Date:

Dear _____[tenant]

I have received reports of trash, including _____, outside your residential home. Not only does trash attract bugs and mice, it degrades the appearance of the property and makes our place look like a pigsty.

I need your help to dispose of this trash properly. If the problem is not corrected within 72 hours, an agent of the manager will remedy the situation and you will be charged the reasonable cost of this cleanup.

So please, please, don't make it tough on everyone else and force us to hire an outside party to clean up your trash. Thanks again for your cooperation. I do appreciate it.

Sincerely,

Manager

FORM 5-33   Letter to tenant when trash is a problem.

Date: _____

Dear _____[tenant]

Management is asking for your help in keeping expenses to a minimum by completing the lower portion of this letter and returning it to the manager with your next rent payment.

The city has what is called a sewer user fee. This is a fee charged (to the owner) for the use of the city's sewer system and is paid in addition to the water bills. The amount of the sewer user fee is determined by the amount of water used during the winter months. Accordingly, the lower the water consumption, the lower the sewer user fee.

continued

FORM 5-34   Leakage letter.

To keep expenses and, eventually, your rent as low as possible, it is requested that you check to see if your toilets run continuously and check each of your water faucets, as well as those not in your living areas but under your control, for leaks. If a leak is discovered, circle the appropriate faucet below, along with any notes about the problem, and return the lower portion of this letter to the manager.

If you find that none of your faucets leak, please circle yes on the last question and return the form. If the form is not returned, it will be necessary to have someone inspect your home.

Thank you, in advance, for your cooperation.

Sincerely,

Manager

Address: _____

Any leaks? _____ Which faucet? _____

Approximate amount of leakage? _____ How long? _____

Kitchen sink	hot	cold
Bathroom sinks	hot	cold
Bathtub/shower	hot	cold
Toilet	cold	

Other (e.g., drain) _____ Specify location: _____

All faucets okay? _____

Checked by:_____ Date checked: _____

FORM 5-34 Leakage letter (continued).

A letter or notice (see Form 5-35) may be used to advise a problem tenant of a garbage handling or disposal violation.

Date: _____

Dear _____[tenant]

We make periodic inspections of the property, including your home and neighborhood. During the last inspection., it was discovered that your garbage was _____. This constitutes a violation of your lease agreement. We realize that it is often difficult to keep garbage in a manner that is not disturbing to neighbors, but keep in mind that messy garbage can attract mice and other animals, such as cats, dogs, and raccoons. It is important to make sure that you keep a tight lid on your garbage or tie it in large plastic bags.

You are responsible for your own garbage. Because of health risks, it is necessary to keep your garbage in a clean and sanitary manner. Your garbage gets picked up on _____. Please bring your garbage to the curb the night before.

FORM 5-35 Garbage violation notice.

We also need your assistance in picking up loose papers around and on your property. Unfortunately, papers from adjoining residences are blown onto your property. Even, though it may not be your garbage, it is important that you pick it up to keep your property clean. We want you to enjoy your property in a manner that is not offensive to your neighbors. We expect that we will not have to contact you about this problem another time. If Management is forced to contact you again because of more garbage violations, you will place yourself in further default of your lease agreement. Default is a serious matter that could result in eviction.

If you miss the weekly garbage pickup, we urge you to take your own garbage to the town dump immediately rather than wait until the following week. Garbage that lies around begins to take on an offensive odor and will attract animals. Don't forget, Management has the right to terminate your lease if you do not comply with this notice. Also, don't forget to retrieve your garbage cans soon after the garbage is picked up.

If you have any questions or we can be of assistance to you, please call us.

THANKS IN ADVANCE FOR YOUR HELP!

Sincerely,

Manager

FORM 5-35   Garbage violation notice (continued).

If the terms of the tenancy require that the landlord pay utilities and a tenant uses excessive utilities, Form 5-36 may be used in an attempt to collect the extra charges for the utilities.

Date: _____

Dear _____[tenant]

As provided in the rental agreement, management pays for the following utilities _____ at your address. The agreement also provides that any time your usage of this utility becomes excessive and exceeds $_____ per month, you are responsible for payment above that amount and that sum is to be considered as additional rent due.

Enclosed is a copy of the last record of your usage, which shows that you went above the amount agreed on. You went over the limits stated in the rental agreement by $_____. Please send us $ _____ as part of your next rent payment to cover the excess amount. Nonpayment of the full rent amount due is a violation of the rental agreement and grounds for termination of the agreement, and appropriate legal action will begin.

Thank you for your cooperation.

Sincerely,

Manager

FORM 5-36   Excessive utility usage.

To prevent your rental property from looking like a junkyard, you must take steps prevent unlicensed and inoperable automobiles from being parked on the property. Form 5-37 may be used to advise a tenant that corrective action is needed.

Form 5-38 may be used to notify a tenant that he or she is in default of the lease but that the default is curable.

Date: _____

Dear _____[tenant]

During the last regular inspection of the rental property, it was noticed that there is a _____ vehicle parked in your space. Your rental agreement states that unauthorized, nonoperational, unregistered vehicles or those not displaying required local or state decals/licenses are not allowed on the rental premises, even on a temporary basis. On our last inspection of the premises, it was noticed that there was a vehicle on your premises with the following description: _____

This vehicle violates your rental agreement for the following reason(s): _____

To be in compliance with your rental agreement and remedy this violation, you are hereby notified that one of the following actions must be done within 72 hours or this violation will lead to a notice to terminate the rental agreement.

_____ The vehicle must be removed by _____ [date]

_____ The vehicle must be in fully operational status and display all required local and state decals/licenses.

Please contact us at the following number, _____, within 72 hours to inform us of your actions regarding this matter. If this matter is not corrected in a timely manner, a towing service will be instructed to remove the vehicle. If you do not wish to have the vehicle towed, please remedy the violation by one of the methods stated above or contact us to make alternative arrangements. The cost of any removal and storage of the vehicle will be the automobile owner's responsibility.

Thank you for your cooperation,

Manager

FORM 5-37   Automobile violation.

Transfer of Ownership

When there is a change of ownership in the property, the tenant should be notified, unless the management company remains in place. Form 5-39 may be used for that purpose. If there is a change in management companies, a similar letter may be used to notify the tenant of the new management company.

Certified Mail, Return Receipt Requested

Date: _____

Dear: _____

Regarding the property located at [address of property], this is to notify you that you are presently in default of the terms of the rental agreement on the subject property. The default is as follows: [describe the conduct that constitutes a violation of the lease].

If you do not remedy the above default within _____ days, legal proceeding, may be commenced against you without any further notice.

I trust you will correct the problem without delay.

Sincerely,

Manager

FORM 5-38   Notice of curable default.

Date: _____

Dear: _____

This letter is to notify you that the property you are currently leasing at _____(address) has transferred ownership. The name of the new owner of the property is _____.

The new owner or a representative should be contacting you shortly if they have not already done so. Please be advised that from this point forward any and all concerns regarding your property should be directed to the new owner or to whomever the owner designates. This includes directing all rental payments, inquiries, requests, or questions to them.

The new owner and or management may be contacted at the following phone number and/or address. Use this information to contact the new owners and find out where to send payments: _____

We have appreciated the opportunity to provide housing for you, and we wish you the best.

Sincerely,

Manager

FORM 5-39   Notice of transfer of ownership.

Property Management Agreement

Many landlords hire property managers to handle their properties. Form 5-40 may be used to enter into a contract with an individual to manage a rental property.

Date:

This agreement is between _____, Owner of residential real property at _____ and _____, Manager of the property. [If the manager is also renting a unit, use the following sentence.] Manager will be renting unit _____ of the property under a separate written rental agreement that is in no way contingent on or related to this agreement.

Manager will begin work on_____.

Manager's duties are set forth below:

Renting Units

[   ] answer inquiries about vacancies

[   ] show vacant units

[   ] accept rental applications

[   ] select tenants

[   ] accept initial rents and deposits

[   ] other (specify)_____

Rent Collection

[   ] collect rents when due

[   ] sign rent receipts

[   ] maintain rent collection records

[   ] collect late rents and charges

[   ] inform owner of late rents

[   ] prepare late rent notices

[   ] serve late rent notices on tenants

[   ] serve rent increase and tenancy termination notices

[   ] deposit rent collections in bank

[   ] other (specify)_____

Vacant Apartments

[   ] inspect unit when tenant moves in

[   ] inspect unit when tenant moves out

[   ] walls, baseboards, ceilings, lights, and built-in shelves

[   ] kitchen cabinets, countertops, sinks, stove, oven, and refrigerator

---

FORM 5-40   Property manager agreement.

[ ] floors, carpets, and rugs

[ ] bathtubs, showers, toilets, and plumbing fixtures

[ ] doors, windows, window coverings, and miniblinds

[ ] clean unit after tenant moves out, including:

[ ] other (specify) _____

Maintenance

[ ] vacuum and clean hallways and entryways

[ ] replace lightbulbs in common areas

[ ] drain water heaters

[ ] clean stairs, decks, patios, facade, and sidewalks

[ ] clean garage oils on pavement

[ ] mow lawns

[ ] rake leaves

[ ] trim bushes

[ ] clean up garbage and debris on grounds

[ ] shovel snow from sidewalks and driveways or arrange for snow removal

[ ] other (specify) _____

Repairs

[ ] accept tenant complaints and repair requests

[ ] inform owner of maintenance and repair needs

[ ] maintain written log of tenant complaints

[ ] handle routine maintenance and repairs, including:

[ ] plumbing stoppages

[ ] garbage disposal stoppages/repairs

[ ] faucet leaks/washer replacement

[ ] toilet tank repairs

[ ] toilet seat replacement

[ ] stove burner repair/replacement

[ ] stove hinges/knobs replacement

[ ] dishwasher repair

[ ] light switch and outlet repair/replacement

[ ] heater thermostat repair

[ ] window repair/replacement

continued

FORM 5-40   Property manager agreement (continued).

[ ] painting (interior)

[ ] painting (exterior)

[ ] replacement of key

[ ] other (specify)_____

Other Responsibilities

_____

Manager will be available to tenants during the following days and times: _____. If the hours required to carry out any duties may reasonably be expected to exceed _____ hours in any week, Manager shall notify Owner and obtain Owner's consent before working such extra hours, except in the event of an emergency. Extra hours worked due to an emergency must be reported to Owner within 24 hours.

Manager will be paid:

[ ] $ _____per hour   [ ] $_____per week

[ ] $_____per month   [ ] Other: _____

Manager will be paid:

[ ] Once a week on every _____   [ ] Twice a month on _____

[ ] Once a month on_____   [ ] Other: _____

Owner may terminate Manager's employment at any time for any reason that isn't unlawful, with or without notice. Manager may quit at any time for any reason, with or without notice.

Owner and Manager additionally agree that: _____.

All agreements between Owner and Manager relating to the work specified in this agreement are incorporated in this agreement. Any modification to the agreement must be in writing and signed by both parties.

Signed at:_____   _____
              City   State   Manager

              _____   _____

Date signed   Owner

FORM 5-40   Property manager agreement (continued).

6

Collecting Delinquent Rent

This chapter contains a discussion of ways to collect delinquent rent. Demand letters, notices to pay delinquent rent, and other collection letters are covered. The legal process of evicting a tenant is discussed in Chapter 7.

Right of Possession on Default in Rent

A landlord has the right upon a default in rent to take possession of the property and cancel the lease. Although the specific rules for how a landlord gets repossession of his or her property from a defaulting tenant vary, generally the rules are as follows (taken from Chapter 83.05 of the Florida Statutes):

> 83.05 Right of possession upon default in rent; determination of right of possession in action or surrender or abandonment of premises.—
>
> (1) If any person leasing or renting any land or premises other than a dwelling unit fails to pay the rent at the time it becomes due, the lessor has the right to obtain possession of the premises as provided by law.
>
> (2) The landlord shall recover possession of rented premises only:
>
> (a) In an action for possession under s. 83.20, or other civil action in which the issue of right of possession is determined;
>
> (b) When the tenant has surrendered possession of the rented premises to the landlord; or
>
> (c) When the tenant has abandoned the rented premises.

(3) In the absence of actual knowledge of abandonment, it shall be presumed for purposes of paragraph (2)(c) that the tenant has abandoned the rented premises if:

(a) The landlord reasonably believes that the tenant has been absent from the rented premises for a period of 30 consecutive days:

(b) The rent is not current; and

(c) A notice pursuant to s. 83.20(2) has been served and 10 days have elapsed since service of such notice.

However, this presumption does not apply if the rent is current or the tenant has notified the landlord in writing of an intended absence.

83.06 Right to demand double rent upon refusal to deliver possession.—

(1) When any tenant refuses to give up possession of the premises at the end of the tenant's lease, the landlord, the landlord's agent, attorney, or legal representatives, may demand of such tenant double the monthly rent, and may recover the same at the expiration of every month, or in the same proportion for a longer or shorter time by distress, in the manner pointed out hereinafter.

(2) All contracts for rent, verbal or in writing, shall bear interest from the time the rent becomes due, any law, usage, or custom to the contrary notwithstanding.

83.07 Action for use and occupation.—Any landlord, the landlord's heirs, executors, administrators, or assigns may recover reasonable damages for any house, lands, tenements, or hereditaments held or occupied by any person by the landlord's permission in an action on the case for the use and occupation of the lands, tenements, or hereditaments when they are not held, occupied by or under agreement or demise by deed; and if on trial of any action, any demise or agreement (not being by deed) whereby a certain rent was reserved is given in evidence, the plaintiff shall not be dismissed but may make use thereof as an evidence of the quantum of damages to be recovered.

83.08 Landlord's lien for rent.—Every person to whom rent may be due, the person's heirs, executors, administrators, or assigns, shall have a lien for such rent upon the property found upon or off the premises leased or rented, and in the possession of any person, as follows:

(1) Upon agricultural products raised on the land leased or rented for the current year. This lien shall be superior to all other liens, though of older date.

(2) Upon all other property of the lessee or his or her sublessee or assigns, usually kept on the premises. This lien shall be superior to any

lien acquired subsequent to the bringing of the property on the premises leased.

(3) Upon all other property of the defendant. This lien shall date from the levy of the distress warrant hereinafter provided.

83.09 Exemptions from liens for rent.—No property of any tenant or lessee shall be exempt from distress and sale for rent, except beds, bed-clothes, and wearing apparel.

83.10 Landlord's lien for advances.—Landlords shall have a lien on the crop grown on rented land for advances made in money or other things of value, whether made directly by them or at their instance and requested by another person, or for which they have assumed a legal responsibility, at or before the time at which such advances were made, for the sustenance or well-being of the tenant or the tenant's family, or for preparing the ground for cultivation, or for cultivating, gathering, saving, handling, or preparing the crop for market. They shall have a lien also upon each and every arti-cle advanced, and upon all property purchased with money advanders. A violation of the command of the writ may be punished as a contempt of court. If the defendant does not move for dissolution of the writ as pro-vided in s. 83.135, the sheriff shall, pursuant to a further order of the court, levy on the property liable to distress forthwith after the time for answer-ing the complaint has expired. Before the writ issues, the plaintiff or the plaintiff's agent or attorney shall file a bond with surety to be approved by the clerk payable to defendant in at least double the sum demanded or, if property, in double the value of the property sought to be levied on, con-ditioned to pay all costs and damages which defendant sustains in conse-quence of plaintiff's improperly suing out the distress.

83.13 Levy of writ.—The sheriff shall execute the writ by service on defendant and, upon the order of the court, by levy on property distrain-able for rent or advances, if found in the sheriff's jurisdiction. If the prop-erty is in another jurisdiction, the party who had the writ issued shall deliv-er the writ to the sheriff in the other jurisdiction; and that sheriff shall execute the writ, upon order of the court, by levying on the property and delivering it to the sheriff of the county in which the action is pending, to be disposed of according to law, unless he or she is ordered by the court from which the writ emanated to hold the property and dispose of it in his or her jurisdiction according to law. If the plaintiff shows by a sworn state-ment that the defendant cannot be found within the state, the levy on the property suffices as service on the defendant.

83.135 Dissolution of writ.—The defendant may move for dissolution of a distress writ at any time. The court shall hear the motion not later than the day on which the sheriff is authorized under the writ to levy on property liable under distress. If the plaintiff proves a prima facie case, or if the defendant defaults, the court shall order the sheriff to proceed with the levy.

Right of a Tenant to Withhold Rent

When a tenant has a right to withhold rent because of the failure of the landlord to maintain or repair, rendering the premises wholly untenantable, it is controlled by state statutes. Normally, when the lease is silent on the procedure to be followed to effect repair or maintenance and the payment of rent relating thereto, yet affirmatively and expressly places the obligation for the same upon the landlord, and the landlord has failed or refused to do so, rendering the leased premises wholly untenantable, the tenant may withhold rent after notice to the landlord. The tenant shall serve the landlord with a written notice declaring the premises to be wholly untenantable, giving the landlord at least 20 days to make the specifically described repair or maintenance, and stating that the tenant will withhold the rent for the next rental period and thereafter until the repair or maintenance has been performed. The lease may provide for a longer period for repair or maintenance. Once the landlord has completed the repair or maintenance, the tenant shall pay the landlord the amounts of rent withheld. If the landlord does not complete the repair or maintenance in the allotted time, the parties may extend the time by written agreement or the tenant may abandon the premises, retain the amounts of rent withheld, terminate the lease, and avoid any liability for future rent or charges under the lease. This section is cumulative to other existing remedies, and this section does not prevent any tenant from exercising his or her other remedies.

Delinquent Notices

The first day the rent is past due, you should automatically post or deliver a written notice. In most instances, the tenant will pay the rent and any late charges. If the rent is not paid within a few days, usually three to five days, you may start the eviction process (see Chapter 7). If you find that you are constantly delivering "pay the rent or leave" notices to certain tenants, you may want to end their tenancy even if they eventually come up with the rent.

The first day rent is in default, serve a form similar to Form 6-1 on the tenant.

If the notice of delinquent rent does not produce results, serve a notice to pay rent or quit. Check your states statutes for the specified number of days residents must be allowed to pay rent or deliver up possession, which should be stated in Form 6-2. Check to see if any additional or specific wording format is required by

---

Certified Mail, Return Receipt Requested

To: _____[name(s) of tenant(s)]

Regarding the property located at [address of property], this is to notify you that you are presently in default of the terms of the rental agreement on the subject property. Presently you owe rent from [date] to [date] for a total past due rent of $_____.

You are hereby directed to pay the past due rent within _____days.

If payment is not received within the above period or possession of the property is not surrendered, legal proceedings may be commenced against you without any further notice.

Sincerely,

_____

Manager

FORM 6-1   Notice of default in rent.

your city or state for this notice to be valid and enforceable. Since notices to pay rent or quit vary among the states, I suggest that you check with a local landlord association or another legal assistance office to obtain a copy of a locally approved form. Forms 6-2 through 6-4 are provided only as suggestions as to the content of the notices. In addition, if this matter goes to court, you will need to submit a proof of delivery of the notice. Use Form 6-6 or Form 6-7 for that purpose.

Date: _____

Dear _____[tenant]

Your rent is delinquent. The total amount due on this date is_____.

This notice is to inform you and all others in possession of the below premises that you are hereby given the option to pay the past due rent or quit and deliver up the premises you hold as our tenant, namely: [Describe premises]

You are to pay the rent and late fee, a total of _____, or deliver up said premises on or within _____days of receipt of this notice, pursuant to applicable state law.

You may reinstate your account by full payment within _____days as provided under the terms of your tenancy or by applicable state law. In the event you fail to bring your rent payments current or vacate the premises, we shall immediately take legal action to evict you and to recover rents and damages for the unlawful retention of said premises together with such future rents as may be due us for breach of your lease.

Sincerely,

Manager

FORM 6-2   Notice to pay rent or quit (Option 1).

Date: _____

Dear _____ [tenant] and all other residents in possession of the premises at the following address:

PLEASE TAKE NOTICE that according to the terms of your rental agreement, the rent is now past due and payable for the above stated address, which you currently hold and occupy. Our records indicate that your rental account is delinquent in the amount itemized as follows:

Rental Period (dates) _____ Rent Due $ _____

Rental Period (dates) _____ Rent Due $ _____

Rental Period (dates) _____ Rent Due $ _____

TOTAL RENT DUE $ _____

Less partial payment of $ _____

Plus late rent fees of $ _____

TOTAL BALANCE DUE OF $ _____

You are hereby required to pay said rent in full within _____ days or to remove from and deliver up possession of the above address, or legal proceedings will be instituted against you to recover possession of said premises, to declare the forfeiture of the Lease or Rental Agreement under which you occupy said premises, and to recover all rents due and damages, together with court costs, legal and attorney fees, according to the terms of your Lease or Rental Agreement.

Dated this day of _____ , 20_____.

Manager

FORM 6-3   Notice to pay rent or quit (Option 2).

Date: _____

Dear _____ and All Others currently residing at _____:

I have registered this letter to make sure that it is delivered to you personally. The reason; In the event of a lawsuit being filed against you, your attorney cannot say that you have not had sufficient notice.

Management is not unreasonable, but we do insist that you live by the rental agreement that you signed. Our other tenants do, and we make no exceptions regardless of your circumstances To prevent legal proceedings beginning by _____, you will have to act quickly, though, and we will require some evidence that you are going to pay the amount due. Otherwise, I will direct our attorney to file a court action to cancel your rental agreement. If the court action is successful, you will be required to leave the premises immediately. In addition to being immediately evicted, you would owe past due rent, attorney fees, and court costs.

I am sure that you do not want this to occur. It is under your control. Please contact me no later than _____ to explain how you are going to remedy the default.

Sincerely,

Manager

FORM 6-4   Pay rent or quit letter (Option 3).

156

Date: _____

To: _____

Dear _____ and all others in possession of the premises located at _____:

THIS IS A NOTICE TO YOU AND ALL OTHERS IN POSSESSION OF THE BELOW PREMISES, THAT YOU ARE HEREBY NOTIFIED TO VACATE, QUIT, AND DELIVER UP THE PREMISES YOU HOLD AS OUR TENANT, NAMELY: [DESCRIBE PREMISES]

You are to deliver up said premises on or within _____days of receipt of this notice, pursuant to applicable state law.

This notice is provided due to nonpayment of rent. The present rent arrearage is in the amount of $_____ according to the below account:

[set forth past due rent and late fees]

You may reinstate your account by full payment within _____ days as provided under the terms of your tenancy or by applicable state law. In the event you fail to bring your rent payments current or to vacate the premises, we shall immediately take legal action to evict you and to recover rents and damages for the unlawful retention of said premises together with such future rents as may be due us for breach of your tenancy agreement.

Manager

Address

FORM 6-5   Pay rent or quit letter (Option 4).

I, the undersigned, being at least 18 years of age, declare under penalty of perjury that I served the above notice, of which this is a true copy, on the above-mentioned tenant(s) in possession in the manner(s) indicated below:

_____ On _____ 20 ___, I handed the notice to the tenant(s) personally.

_____ On _____, 20 ___, after attempting personal service, I handed the notice to a person of suitable age and discretion at the residence/business of the tenant(s), AND I deposited a true copy in the U.S. Mail, in a sealed envelope with postage fully prepaid, addressed to the tenant(s) at his/her/their place of residence [date mailed, if different from above date].

_____ On_____, 20 _____, after attempting service in both manners indicated above, I posted the notice in a conspicuous place at the residence of the tenant(s), AND I deposited a true copy in the U.S. Mail, in a sealed envelope with postage fully prepaid, addressed to the tenant(s) at his/her/their place of residence. [date mailed, if different from above date].

Executed on _____, 20___ , at the County/City of

State of_____

Served by _____

FORM 6-6   Proof of service of notice to pay rent or quit (Option 1).

I, the undersigned, being at least eighteen years of age, declare under penalty of perjury that I served notice to pay rent or quit tenancy, of which this is a true copy, on the above-named tenant in the manner indicated below on _____, 20_____.

_____ I personally delivered a copy of the notice to tenant.
_____ I posted a copy on the door of the premises and
_____ I mailed a true copy of the notice to tenant by certified mail.
_____ I mailed a true copy of this notice to tenant by first-class mail.

Executed on _____, 20_____, at _____

By _____

FORM 6-7   Proof of servcie of notice to pay rent or quit (Option 2).

Late Fees

Many states have regulations regarding the amount of late fees a landlord may impose. If your state does not regulate late fees, your late fees should be reasonable. Late fees normally should not exceed 5 percent of the monthly rent. They should not be applied until the rent is three to five days late. Although late fees may be increased for each day the rent remains unpaid, there should be an upper limit. For example, a late fee of $10 that is due after the first three days and increases $5 per day up to a maximum of 5 percent probably would be considered reasonable. Some landlords try to hide late fees by giving a "discount" when rent is paid early or on time. The courts generally consider this a method to charge excessive late fees. Do not get in the habit of waiving late fees, because the tenant will take that as an indication that late payments are acceptable.

Often, a tenant will pay the rent late without paying the late fee. Form 6-8 may be used to inform the tenant of the late fee.

Date: _____

Dear _____

Thank you for your rent payment. As stated in your rental agreement, however, when rent payments are not received by _____, you must pay additional rent because of a late charge due or because you did not qualify for the rent discount. The required additional amount was not included in your payment and is therefore now due.

Please send the additional required rent amount of $ _____ at once to bring your credit balance up to date and remove it from the delinquent list. This amount must be paid within _____ days from the date of this notice.

Thank you for your prompt cooperation.

Sincerely,

Manager

FORM 6-8   Late rent fee due.

Bounced Check Charges

A landlord may charge an extra fee if a tenant's check does not clear the bank. This is an item that should be in the rental agreement. Like late charges, returned check fees must be reasonable. The local consumer protection office can provide you with information about what fees may be charged for returned checks. Information about state consumer protection agencies may be obtained from the Federal Citizen Information Center at www.consumeraction.gov. Use Form 6-9 to notify a tenant of a returned check.

Partial Rent Payments

It is bad business practice to allow tenants to make partial or delayed rent payments. If a tenant has a good payment record and you wish to keep the tenant,

---

Returned Check Notice

Date: _____

Dear_____,

Your bank has refused to pay your check dated _____ in the amount of $ _____, and the check is now being returned to us. Hopefully, this matter was a simple mistake that can be quickly corrected. Unfortunately, however, because of the returned check, your rent is past due and delinquent.

It is critical that you immediately and without delay of any kind make the necessary arrangements to deliver us a money order or a certified check to bring your rent up to date.

The amount due on your account currently is:

Rent due _____

Late rent fee due _____

Loss of early rent discount (if any) _____

Returned check charge _____

Total amount now due_____

Again, I must warn you that the above amount must be paid within ____ days or eviction proceedings will commence. I thank you for your cooperation in the matter.

Sincerely,

[Your Name]

P. S. Please do not delay or ignore this notice. The negative effect that this matter can have on your overall credit rating can be devastating. Bring your money order or certified check in before _____ for your own protection if you want to avoid the added cost of a lawsuit.

FORM 6-9   Notice of returned check.

an exception may be made. In those cases, get a written agreement about when the rent will be fully paid and, in the agreement, indicate that this is a one-time exception. A sample agreement is shown in Form 6-10. If the tenant does not pay the rent as agreed, take the necessary steps to terminate the tenancy.

Form 6-10 may be used to accept partial rent or late rent from a tenant. **Caution:** Do not get in a habit of using this form. (An electronic copy of the form is included on the CD.)

If you decide to allow a tenant to catch up on the rent by using a schedule of payments, the worksheet shown in Form 6-11 may be used.

This agreement between _____ "Tenant(s)" and _____ "Manager" is an agreement for delayed or partial rent payment for the months listed. This agreement covers only the period indicated and does not modify any provisions in the lease.

1. _____ (Tenant(s)) has/have paid _____ on _____, _____, which was due on _____, _____.

2. _____ (Manager) agrees to accept all the remainder of the rent on or before _____, _____, and to hold off on any legal proceeding to evict _____ (Tenant(s)) until that date.

Date_____   Manager_____

Date_____   Tenant _____

Date_____   Tenant _____

FORM 6-10   Agreement for delayed or partial rent payments.

Date: _____

I/We _____ (tenant(s)) agree that I/we owe the below listed past due rent:

Previous balance (prior to current month): $ _____

Current month (now past due): $ _____

Late charges $ _____

Next month (month of _____, 20xx) rent: $ _____

Following month (month of ____20xx) rent: $ _____

Total Rent Due within Next 60 Days: $ _____

Tenant(s) agrees to pay $_____ per (week, bi-weekly, or month) until the rent is current. The first payment is due on _____ (date) and the same day each ____ thereafter.

FORM 6-11   Rent payment schedule worksheet.

The resident agrees to pay rent monies due according to the above payment schedule. If the resident fails to pay amount due on or before any of the agreed dates, the owner has the right to continue the legal eviction procedure against the resident without having to serve another pay or quit notice. The resident already has been served. The resident has been given extra time to pay only as a courtesy. By granting this extension, the landlord does not waive any current or future rights granted in the rental agreement, especially as it relates to rights to terminate this agreement and eviction for failure to timely pay rent.

Tenant(s): _____ Date: _____

Manager: _____ Date: _____

FORM 6-11   Rent payment schedule worksheet (continued).

Collecting from a Cotenant or Guarantor

When a cotenant on the lease has moved or no longer is on the premises, but still is liable under the terms of the lease for the rent, Form 6-12 may be used to demand payment from the cotenant.

When an individual has guaranteed payment of the rent, Form 6-13 may be used to place a demand on the guarantor for payment of the past due account.

Certified Mail, Return Receipt Requested

Date: _____

To: _____[name and address of cotenant]

Dear _____(cotenant)

In the lease of property entered into on _____ date between the Landlord, you, and _____ [Tenant], you agreed to the terms of the lease and stated that you would be responsible along with _____ (Tenant) to pay the rent.

Please be advised that the sum of $ _____ is owed to the undersigned for the following:

Since this debt was incurred in respect to the leased property in which you were a Cotenant, demand is hereby made upon you for the payment of $_____.

If payment or satisfactory arrangements for payment are not made within 15 days, I will take the necessary legal action to collect the sum due me, including, if applicable, court costs and attorney fees.

Sincerely,

Landlord

FORM 6-12   Demand on cotenant for payment.

Certified Mail, Return Receipt Requested

Date: _____

To: _____[name and address of guarantor]

By attachment to the lease of property between [Landlord] and [Tenant] entered into on [date lease was signed], you guaranteed payment of rent and related charges for [name of Tenant].

Please be advised that the sum of $_____ is owed to the undersigned for the following charges:

Since this debt was incurred in respect to the lease in which you agreed to act as the guarantor, demand is hereby made upon you for the payment of $_____.

If payment or satisfactory arrangements for payment are not made within _____ days, I will take the necessary legal action to collect the sum due me, including, if applicable, court costs and attorney fees.

Sincerely,

Landlord

FORM 6-13   Demand on guarantor for payment.

Collecting Past Due Rent after the Tenant Has Vacated

Because debt collection has a history of abuse, there are both state and federal statutes setting forth debt collectors' responsibilities and prohibiting certain acts. For example, a debt collector may not collect or attempt to collect a consumer debt by force or threat of force or use criminal means to cause harm to the debtor or the debtor's reputation or property. When you attempt to collect past due rent after a tenant has left, you are considered a debt collector and are subject to certain restrictions.

In most states, debt collectors are prohibited from trying to collect a debt by using profane or obscene language, placing telephone calls without disclosing their identity, calling collect, or causing the telephone to ring repeatedly to annoy the person being called. Collectors also cannot telephone or see the debtors with a frequency that would constitute harassment.

Contacting debtors' employers also is restricted. In most states, creditors are not allowed to inform debtors' employers about debtors' payment of a consumer debt. An exception to this is a communication necessary to the collection of the debt if it is made only to verify debtors' employment, locate debtors, or garnish the wages of debtors.

Debt collectors may not communicate with debtors in the name of an attorney or counselor at law or upon stationery bearing the name of an attorney or counselor at law, unless such communications are previously authorized by an attorney.

Collectors may not threaten to increase consumer debt by the addition of attorney fees, investigative fees, or service or finance charges if such fees or charges may not be legally added to an existing obligation. Collectors may not falsely represent themselves as being representatives of a credit reporting agency.

The Federal Fair Debt Collection Practices Act of 1978 supplements state restrictions. Basically, the act prohibits telephone calls from being made to debtors at unusual or inconvenient times; this usually is interpreted to mean calls before 8 a.m. or after 9 p.m. Repeated calls are prohibited, even if they are made during convenient hours. If a debtor is represented by an attorney and requests that creditors communicate only with the attorney, then all communications must be with the attorney. Creditors may contact debtors' places of employment only to obtain the debtors' current addresses. Creditors may not call neighbors, relatives, or third parties of the debtors except in a honest effort to locate them.

If debtors write stating that they do not intend to pay the debt, collectors must stop all communications with the debtors except to inform them of any legal action being taken.

Form 6-14 may be used as a collection letter in an attempt to collect past due rent.

Date: _____

To: _____[Name and address of debtor]

Re: Your account due from your tenancy at_____[address]

Dear: [name of debtor]:

There is still a balance due on your account of $ _____. This amount includes:

Past due rent	$_____
Accumulated late charges	$_____
Damages to the property	$_____

You are legally responsible for payment of the above-stated sum. Please contact me regarding when and how you intend to resolve this matter.

If I have not received a satisfactory response from you within ____ days, without further notice, the account may be

___ referred to a collection agency.

___ referred to our attorney with instructions to commence legal action for collection of the delinquent amount.

___ considered for a suit in small claims court.

As I am sure you are aware, if this matter goes to suit, all court costs, process servers' fees, sheriff's fees, attorney fees where permitted, and other postjudgment costs will be added to the amount you already owe. You can avoid the unnecessary inconvenience and added expenses of a lawsuit by making immediate payment to us within _____ days.

Sincerely,

Manager

FORM 6-14   Past due rent collection letter.

Before forwarding a case to a local attorney, you should consider whether that would be in your best interest. Often deadbeat tenants have no money, and even if you get a judgment against them, you may not be able to collect on it. Consider these factors before you incur additional legal expense. If a debt collection agency will take it on a contingency basis (for a percentage of the debt collected), you should consider that. In trying to collect rent from deadbeat tenants, it is best to remember an old gambler's adage: Don't throw good money after bad money. In other words, do not waste additional money unless there is a likelihood that your collection efforts will be successful. If you transfer the debt to a debt collection agency, the agency probably will want 40 to 50 percent of the amount collected as its fee. The fee is high because the likelihood of collection is low, but 50 percent of the debt is better than none of it. You may use a collection transmittal letter similar to the one in Form 6-15 to transmit the collection to a collection agency.

Often, a former tenant will dispute the amount due or attempt to compromise with you on the balance. It is against human nature to accept less when you know that the deadbeat owes the full amount, but a settlement is always more advantageous than the cost of a court case. Forms 6-16 and 6-17 may be used to achieve a compromise on an account. **Note:** Do not waive your rights to the full amount until you have the lesser amount in hand.

Before you take legal action on a delinquent debt, you may use Form 6-18 to provide the former tenant one last chance to correct this delinquency.

Date: _____

To: _____[attorney or collection agent]

Dear Madam/Sir:

The below-listed accounts are being turned over to your office for collection in accordance with your standard fee schedule. Also enclosed are the supporting documents for each account.

If additional information is required, please contact [name of contact person and telephone number].

We would appreciate your expedited efforts in collecting these accounts.

List of accounts being forwarded:

[list accounts here and attach supporting documents to this letter]

Sincerely,

Manager

FORM 6-15   Collection transmittal letter.

Date: _____

By this agreement, [name of Creditor] Creditor and [name of Debtor] Debtor resolve and forever settle and adjust the below-listed claim. Both parties agree that there is a bona fide dispute regarding the amount due the Creditor on this account. Accordingly, the parties agree that the Debtor shall pay to the Creditor the sum of $_____ no later than [date] as payment in full on the below-described account or claim.

Should Debtor fail to pay the agreed sum by the above-listed date, Creditor has the right to pursue the full amount claimed and is no longer under obligation to take the agreed sum as payment in full. If Debtor pays the agreed amount on or prior to the above-listed date, Creditor will accept the payment as payment in full.

This agreement covers the below-described account:

[describe the account or claim in this space]

This agreement shall be binding on all parties involved, their assigns, successors, and personal representatives.

FORM 6-16   Settlement of disputed account balance.

For good and valuable consideration, [name of Creditor (landlord)] Creditor and [name of Debtor (tenant(s)] Debtor hereby agree to compromise and discharge the debt owed to the Creditor by the Debtor according to the following terms

1. The Debtor acknowledges that the sum of the present debt due the Creditor is $_____.

2. The Creditor agrees to accept the sum of $ _____as payment in full and agrees to discharge, release, and accept as satisfaction of all monies presently due.

3. Agreement of the Creditor to accept a lesser sum is binding only if payment by the Debtor is made within ____days of the signing of this agreement.

4. If Debtor fails to pay the agreed sum within _____days of the signing of this agreements, the Creditor shall have the right to pursue his/her claim for the full amount.

5. In the event of default, the defaulting parties agree to pay reasonable attorney fees and costs.

6. The agreement shall be binding on parties, their heirs, assigns, successors, and personal representatives.

Signed this _____day of _____20_____

_____   _____
Debtor   Debtor

_____
Creditor

FORM 6-17   Compromise.

Date: _____

To: _____[name and address of debtor]

Re: Your past due account

Dear: _____[name of debtor]

We have made numerous requests for payment on your long overdue account. The balance is currently $_____.

Since you have failed to pay this account, we are by copy of this letter forwarding the account to our attorney. You may, however, still avoid legal action if you contact us within the next 10 days and make satisfactory arrangements for payment.

This is your final opportunity to avoid legal action.

Sincerely,

Manager

FORM 6-18   Final notice before legal action.

If you have made an agreement to collect the delinquent rent or other charges and the debtors (former tenants) have defaulted on their agreement, you may use Form 6-19 to advise them of the consequences of their default.

Using Small Claims Court to Collect Delinquent Rent

There are small claims courts in most states. In this section, the basic procedures of small claim courts and ways to use them to collect overdue rental accounts are discussed. Because there are some differences between states, you should check with the local court clerk to determine the specific rules in your state. These courts were established to provide citizens with a convenient method to collect

Date: _____

To: _____[name and address of debtor (former tenants)]

Dear: _____[name of debtor]

This is to advise you that you are in default of the (monthly)(weekly) payment for your past due rent and other charges associated with your tenancy at _____(address).

Accordingly, unless the account is current within _____ days after you receive this letter, I will have no alternative but to forward the matter to our attorney to take action necessary to collect the balance due on the account.

Sincerely,

Manager

FORM 6-19   Notice of default on settlement agreement.

amounts due without having to resort to the complicated and complex rules of procedure and evidence that prevail in regular courts.

Many states prohibit attorneys from appearing in small claims courts. In those which do allow attorneys, the modest jurisdictional amounts make it uneconomical for attorneys to appear. If your losses are above the maximum limit in your state, you may reduce the amount claimed to the maximum limit and bring your case in small claims court.

You can use the court to collect accounts that are too small to refer to an attorney and to reduce the legal expenses in marginal accounts by collecting them yourself.

Venue

Venue refers to the location of the specific court in which you may bring suit. In all states, you may sue the defendant in the county where she or he resides or has a place of business. In most states, you also may sue the defendant in the county in which the damage or injury occurred or in which the defendant was to perform the obligation. In most states, you may sue the defendant in the county in which the contract was entered into. Generally, since the rental debt was incurred in your county, the defendant may be sued in your county. Make sure to bring the suit in the proper court. Otherwise a delay will be caused by the need to refile in the appropriate court.

Cost

Filing fees for small claims courts vary from $50 to $100. In some states, if the plaintiff files more than six small claims actions a year, filing fees are higher. The only other cost involved, other than the loss of time from work to file and try the case, is the cost for service of the summons on the defendant. In most states, the defendant may be served by registered mail. Thus, this expense is small. In states that require personal service, either a professional process server or a police officer can serve the summons. The usual cost in the latter situation is about $30.

Starting the Case

A small claims case is started by filing a petition with the proper court. When you file, check with the clerk's office to make sure you are bringing the case in the correct court and at the proper location. Usually, filing a case consists of completing a simple form and paying the required filing fee. Most small claims courts have a person who will help you fill out the form and answer your questions. After the case is filed, the summons (notice of pending court case) must be served on the defendant either by registered mail or by a process server. Ask the court clerk what the normal methods of service are in your county.

When you file the case, you should obtain a date for the hearing from the court. If the date the clerk suggests is inconvenient, ask for a more convenient one. Remember to leave enough time to serve the defendant and permit the defendant to have the required notice time. In most states, you are required to give the defendant at least 15 days' notice before the court date.

Changing a Court Date

If the defendant or plaintiff has problems going to court on the scheduled date and requests a different date, the court usually will allow at least one delay. After the first delay, however, any person requesting another one must provide sufficient justification to warrant it. To request a delay, ask the clerk for the proper procedure in your district or county.

If either party fails to appear at the scheduled time or has received improper notice, the court usually will rule in favor of the other party. If a default occurs, that is, the defendant fails to appear—you may be required to prove that the defendant was served properly.

The Hearing

On the scheduled hearing date, you should be on time and in the right courtroom. Check this out ahead of time. Bring any documents and witnesses you need to prove your claim. The hearings are informal, without the need to comply with the strict rules of evidence required in other civil court proceedings. The judge will allow the plaintiff (you) to state the facts surrounding the complaint and then allow the defendant to tell his or her side of the case. After listening to both sides, the judge will make a decision on the merits of the case. He or she will announce his decision or tell you that you will receive his or her decision by mail in a few days. In most states, persons are notified by mail. Remember to ask the judge to award you your costs if bringing the suit.

In most states, the allowable costs are your filing fee, the costs to serve notice on the defendant, the witnesses' fees, and the cost of preparing documents for the case. There are no rights to a jury trial in small claims court. The decor of the court depends on the judge. Most judges in small claims courts are relaxed and informal. Occasionally, you will have a judge who demands a certain degree of formality. Always be polite to the judge, and do not argue with him or her.

If you bring witnesses, discuss their testimony with them before going into the courtroom. By this I mean that you should be very familiar with the testimony they are going to present. Do not, however, suggest or tell the witnesses what to say in court.

Default Judgment

If the defendant fails to appear on the scheduled date, the judge will require you to prove that the defendant was properly notified of the hearing. The judge also may ask you about some of the basic facts of the case. If the judge is satisfied that your claim is proper, he or she will enter a default judgment in your favor. If you fail to prove that the defendant was given proper notice, in most cases the judge will reschedule the case.

After a default judgment against the defendant, she or he has a short period to appear in court and explain his or her absence. To set aside a default judgment, the defaulting party must establish a sufficient excuse for failing to appear at the scheduled time and also show that she or he should prevail in the lawsuit. If both requirements are met, a new hearing date will be set.

Small Claims Courts for the State of New York

- Dollar Limit: $3,000.
- Where to Sue: Where defendant resides, is employed, or maintains a business office.
- Service: Certified or registered mail, court-approved adult. If after 21 days not returned as undeliverable, notice presumed.
- Hearing Date: Set by court.
- Attorneys: Allowed; required for most corporations.
- Transfer: Within court's discretion to appropriate court.
- Appeals: By defendant only for review of law, not facts, or by plaintiff if "substantial justice" was not done; to County Court or Appellate Terms within 30 days.

To find out the rules in your state, visit www.consumeraffairs.com.

Appeals

In some states, including California, only the defendant can appeal a small claims judgment. This limitation is based on the concept that the plaintiff, by bringing the case in small claims court, agrees to abide by that court's decision. In most states, either party unhappy with the decision may appeal by giving notice or filing an appeal bond within a few days after the decision is announced or mailed. The time in which the appeal must be filed varies from 15 to 30 days. If an appeal is not filed within that time, the judgment is considered final.

In 15 states, an appeal from the small claims court goes to the district or superior court, and the case is tried de novo. "De novo" means that the case is completely retried in the higher court. The judge makes a decision that is based only on the evidence presented before his or her court. In the other states, the appellate court does not hear any evidence and decides the merits of the appeal on the basis of the record of the trial and the briefs submitted by the parties.

Enforcing a Judgment

After you win a case in court and the judge orders the opposing party to pay a sum of money to you, the next step is to collect the money. In most cases, the threat of court intervention will cause the losing party to pay the judgment. If that is not sufficient, you must execute the judgment to get your money. In most states, a court judgment creates a lien on the property of any person who is ordered by a court to pay a sum of money (judgment debtor). The extent of the lien and the mechanics of enforcing it vary from state to state.

A judgment lien operates as a general lien on all the debtor's property, but it isn't a specific lien on particular property. It is, in reality, a right to levy on the property of the judgment debtor. In most states, statutes provide for a single writ by which a person with favorable court judgment may seize any property of the debtor and have it sold to satisfy the debt.

To obtain a writ of execution, see the clerk of the court that issued the judgment and request that he or she issue one. No hearings or other court proceedings are required. After the clerk issues you the writ, take it to the sheriff's office or to another authorized authority. If in doubt about this procedure, ask someone in the clerk's office. The clerk may charge a small fee to issue the writ of attachment.

The writ is directed to the sheriff and orders him or her to levy on the property of the judgment debtor and, after due notice, to sell such property at a public sale. The writ will have a "return date" on it. The sheriff is ordered by the court to return the writ to the court by that date with an endorsement stating that the property listed in the writ was sold or that it was impossible to find leviable assets.

If no property that belongs to the judgment debtor can be found, in most states the debtor may be called to court and examined under oath by the other party regarding his or her property (a debtor's examination). False statements regarding the status of the debtor's property are criminal offenses in all states.

Execution Sales

After you obtain a writ of execution and have it levied on the property of the debtor, the next step is the sale of the property and the distribution of the proceeds. Most states require that an appraisal of the property be made before the sale. If the sale brings less than a stated percentage of the appraised value, the sale must be canceled or the required percentage must be credited against the debt.

The proceeds of the sale are applied first to the fees and expenses of the sale and then to the judgment debt. If any money remains, it goes to the judgment debtor. At an execution sale, unlike a judicial sale, no specific property is designated and the court gives no directions regarding the sale. At the sale, however, the buyer buys only the interests the judgment debtor has in the property. There are no implied warranties on anyone's part. It is a sale "as is." If there are preexisting liens or mortgages on the property, they remain a charge against the property. Another problem with an execution sale is that if the purchaser loses the property because it did not belong to the debtor or there was a superior claim to it, the buyer is not entitled to a return of his or her purchase money.

Right of Redemption

In most states, a judgment debtor has a right of redemption of any real property sold at an execution sale. This means that within a stated period of time, the judgment debtor may reclaim the real property by refunding to the buyer the amount that he or she originally paid. In some states, the debtor also may redeem personal property by repaying the purchase price. The usual period of redemption for real property is four to six years; it is six months to one year in states that allow redemption of personal property.

Garnishment

Garnishing a judgment debtor's property that is possessed by a third person is another method that may be used to collect a judgment debt. The most common method is to garnish the wages of an employee by serving an order of garnishment on his or her employer. Unlike a writ of execution, which is issued by the clerk, a garnishment order requires a court order and, in most states, a court hearing. In most states, if an employee's wages are being garnished, there are limits and restrictions on the percentages of his or her wages that are subject to garnishment.

Exempt Property

In all states, certain properties of a judgment debtor may not be attached and sold at an execution sale. The most commonly exempt property is the homestead of the debtor. In some states, the debtor must have registered or recorded the property as his or her homestead to protect it from a judgment creditor. Other property commonly exempted includes the family automobile, personal clothes, tools of one's trade, and items such as the family Bible. Because the list of exempt property varies among the states, check with your court clerk's office for a list of exempt property in your state.

7

Ending the Tenancy

In this chapter, we look at ending the landlord–tenant relationship, including, what to do when notice of termination is received from tenants, when it is necessary to terminate a tenancy for nonpayment of rent, requirements for the return of the deposit, and other recommended actions to take when a tenancy is ended.

Breach of Lease by Tenant

Generally, if a tenant breaches the lease, the landlord may terminate the tenancy and sue for damages under breach of contract theory; elect to continue the tenancy and sue periodically for rent as it accrues; or terminate the lease, retake possession, and absolve the tenant from all liability. If the landlord chooses to terminate the tenancy, the landlord must mitigate damages. The most common method of mitigating damages is by making a good faith effort to rerent the premises.

Damages for Breach of Lease

In general, upon a renter's default or breach of the rental agreement, the landlord has three options: The landlord can (1) remain out of possession, treat the lease as subsisting, and collect rent; (2) give notice to the tenant, resume possession of the premises, and attempt to mitigate damages by rerenting the premises; or (3) reenter, resume possession, and effectively terminate the lease. (*Brywood Ltd. Partners, L.P. v, H.G.T., Inc.*, 866 SW2d 903.)

General Rules Regarding the Ending of a Tenancy

The general rules set forth in this section were taken from the Model Landlord and Tenant Act. They apply in most states and apply in the others with slight variations. They are listed here to give landlords an idea of the requirements involved in ending a tenancy. Check your local statutes for specific requirements.

Holding Over after Term, Tenancy at Sufferance

When any tenancy created by a lease or any instrument in writing, the term of which is limited, has expired and the tenant holds over in the possession of said premises without renewing the lease by some further instrument in writing, then such holding over shall be construed to be a *tenancy at sufferance*. The mere payment or acceptance of rent is not be construed to be a renewal of the term, but if the holding is continued with the written consent of the lesso,r then the tenancy shall become a tenancy at will.

Right of Possession upon Default in Rent

If any person leasing or renting any land or premises fails to pay the rent at the time it becomes due, the landlord has the right to obtain possession of the premises as provided by law.

The landlord shall recover possession of rented premises only:

- In a legal action for possession, or other civil action in which the issue of right of possession is determined;
- When the tenant has surrendered possession of the rented premises to the landlord; or
- When the tenant has abandoned the rented premises.

In the absence of actual knowledge of abandonment, it is presumed that a tenant has abandoned the rented premises if:

- The landlord reasonably believes that the tenant has been absent from the rented premises for a period of 30 consecutive days;
- The rent is not current; and
- A notice of belief of abandonment has been served and 10 days have elapsed since service of such notice.

However, this presumption does not apply if the rent is current or the tenant has notified the landlord in writing of an intended absence.

Causes for Removal of Tenants

Any tenant or lessee at will or sufferance, or for part of the year, or for one or more years, of any houses, lands, or tenements, and the assigns, under tenants or legal representatives of such tenant or lessee, may be removed from the premises in the manner hereinafter provided in the following cases:

- Where such person holds over and continues in the possession of the demised premises, or any part thereof, after the expiration of the person's time, without the permission of the person's landlord.
- Where such person holds over without permission as aforesaid, after any default in the payment of rent pursuant to the agreement under which the premises are held, and 3 days' notice in writing requiring the payment of the rent or the possession of the premises has been served by the person entitled to the rent on the person owing the same. The service of the notice shall be by delivery of a true copy thereof, or, if the tenant is absent from the rented premises, by leaving a copy thereof at such place.
- Where such person holds over without permission after failing to cure a material breach of the lease or oral agreement, other than nonpayment of rent, and when 15 days' written notice requiring the cure of such breach or the possession of the premises has been served on the tenant. This applies only when the lease is silent on the matter or when the tenancy is an oral one at will. The notice may give a longer time period for cure of the breach or surrender of the premises. In the absence of a lease provision prescribing the method for serving notices, service must be by mail, hand delivery, or, if the tenant is absent from the rental premises or the address designated by the lease, by posting.

Waiver of Right to Proceed with Eviction Claim

The landlord's acceptance of the full amount of rent past due, with knowledge of the tenant's breach of the lease by nonpayment, shall be considered a waiver of the landlord's right to proceed with an eviction claim for nonpayment of that rent. Acceptance of the rent includes conduct by the landlord concerning any tender of the rent by the tenant that is inconsistent with reasonably prompt return of the payment to the tenant.

Removal of Tenant

The landlord, the landlord's attorney or agent, applying for the removal of any tenant, shall file a complaint stating the facts that authorize the removal of the tenant, and describing the premises in the proper court of the county where the premises are situated and is entitled to the summary procedure provided.

Right of Action for Possession

If a rental agreement is terminated, and the tenant does not vacate the premises, the landlord may recover possession of the dwelling unit as provided by state law. A landlord, the landlord's attorney, or the landlord's agent, applying for the removal of a tenant shall file in the county court of the county where the premises are situated a complaint describing the dwelling unit and stating the facts that authorize its recovery. A landlord's agent is not permitted to take any action other than the initial filing of the complaint, unless the landlord's agent is an attorney. The landlord is entitled to the summary procedure, and the court shall advance the cause on the calendar.

A landlord may not recover possession of a dwelling unit except:

- In a legal action for possession under subsection (2) or other civil action in which the issue of right of possession is determined;
- When the tenant has surrendered possession of the dwelling unit to the landlord; or
- When the tenant has abandoned the dwelling unit.

In the absence of actual knowledge of abandonment, it shall be presumed that the tenant has abandoned the dwelling unit if he or she is absent from the premises for a period of time equal to one-half the time for periodic rental payments. However, this presumption shall not apply if the rent is current or the tenant has notified the landlord, in writing, of an intended absence.

Choice of Remedies upon Breach by Tenant

If the tenant breaches the lease for the dwelling unit, and the landlord has obtained a writ of possession, or the tenant has surrendered possession of the dwelling unit to the landlord, or the tenant has abandoned the dwelling unit, the landlord may:

- Treat the lease as terminated and retake possession for his or her own account, thereby terminating any further liability of the tenant; or
- Retake possession of the dwelling unit for the account of the tenant, holding the tenant liable for the difference between rental stipulated to be paid under the lease agreement and what, in good faith, the landlord is able to recover from a reletting; or
- Stand by and do nothing, holding the lessee liable for the rent as it comes due.

If the landlord retakes possession of the dwelling unit for the account of the tenant, the landlord has a duty to exercise good faith in attempting to relet the premises, and any rentals received by the landlord as a result of the reletting shall be deducted from the balance of rent due from the tenant. "Good faith in attempting to relet the premises" means that the landlord shall use at least the same efforts to relet the premises as were used in the initial rental or at least the same efforts as the landlord uses in attempting to lease other similar rental units but does not require the landlord to give a preference in leasing the premises over other vacant dwelling units that the landlord owns or has the responsibility to rent.

Defenses to Action for Rent or Possession

In a court action by the landlord for possession of a dwelling unit based upon nonpayment of rent or in an action by the landlord seeking to recover unpaid rent, the tenant may defend upon the ground of a material noncompliance with the lease, or may raise any other defense, whether legal or equitable, that he or she may have, including the defense of retaliatory conduct.

The defense of a material noncompliance with the terms of the lease may be raised by the tenant if 7 days have elapsed after the delivery of written notice by the tenant to the landlord, specifying the noncompliance and indicating the intention of the tenant not to pay rent by reason thereof. Such notice by the tenant may be given to the landlord, the landlord's representative, a resident manager, or the person or entity who collects the rent on behalf of the landlord.

A material noncompliance by the landlord is a complete defense to an action for possession based upon nonpayment of rent, and, upon hearing, the court or the jury, as the case may be, shall determine the amount, if any, by which the rent is to be reduced to reflect the diminution in value of the dwelling unit during the period of noncompliance.

Restoration of Possession to Landlord

In an action for possession, after entry of judgment in favor of the landlord, the clerk shall issue a writ to the sheriff describing the premises and commanding the sheriff to put the landlord in possession after 24 hours' notice conspicuously posted on the premises.

Power to Award Possession and Enter Money Judgment

In an action by the landlord for possession of a dwelling unit based upon nonpayment of rent, if the court finds the rent is due, owing, and unpaid and by reason thereof the landlord is entitled to possession of the premises, the court, in addition to awarding possession of the premises to the landlord, shall direct, in an amount that is within its jurisdictional limitations, the entry of a money judgment with costs in favor of the landlord and against the tenant for the amount of money found due, owing, and unpaid by the tenant to the landlord. However, no money judgment shall be entered unless service of process has been affected by personal service or, where authorized by law, by certified or registered mail, return receipt, or in any other manner prescribed by law or the rules of the court; and no money judgment may be entered except in compliance with the Rules of Civil Procedure. The prevailing party in the action may also be awarded attorney's fees and costs.

Retaliatory Conduct

It is unlawful for a landlord to discriminatorily increase a tenant's rent or decrease services to a tenant, or to bring or threaten to bring an action for possession or other civil action, primarily because the landlord is retaliating against the tenant. In order for the tenant to raise the defense of retaliatory conduct, the tenant must have acted in good faith. Examples of conduct for which the landlord may not retaliate include, but are not limited to, situations where:

- The tenant has complained to a governmental agency charged with responsibility for enforcement of a building, housing, or health code of a suspected violation applicable to the premises;
- The tenant has organized, encouraged, or participated in a tenants' organization; or
- The tenant has complained to the landlord regarding a condition that is unhealthy.

Evidence of retaliatory conduct may be raised by the tenant as a defense in any action brought against him or her for possession. Retaliatory conduct defense does not apply if the landlord proves that the eviction is for good cause. Examples of good cause include, but are not limited to, good faith actions for nonpayment of rent, violation of the rental agreement or of reasonable rules, or violation of the terms.

"Discrimination" means that a tenant is being treated differently as to the rent charged, the services rendered, or the action being taken by the landlord, which shall be a prerequisite to a finding of retaliatory conduct.

Prohibited Practices

A landlord shall not cause, directly or indirectly, the termination or interruption of any utility service furnished the tenant, including, but not limited to, water, heat, light, electricity, gas, elevator, garbage collection, or refrigeration, whether or not the utility service is under the control of, or payment is made by, the landlord.

A landlord may not prevent the tenant from gaining reasonable access to the dwelling unit by any means, including, but not limited to, changing the locks or using any bootlock or similar device.

A landlord may not discriminate against a servicemember in offering a dwelling unit for rent or in any of the terms of the rental agreement.

A landlord shall not prohibit a tenant from displaying one portable, removable, cloth or plastic United States flag, not larger than 4½ feet by 6 feet, in a respectful manner in or on the dwelling unit regardless of any provision in the rental agreement dealing with flags or decorations. The landlord is not liable for damages caused by a United States flag displayed by a tenant. Any United States flag may not infringe upon the space rented by any other tenant.

A landlord of any dwelling unit governed by this part shall not remove the outside doors, locks, roof, walls, or windows of the unit except for purposes of maintenance, repair, or replacement; and the landlord shall not remove the tenant's personal property from the dwelling unit unless such action is taken after surrender, abandonment, or a lawful eviction.

Orders to Enjoin Violations

A landlord who gives notice to a tenant of the landlord's intent to terminate the tenant's lease pursuant due to the tenant's intentional destruction, damage, or misuse of the landlord's property may petition the county or circuit court for an injunction prohibiting the tenant from continuing to violate any of the provisions of the lease.

Termination of Rental Agreement by a Servicemember

Any servicemember may terminate his or her rental agreement by providing the landlord with a written notice of termination to be effective on the date stated in the notice that is at least 30 days after the landlord's receipt of the notice if any of the following criteria are met:

- The servicemember is required, pursuant to a permanent change of station orders, to move 35 miles or more from the location of the rental premises;
- The servicemember is prematurely or involuntarily discharged or released from active duty; or
- The servicemember is released from active duty or state active duty after having leased the rental premises while on active duty or state active duty status

and the rental premises is 35 miles or more from the servicemember's home of record prior to entering active duty or state active duty;

- After entering into a rental agreement, the servicemember receives military orders requiring him or her to move into government quarters or the servicemember becomes eligible to live in and opts to move into government quarters;
- The servicemember receives temporary duty orders, temporary change of station orders, or state active duty orders to an area 35 miles or more from the location of the rental premises, provided such orders are for a period exceeding 60 days; or
- The servicemember has leased the property, but prior to taking possession of the rental premises, receives a change of orders to an area that is 35 miles or more from the location of the rental premises.

The notice to the landlord must be accompanied by either a copy of the official military orders or a written verification signed by the servicemember's commanding officer.

In the event a servicemember dies during active duty, an adult member of his or her immediate family may terminate the servicemember's rental agreement by providing the landlord with a written notice of termination to be effective on the date stated in the notice that is at least 30 days after the landlord's receipt of the notice. The notice to the landlord must be accompanied by either a copy of the official military orders showing the servicemember was on active duty or a written verification signed by the servicemember's commanding officer and a copy of the servicemember's death certificate.

Upon termination of a rental agreement by the servicemember, the tenant is liable for the rent due under the rental agreement prorated to the effective date of the termination payable at such time as would have otherwise been required by the terms of the rental agreement. The tenant is not liable for any other rent or damages due to the early termination of the tenancy.

Constructive Eviction

Landlords should be careful to avoid a situation in which the residential unit is unsuitable for habitation. In other words, a landlord may provide housing that is so substandard that the landlord has legally evicted the tenant. For example, if the landlord refuses to provide heat or water or refuses to clean up an environmental health hazard, the tenant has the right to move out and stop paying rent without incurring legal liability for breaking the lease. In a constructive eviction case, if the tenant establishes that the premises were not livable and the landlord failed to take reasonable action to cure the problem, the landlord will be considered as having breached the lease.

Failure to Take Possession

When tenants enter into a valid rental lease and then change their minds and never take possession of the unit, this constitutes a breach of contract. The measure of damages recoverable for their breach is the excess, if any, of the agreed rent over the actual rental value of the premises, together with any special damages the landlord may incur. For example, the cost of readvertising the unit is considered a special damage that has resulted from the breach. As a general rule, if the landlord makes alterations in the property to adapt to the special needs or request of the prospective renter, the cost of those alterations also may be recovered as special damages. Other possible damages include the loss of rent when the unit is vacant because of the breach or when it is necessary to rent the unit for a lower rent.

It is the landlord's duty, on the tenant's failure to occupy, to mitigate damages by accepting or procuring another renter. **Note:** Even when the landlord has a duty to mitigate damages, the burden of proving failure to mitigate is on the individuals who breached the lease, and they also must show the amount by which their damages were increased by the landlord's failure to mitigate. Even when the landlord fails to execute his or her duty to minimize all possible damages to the proposed renter as soon as the breach is committed, the landlord is at least entitled to nominal damages for the breach of the agreement.

This agreement is entered into on the following date: _____ , between _____ (Resident), who leases the premises at the following address: _____, and _____ (management).

Resident has asked for permission to break or cancel the rental agreement between the parties on short notice and/or prior to the expiration date of the agreement. Resident wishes to move out by the following date, _____, even though he/she will not be able to give proper notice as required in the rental agreement. In exchange for Owner agreeing to cancel the agreement, Resident agrees to the following terms:

- To provide Manager with written notice of intent to vacate.

- To pay the current month's rent of $ _____ plus an additional amount of $ _____.

- These payments will be paid by the following date: _____.

- To promptly return the keys to Manager and completely move and vacate the premises on or before the following date: _____, which shall be considered the cancellation date of this agreement.

- To provide a forwarding address to Owner prior to vacating the apartment.

continued

FORM 7-1 Agreement to cancel lease.

- To leave the apartment in a clean condition and free of any and all damages.
- To allow Manager to show the premises to any prospective resident with as little as one hour's notice any time during the following hours: _____.
- If Resident can't be reached after Manager has made a good faith effort to do so, Manager or an agent may enter and show the rental.
- To hereby forever release any claims or causes of action that Resident may have or that shall arise in the future against Management, its officers, directors, employees, or agents arising out of the rental agreement.
- Other:_____.

If Resident fulfills the obligations agreed to above, Management agrees to:

- Release Resident from any further obligation to pay rent.
- Not report any poor performance or unfavorable information regarding Resident to any credit or tenant reporting agencies.
- Return the security deposit, provided that Resident has complied with the above terms, and provided that there are no unpaid outstanding charges of any kind due from Resident and that there are no damages to the property.
- In the event Resident does not fulfill the terms above or is in default under any of the terms of the rental agreement, management shall have the right to keep and apply the aforesaid cancellation fee toward any damages arising as a result of such default.

Date: _____   Resident's Signature: _____

Date: _____   For Management: _____

FORM 7-1   Agreement to cancel lease (continued).

Canceling the Lease

Although, as landlord, you have a right to enforce the terms of a lease, sometimes it is better to allow a problem tenant to move. Form 7-1 may be used to cancel the lease in a case where both parties wish to end the tenancy.

Return of Security Deposit

As was discussed earlier, state law generally requires that the security deposit be returned within a certain number of days after the tenancy ends and that the tenants receive an itemized statement of any charges applied against the deposit. Form 7-2 may be used to note the setoffs against the deposit.

Tenant Obligations in Terminating the Tenancy

Form 7-3 may be used to inform tenants of their obligations under the lease as they terminate the tenancy.

Date: _____

Dear: _____(former tenants)

This letter is to notify you of the itemization of the security deposit returned to you for the property you occupied at_____.

You officially vacated the apartment (keys returned, etc.) on the following date: _____.

    Amount of security deposit: $ _____

    Interest on deposit (if applicable or required by law): $ _____

    The following deductions were applied:

        Total amount deducted: $ _____

Balance of deposit returned: $ _____

Amount due management (if balanced owed exceeded the security deposit) $ _____

Please contact us within _____ days (if you have any questions) to arrange to pay balance due to prevent damage to your credit history.

Sincerely,

Manager

FORM 7-2   Itemization of security deposit return.

Date: _____

Dear:_____(tenants)

Your Intent to Vacate Notice has been received, and we appreciate that you are following the steps necessary so that you can be entitled to have as much security deposit as possible refunded back to you.

This letter is sent to remind you that your rental agreement requires that the premises be left clean and undamaged. This includes the obligations below:

■ Remove any unwanted items from the building and set them outside for trash pickup on the appropriate day prior to your final move-out. Please note that you may need to contact the appropriate sanitation office at the following number to make special arrangements for removal of large items. If you leave any items in the premises or outside that have not been removed after you vacate, the owner will have items removed and you will be held responsible for the cost of removal, which will be deducted from your security deposit.

■ Please have the property looking clean and neat several days before you vacate so that it looks presentable when we show it to prospective residents. We ask for your complete cooperation in allowing us to show the property. If we attempt to contact you for a showing and can't reach you, we ask for permission to enter the premises. Feel free to recommend any persons you know who may wish to move into the premises you are vacating. Have them call us at the following number: _____.

continued

FORM 7-3   Move-out and reminder letter.

- Remove all food and items from the cabinets and the refrigerator.

- Clean all the appliances, including the stove, oven, and refrigerator. Replace any missing or burned-out lightbulbs.

- Remove all items from the walls and sweep or vacuum all floors.

The property will be inspected after you have alerted us that the property has been vacated. We will check to ensure that it has been left clean and undamaged. If we have to hire someone to clean or repair damages, you will be notified of any charges to your deposit. Hopefully that will not be necessary.

Thank you for your cooperation.

Sincerely,

Manager

FORM 7-3   Move-out and reminder letter (continued).

Form 7-4 may be used to notify a tenant whose lease has been terminated.

Court Cases

Often, information regarding local court rules and procedures are posted on the state court's web site. For example, the official website of the New Jersey state courts provides the following information regarding landlord–tenant cases in New Jersey courts.

Landlord and Tenant Complaints

Most disputes between landlords and tenants are resolved by the Landlord/Tenant Section of the New Jersey Superior Court, Special Civil Part. The Landlord/Tenant Section is one of the three sections of the Special Civil Part. Following is a general list of some of the reasons a landlord may file a complaint in court:

- Failure to pay rent.
- Continued disorderly conduct.
- Willful destruction or damage to property.
- Habitual lateness in paying rent.
- Violation of rules and regulations, after written notice to comply, as outlined in a lease or other document.
- Tenant's conviction for a drug offense.

   Before filing some complaints, a landlord must give a tenant written notice to stop particular conduct. Only when a tenant continues that conduct after notice to stop can a landlord try to have the tenant evicted. Also, complaints

To:_____

And All Tenant(s) in Possession

You are hereby required within thirty (30) days from this date to vacate, remove your belongings, and deliver up possession of the premises now held and occupied by you, being those premises located at:

House number:_____ Street:_____ Apartment number: ____

City: _____ State: _____ Zip:_____.

This notice is intended for the purpose of terminating the lease agreement by which you now hold possession of the above premises. Should you fail to vacate and comply, legal proceedings will be instituted against you to recover possession, to declare said lease/rental forfeited, and to recover rents, damages, attorney fees, and court costs for the period of the unlawful detention.

Please be advised that your rent for said premises is due and payable up to and including the date of termination of your tenancy under this notice. This notice complies with the terms and conditions of the lease or rental agreement under which you presently hold said property. Please contact the office of the manager if you have questions regarding this notice or the requirements and procedure for getting back any deposits to which you are entitled.

Dated this _____ day of _____ , 20 _____.

Manager

PROOF OF SERVICE

I, the undersigned, being of legal age, declare under penalty of perjury that I served the notice to terminate tenancy, of which this is a true copy, on the above-mentioned tenant in possession, in the manner indicated below:

On _____, 20_____, I served the notice to the tenant in the following manner:

Executed on _____ , 20 _____ , at _____

By: _____ Title: _____

FORM 7-4 Notice to terminate tenancy.

for other than nonpayment of rent generally require notice terminating the tenancy. You may wish to contact an attorney for more information.

A landlord or a tenant that is a corporation must be represented by a New Jersey attorney in all matters filed in the Landlord/Tenant Section. No landlord or tenant may send a representative other than a lawyer to court.

Filing a Complaint

A Landlord/Tenant complaint form is available from the Office of the Clerk of the Special Civil Part in the county where the rental premises are located. The complaint can be sent to the court through the mail or delivered in person. When filing a complaint, you must:

- Give your full name, address, and telephone number. To ensure proper service of the complaint, give the correct name(s) and address(es) of the person(s) named in the complaint as defendant(s). It is important that the defendant be properly identified as an individual, a sole proprietorship, a partnership, or a corporation.
- Give all information for the type of complaint you're filing, as indicated on the form.
- Sign the completed form.
- Pay the correct filing and service fees when filing the complaint with the Office of the Clerk of the Special Civil Part.

Where to File a Complaint

A complaint must be filed with the Office of the Special Civil Part Clerk in the county where the rental premises are located.

Filing Fees

The cost for filing a complaint in the Landlord/Tenant Section is:
$20.00 for one defendant. $2.00 for each additional defendant.

In addition, you must pay a mileage fee for delivery of the complaint by a Court Officer. The staff of the Special Civil Part can inform you of the mileage fee.

Preparation for Trial

If you are the landlord, you must come to court and prove the statements made in the complaint are true. Arrange to have in court any witnesses you need to prove your case. *A written statement, even if made under oath, cannot be used in court.* Only actual, in-court testimony of the witnesses will be allowed. Prepare your questions in advance.

Bring to court records of any transactions that may help you prove your case. Such records may include leases, estimates, bills, rent receipt records, dishonored checks, letters, photographs, and other documents proving your claim.

The Day of Trial

Both the landlord and the tenant must come to court at the time and date stated on the complaint unless otherwise notified by the court. Bring all evidence and witnesses needed to present your case. Both the landlord and tenant will be able to present their cases.

If the court decides in favor of the tenant, the case will be dismissed. If the court decides in favor of the landlord, a "judgment for possession" will be granted. A judgment for possession allows the landlord, within time limits, to have the tenant removed from the premises by a Court Officer.

If the landlord's complaint is for nonpayment of rent, and the tenant offers to pay all the rent due plus court costs before or on the day of the court hearing, the landlord must accept the rent, and the case will be dismissed. If the landlord doesn't accept the money, it may be deposited with the Clerk of the Special Civil Part. The judgment then will be voided, and the tenant does not have to move out of the premises.

Judgment for Possession

If a landlord is granted judgment for possession, the landlord may apply to the Clerk of the Special Civil Part for a warrant for possession, which allows the landlord to force the tenant to move out of the premises. The fee for a warrant for possession is $15.00 plus double the amount of the mileage fee. The warrant for possession may not be issued until three (3) business days (not counting the court day) after the judgment for possession is granted. The warrant for possession will be issued to a Court Officer to serve on the tenant.

The Court Officer must give a residential tenant three (3) business days to move all persons and belongings from the premises. If the tenant does not move after three (3) business days from which the warrant for possession was served, the landlord may arrange with the Court Officer to have the tenant evicted or locked out. The Court Officer will tell the landlord the fee charged for an eviction.

Following the eviction, the landlord must let the tenant remove personal belongings from the premises. A landlord cannot keep a tenant's belongings, but can arrange for their storage.

A landlord must apply for a warrant for possession within 30 days from the date of the judgment for possession unless the judgment is stopped through a court order or other written agreement signed by the landlord and the tenant.

A tenant may ask the court for permission to stay in the premises due to special difficulties that moving out may cause. If permission is granted, the tenant may not stay in the premises for more than six months. All rent due ordinarily must be paid for permission to be granted by the court.

Personal Property

It is not unusual for tenants to leave personal property in the unit after they have moved out. Form 7-5 may be used to notify tenants about the left property.

Notice by Tenant

It is often advisable to have a standard notice that tenants may use to notify management that they intend to vacate the premise. A form similar to Form 7-6 may be used for this purpose. It is recommended that these forms be available in your management office. When a tenant indicates that he or she will be moving, provide the tenant with a copy of the form and indicate that you need the tenant to complete it to complete the notice of intent to vacate.

If a tenant gives a shorter notice than is required by the lease, Form 7-7 may be used to response to the short notice period.

Date: _____

Dear: _____[former tenants]

When you vacated the rental dwelling at _____, the following personal property was left behind in the dwelling:

These items have been placed in storage for _____days. You may claim this property by contacting _____.

These items must be claimed as well as storage and moving charges paid within _____ days of this notice or the property will be either sold or disposed of, which is allowed by local law.

Sincerely,

Manager

FORM 7-5   Notice to reclaim personal property.

Date: _____

From:_____, Resident

To: Manager

This letter is to notify you that I/we will be moving from the following address: _____

I/we will move out and vacate the premises no later than the following date: _____

___ This notice provides you with at least ____ days written notice as required in the rental agreement.

FORM 7-6   Resident's notice of intent to vacate.

___ Special arrangements are requested. Those arrangements include _____, and I agree to pay an additional buy-out fee, if applicable, to get the rental agreement cancelled early and/or without sufficient advance notice provided to the manager. I plan to fully cooperate with the management in regard to the following:

I agree to:

___ allow management to show the premises to any prospective residents, and I understand that if I can't be reached after Manager has made a good faith effort to do so, Manager or an agent may enter and show the rental.

___ promptly return the keys to Manager and completely move and vacate the premises on or before the date stated above.

___ leave the rental in a clean condition and free of any and all damages.

___ provide a forwarding address to Owner prior to vacating the rental so that the security deposit can be returned, provided that I have complied with the above terms, that I have no unpaid outstanding charges of any kind, and that there are no damages to the property.

Resident's Signature: _____ Date: _____

FORM 7-6 Resident's notice of intent to vacate (continued).

Date: _____

Dear: _____(tenant)

_____(address)

Your request for permission to vacate the above address without giving proper notice has been received. Under the terms of the lease, you are required to give a minimum 30-day written notice prior to the date you desire to move out in order to receive your security deposit back.

We understand that sometimes circumstances arise that you are unable to plan for. The reason 30-day notices are required is to give both parties advance notice to plan for the change. In our case, a 30-day notice gives us time to find another tenant to take your place. Without sufficient time, we may have days go by with a vacant dwelling and loss of income, which is why your security deposit is not refunded. However, if you assist us by recommending a friend or coworker to take over the residential unit as soon as you move out, we do not lose rental income and we can, therefore, return your deposit to you, minus a small transfer fee of only $50.

We will also do all we can to get the place rerented promptly. If we do so prior to your moving, we will return your deposit to you minus the transfer fee plus advertising costs we incurred. This will still provide you with a return of part of your deposit that I'm sure will be helpful to you, wherever you are going.

Thank you for your cooperation.

Manager_____

FORM 7-7 Response to vacating with short notice.

When a notice that a tenant is vacating his or her rental unit is received, it is advisable to communicate with the tenant and acknowledge receipt of the notice. Form 7-8 may be used for that purpose.

_____[Date]

_____[Tenant]

_____[Street Address]

_____[City and State]

Dear _____[Tenant],

I have received your notice of intent to vacate your rental home. I hope you have enjoyed living here. In order that our relationship may end on a positive note, this move-out letter describes how management expects your unit to be left and what the procedures are for returning your security deposit.

You are expected to leave your rental unit in the same condition it was when you moved in, except for normal wear and tear. I have attached a copy of the Landlord/Tenant Checklist you signed at the beginning of your tenancy. I'll be using the same form to inspect your unit when you leave.

Specifically, here's a list of items you should thoroughly clean before vacating:

[ ] Floors

[ ] Sweep wood floors

[ ] Vacuum carpets and rugs (shampoo if necessary)

[ ] Walls, baseboards, ceilings, and built-in shelves

[ ] Doors, windows, and window coverings

[ ] Kitchen cabinets, countertops and sink, stove, and oven—inside and out

[ ] Refrigerator—clean inside and out, empty it of food, and turn it off, with the door left open

[ ] Mop kitchen and bathroom floors

[ ] Bathtubs, showers, toilets, and plumbing fixtures

[ ] Other _____

If you have any questions as to the type of cleaning, please let me know.

It is important that you do not leave anything behind—that includes bags of garbage, clothes, food, newspapers, furniture, appliances, dishes, plants, cleaning supplies, or other items that belong to you.

You are required to transfer or disconnect phone and utility services, cancel all newspaper subscriptions, and send the post office a change of address form.

Once you have cleaned your unit and removed all your belongings, please call me at _____ to arrange for a walk-through inspection and to return all keys.

FORM 7-8   Move out letter.

> Please be prepared to give me your forwarding address where we may mail your security deposit.
>
> It's our policy to mail all deposits to the address you provide at the time you move out. If any deductions are made for past due rent or because the unit is damaged or not sufficiently clean, they will be explained in writing.
>
> If you have any questions, please contact me at _____.
>
> Sincerely,
>
> Manager _____

FORM 7-8 Move out letter (continued).

Notice of Noncurable Default

If a tenant has committed a breach of the lease, and it is of such a serious nature that the landlord exercises his or her option to terminate the lease, Form 7-9 may be used.

The notice shown in form 7-10 may be used to notify a tenant of your decision to terminate the lease.

Belief of Abandonment of the Rental Unit

If it appears that the tenant has abandoned the rental unit, Form 7-11 should be served on the tenant by posting it on the door of the unit and mailing a copy by certified mail, return receipt requested.

> Certified Mail, Return Receipt Requested
>
> Date: _____
>
> To: _____[name(s) of tenant(s)]
>
> Regarding the property located at [address of property], this is to notify you that you are presently in default of the terms of the rental agreement on the subject property. The default is as follows:
>
> [describe the conduct that constitutes a violation of the lease]
>
>
> The default constitutes a forfeiture of your rights under the lease. Accordingly, unless you surrender possession of the subject property within _____ days, legal proceedings may be commenced against you without any further notice.
>
> Sincerely,
>
> Manager

FORM 7-9 Notice of noncurable default.

Certified Mail, Return Receipt Requested

Date: _____

_____[Tenant's name and address]

Re: Notice of Termination of Lease

To: _____[Tenant]

This is to officially notify you that we are exercising our option to cancel your lease and to direct you to deliver up possession of the property located at [address of property]. This termination of the lease is based on _____, which you presently occupy, on [date the possession of property will be surrendered].

Sincerely,

Manager

FORM 7-10   Lessor's notice of termination of lease.

Certified Mail, Return Receipt Requested

Date: _____

_____[Tenant's name(s) and address(es)]

Re: Notice of belief of abandonment of leased property located at:

To: _____[tenant(s)]

The rent on the above property is past due and owing since [date rent was due]. It also appears that you have abandoned the said property, since there are no possessions of yours located on the property.

Please be advised that unless I receive a written notice from you within the next 15 days both (1) stating that it is your intent not to abandon the property and (2) providing me with an address whereby legal process may be served on you by certified mail, I will consider the property has been abandoned and will reclaim possession of the property.

Sincerely,

Landlord

FORM 7-11   Notice of belief of abandonment of leased property.

8

Insurance

This chapter will examine the insurance requirements and contains suggestions regarding insurance coverage.

Insurance Contract

Insurance is a contract between the insured and the insurance company. Under this contract, the insured (landlord) agrees to pay premiums, and if he or she suffers a loss, the insurance company is obligated to pay for the damages. There are so many types of insurance policies that a discussion of every type would be impossible here. For a price, almost any type of risk can be insured. Only those policies most commonly used by landlords are discussed here.

Property insurance is the most common type of business insurance and covers the risks of fire, theft, wind, hail, and so forth. The next most common type, liability insurance, protects a business owner against third-party claims for losses and damages caused by an activity of the business. A third type, business interruption insurance, protects a business owner when he or she cannot conduct business as usual because of fire or another cause.

Insurance is a highly regulated business. In every state, insurance boards, commissioners, or superintendents regulate and supervise the transaction of insurance business in that state.

Insurance Agent

Dealing with an insurance agent is in many respects similar to dealing with an attorney. Your first goal is to select the right agent. Ask businesspersons in your area to recommend a reliable agent. It pays to shop around. Find an independent agent who can get quotes from more than one insurance company. Stay clear of an agent who tries to sell you a package deal without first taking the time to analyze your business needs.

After you have chosen an agent, tell the agent your specific needs. Mention any unusual risks that may be present. Be frank with the agent, because you want his or her advice and recommendations to be based on sound information. Remember that he or she represents the insurance company, too. Review your coverage with the agent when any major changes occur or at least once a year.

Insurance Coverage

Like other businesses, insurance companies are designed to operate at a profit. Because less than 60 percent of the premiums are returned to policyholders in payments for losses, over the long run the average businessperson will pay more in premiums than he or she will recover as insurance payments for losses. In many ways, insurance coverage is a gamble. If every possible risk is covered, the insurance premiums will be a heavy burden on a landlord. In determining the amount and types of insurance coverage your rental business needs, the goal is to have just the right amount. The only problem is that you never know if you have the right amount and the right type of coverage until a loss occurs. With this in mind, a landlord should try to determine the risks of a certain type of loss and weigh the risks against the premiums charged.

One way to reduce insurance expenses is by self-coverage. Because most losses are small, a landlord may wish to self-insure for small losses and have outside insurance protection for casualties that would destroy the business. Another way to keep the cost of insurance premiums down is to have a higher than normal deductible.

Keep in mind that the higher the deductible, the lower your premiums.

In deciding what types of coverage and policy limits you need, balance the cost of the premium against the odds of the risk covered and the effects of the loss on your business. If you can absorb the loss without too many problems, don't insure against it. Be sure to insure against a single catastrophe that could destroy your business.

If you lease your building, insurance on the structure probably is covered by its owner. If the building is destroyed, the owner's insurance will pay him or her for the loss, but you will be without a place to do business. In this case, you should insure not only your supplies, inventory, and equipment but also the cost involved in relocating the business.

Another aspect to be concerned about is the liability that can be incurred if your business operations cause the fire or other damage. The building owner's insurance company may sue you after it has paid the claim. Check your liability policy for this type of coverage.

If you own your building, you need property insurance to protect your investment. If you insure the property for more than its value or replacement cost, you still will recover only the value of the property or its replacement cost if it is totally destroyed. Therefore, you have paid extra premiums for overinsurance. Most buildings are insured for much less than their present value or replacement cost. The average person insures the building for its original cost without providing for any increases in the value of the building or increasing replacement costs. This can cause a problem with the "coinsurance" clauses discussed later in this chapter. Many insurance companies sell property insurance whose face value increases with inflation or the increasing cost of replacement. This coverage is more expensive; to offset the increased cost, the owner may want to increase the deductible.

If you have a large inventory, consider the effects on your business if it were destroyed. In most cases, your business insurance would cover the loss of inventory and supplies. Most landlords operate with a small inventory of products, and so this insurance may not be needed. Ask your agent for recommendations regarding your particular situation.

Liability insurance is almost a necessity for landlords. Although the chances of someone being hurt as a result of your operations may be low, one such claim can destroy most businesses.

The dollar amount of your policy is an important factor to consider in liability coverage. If you conduct your rental business in California, Florida, or New York, I recommend that you get higher than usual coverage for liability than you would in states where large recoveries are not as common. For example, million-dollar judgments are not unusual in those states but are very unusual in Texas, Arizona, Oklahoma, and Virginia.

The policy should cover liability to people injured on the business premises. Company automobiles and trucks also should be covered by your liability policies. In some cases, an employee who uses his or her own car for business purposes can expose your business to liability if an accident occurs while he or she is using the car. Coverage is needed for these situations, too.

A landlord also should consider getting business interruption insurance. Key factors to consider here are how long the loss of your building would put your company out of operation, whether you could relocate with a minimum of expense, and what impact any business stoppage would have on the earnings of the company. Most policies covering business interruption use the "gross earnings" approach. Under this approach, the company's estimated gross earnings during any period of interruption are estimated. The insurance company then pays 50 to 80 percent of the gross earnings, depending on the terms of the policy. Gross earnings under these policies are defined as profits plus all continuing expenses.

If you purchase business interruption insurance, make sure to get a clear explanation of what business interruptions are covered. For example, most policies cover interruptions caused by the destruction of a business building, but will interruptions caused by strikes, work stoppages, computer system failure, lack of raw materials, and the like, be covered?

In some cases, instead of business interruption insurance, it may be more appropriate for your business to have "extra expense" insurance. If you could continue the business in temporary quarters but at additional costs, this type of coverage may be cheaper. Extra expense coverage protects against the loss of future income because of the added expense of doing business at a location other than the present one. It does not provide protection for current income while you are out of business.

Many businesses are being insured against employee thefts and misconduct. If your employees are in positions of trust and can do substantial damage to your business, seriously consider this type of coverage.

It is very hard to get the right amount of coverage. Too much, and the premiums will diminish your profits; too little, and you are playing Russian roulette. Discuss the extent and types of coverage you need with your attorney, insurance agent, and other business associates. Get their advice but base the decision on your best business judgment. It is also important to review your insurance needs constantly to ascertain if your coverage is appropriate for your current needs.

Coinsurance Clauses

Most property insurance policies have "coinsurance" clauses. If you insure the property for less than 80 percent of its value, the insurance company will consider you a coinsurer. The percentage may vary, but the principles are the same. If you own a building valued at $100,000 and insure it for $80,000, the insurance company will pay the full amount of any loss up to the policy limit of $80,000. If, however, you insure the building for only $40,000 (40 percent), the insurance company will consider you a coinsurer only for the amount necessary to constitute the 80 percent: 40 percent. If a loss of $20,000 occurs in this latter situation, the insurance company will pay only $10,000 because you are carrying only half of the 80 percent coverage required by the policy.

To determine whether a building is insured for 80 percent, the deductible portion of your policy is included as part of the insured coverage. For example, if the building is valued at $100,000, is insured for $80,000, but has a $5,000 deductible, you still have coverage for 80 percent of the building's value even though you can recover a maximum of $75,000 if the building is totally destroyed. If your loss is

$5,000 or less, you will not recover anything on your policy. The premiums will be much lower because most damages are for less than $5,000.

In most cases, it is better for the business if you insure the property for 80 percent or more of its value and have a higher deductible rather than insure it for less than 80 percent of its value. Not only will the premiums be cheaper, your coverage when major damages occur will be more. For example, if you insure the building for 40 percent of its value with a $100 deductible, you become an equal coinsurer of the building. If the loss amounts to $20,000, the insurance company will pay $9,900 (50 percent of the loss minus the deductible). If, however, the building is insured for $80,000 with a $5,000 deductible and the loss is $20,000, you will receive $15,000, not $9,900, and your premiums probably will be lower.

The Policy

As noted earlier, an insurance policy is a contract between the insured (policyholder) and the insurer (insurance company) and is governed by the contract laws of the state in which the policy is written. The insurance industry is highly regulated; therefore, most states have prescribed clauses and provisions that must be in each policy. An insurance policy is invalid if it violates a state statute or is contrary to public policy. For example, insuring property such as illegal drugs would be against public policy. The average businessperson won't have these problems but could have problems with the contract language and standard clauses, such as the coinsurance clause discussed earlier.

Have your agent explain the terms and phrases in your policy that you do not understand. If there is a conflict between what the agent tells you and the terms of the policy, make the agent explain it to you in writing. Also, tell the agent that you consider what he or she said to be a modification to the policy because it conflicts with its terms.

Modification, Cancellation, and Termination of Coverage

Like other contracts, an insurance contract can be modified by the agreement of both parties. In many cases, the insurance company reserves the right to cancel or modify the policy upon written notice and to refund the unearned part of the premiums. The policy must clearly state this right. The insurance company usually also reserves the right to cancel the policy when premiums are not paid on time or when a false application for insurance is discovered. Know the rights you and the insurance company have under the policy to cancel your coverage.

If you feel that the insurance company has wrongfully cancelled your policy, check with your attorney. The courts generally hold that the policyholder has three courses when an insurance company wrongfully cancels a policy: The hold-er can (1) consider the policy at an end and recover any damages he or she has suffered, (2) bring court action and request that the court order the reinstate-ment of the policy, (3) offer to pay the premiums and, when the offer is refused, consider the policy as being in effect. Then, if any losses occur, the policyholder can sue for the losses. This last remedy is not recommended, because you won't know until after a loss whether the policy is in force.

The insurance application can constitute just grounds for the company to can-cel the policy if fraud or misrepresentations are a material part of the contract. For example, saying that a company truck was red in the application when in fact it was white was held by one court not to be a material misrepresentation. In one case, the insurance policy on an automobile was declared void for a material mis-representation. The insured had stated that he was using the automobile only for personal use, when in fact he was using it in his residential rental business.

Making a Claim against the Insurance Policy

The terms of the contract determine the rights and obligations of the policy-holder and the insurance company after a loss occurs. Most policies require the policyholder to provide notice and proof of the loss within a certain time. If no time limit is stated in the policy, the notice and proof of the loss must be report-ed within a reasonable time, preferably as soon as possible. Keep a copy of the notice, in case it is disputed, and request a claim form from your agent. If the loss is large, consult your attorney immediately.

The best approach to take in dealing with insurance companies is to prepare your claim as if it were going to be disputed. By doing this, you reduce the chances of being unable to prove your claims in court later on. Take pictures of the damaged property, make detailed notes, get statements from witnesses, and collect bills or other documents that establish the value of the destroyed or stolen goods. If the police were called, get a copy of the police report.

You will be in a better position to talk settlement with an adjuster if you have documented your losses. If there is any question of criminal misconduct, report it to the police. A standard clause in many insurance policies requires that any possible criminal misconduct be reported to the police. By doing this, you get an additional record of the loss with the police report.

Submit a claim if it is questionable that the loss is covered by your insurance policy. If you feel the loss is covered, and the agent or company states that it is not, consult your attorney. I have learned that if one is aggressive, insurance compa-nies are more likely to pay doubtful claims. If you have a substantial amount of insurance with the company, it may pay doubtful claims to keep your business.

Dealing with an Adjuster

Because of the nature of their work, most adjusters are basically conservative, and approach most claims with the goal of denying them or making as low a settlement as possible. Remember, they don't get bonuses for making liberal settlements. Most adjusters are pressured by their supervisors to close cases promptly. This pressure to close quickly may work to your advantage if your claim is well documented.

Adjusters have the authority to settle claims within certain limits. For claims above their preauthorized limits, they have to check with their office. In the first meeting with the adjuster, his or her only objective is to determine the type of case, its probable range of settlement, and any other problems associated with it. If the amount of loss is clear, and there is no question of liability, a settlement may be made at the first meeting.

If the insurance company disputes the amount, have your attorney negotiate for you. Studies have shown that adjusters offer higher settlements when dealing with an attorney. In one insurance company studied, the average recovery of clients represented by attorneys was 4 to 12 times higher than the recovery for those without legal representation.

If You Are Sued for More than Policy Limits

There usually is no need for an attorney when liability cases are involved, if the insurance company had agreed to represent you and there is no question of coverage. However, if the suit is for more than the face amount of your policy, consult an attorney to ensure that your rights are represented.

The insurance company has a duty under the policy to protect your interests. Therefore, if the company refuses a reasonable offer to settle within the policy limits, it may be required to pay the entire judgment, even the part above the policy limits. This requirement is based on the premise that the insurance company has a duty to protect you and should do so by settling within the policy limits.

The business of insurance coverage is tricky and sometimes very technical. Therefore, see an attorney any time you are sued and there is a possibility of recovery in excess of policy limits.

Renter's Insurance

Many landlords now require tenants to obtain renter's insurance, especially in high-end rental units. If your property is not subject to rent regulations, normally you may require that the tenant obtain renter's insurance within 10 or 20 days after move-in. The following clause may be inserted in your rental agreements:

Renter's Insurance
Within ten days of the signing of this agreement, tenant will obtain renter's insurance covering loss of tenant's property and personal liability protection. The tenant agrees to provide proof of purchase to the rental manager and further agrees to maintain the required insurance throughout the duration of the tenancy, and to furnish the rental manager with proof of insurance on a yearly basis.

You may wish to establish a relationship with a local insurance agency that will provide discount insurance to your tenants. As part of the move-in package, information regarding the insurance will be provided to new tenants.

Research indicates that tenants whose property is insured are less likely to sue the landlord when that property is destroyed by fire or flood. In addition, when a tenant's child damages a neighbor's property, it is better to have the neighbor deal with the tenant's insurance adjuster than to have the neighbor look to the landlord for reimbursement.

Terrorism Insurance

After September 11, 2001, many insurance companies' property insurance contracts excluded damage to property caused by acts of terrorism. If your property insurance has a "terrorism" exclusion, you may wish to consider terrorism insurance. Congress passed the Terrorism Risk Insurance Act (15 U.S. Code 6701) to help property owners get access to terrorism insurance. The insurance program is similar to federal flood insurance and provides coverage for losses resulting from terrorist acts. The act requires insurance companies to allow you to purchase such coverage, but also allows them to charge additional premiums for the coverage.

9

Low-Income Housing Programs

Section 8 and Low-Income Housing Programs

The major low-income housing program is the federally funded program established under the United States Housing Act of 1937, 42 U.S. 143(f). Section 8 of that act provides that the program will pay part of a low-income tenant's rent under certain conditions. The program is administered by the U.S. Department of Housing and Urban Development (HUD). Under this program, a local public housing agency, the landlord, and the tenant enter into a one-year written agreement that is supplied by the local public housing agency. The amount of rent the tenant pays depends on his or her income. The housing agency then pays the landlord the difference between what the tenant pays and a reasonable rental rate for the residential unit.

Generally, a landlord has the freedom to choose whether to participate in the Section 8 housing program. Some states, however, provide that if a current tenant becomes eligible for the program, the landlord may not refuse to accept the vouchers and must participate in the program for at least the present tenant (see *Franklin Tower One v. N.M.*, 157 N.J. 602 [New Jersey 1999]). A few other states, such as Connecticut, provide that landlords may not refuse to rent to a tenant who will be paying with program vouchers. If you, as a landlord, wish to participate in a Section 8 program or a similar low-income program, check with your local housing agency. Before refusing to accept vouchers from a potential tenant, check with the agency about to whether state law requires you to accept low-income tenants who are in Section 8 or a similar program.

There are several advantage to participating in a Section 8 programming, the following include:

- The public agency generally pays a substantial portion of the rent and pays on time, so that you are guaranteed to receive the majority of the rent each month, and generally the part that the tenant pays will be small enough that the tenant will not have problems paying.
- If you are required to evict the tenant for nonpayment of rent, in many cases that sum will be recoverable from the housing agency.

The disadvantages of participating in a subsidized program include the following:

- The added paperwork required for the program.
- You generally are required to accept the agency's determination of the market rate for rental of the unit.
- It is difficult to evict the tenant for reasons other than nonpayment of rent.

Section 8 Questions and Guidelines

What families are eligible to apply for tenant-based vouchers?
Very lo- income families (i.e., families with incomes below 50 percent of area's median income) and a few specific categories of families with incomes up to 80 percent of the area's median income. This includes families that are already assisted under the 1937 U.S. Housing Act, such as families physically displaced by public housing demolition, and owners opting out of project-based Section 8 housing assistance payments (HAP) contracts. (HUD determines median income levels for each area annually.)

How does a family obtain an apartment once it has a voucher?
It is the responsibility of a family to find a unit that meets its needs. If the family finds a unit that meets the housing quality standards, the rent is reasonable, and the unit meets other program requirements, the Public Housing Agency (PHA) executes a contract with the property owner. This contract authorizes the PHA to make subsidy payments on behalf of the family. If the family moves out of the unit, the contract with the owner ends, and the family can move with continued assistance to another unit.

Do families have to lease a unit in the jurisdiction where the PHA issued the voucher?
No. A family may choose a unit anywhere in the United States where there is a PHA that administers a tenant-based housing choice voucher program. However, the family may use the voucher to lease a unit only in an area where the family is income-eligible for admission to the program.

What regulations cover this program?
The regulations are found in 24 CFR Part 982.

Contact Numbers for HUD Programs

HUD's Local Offices
HUD is organized in 10 regions. Each region is managed by a regional director, who also oversees the regional office. Each field office within a region is managed by a field office director, who reports to the regional director.

See the CD for a listing of HUD offices. Staff who answer the main office telephone will be able to respond to your calls or direct them to the appropriate person.

Voucher Program

The following tenancy addendum must be attached to leases that are involved in the voucher program.

1. Section 8 Voucher Program
   a. The owner is leasing the contract unit to the tenant for occupancy by the tenant's family with assistance for a tenancy under the Section 8 housing choice voucher program (voucher program) of the United States Department of Housing and Urban Development (HUD).
   b. The owner has entered into a Housing Assistance Payments Contract (HAP contract) with the PHA under the voucher program. Under the HAP contract, the PHA will make housing assistance payments to the owner to assist the tenant in leasing the unit from the owner.
2. Lease
   a. The owner has given the PHA a copy of the lease, including any revisions agreed by the owner and the tenant. The owner certifies that the terms of the lease are in accordance with all provisions of the HAP contract and that the lease includes the tenancy addendum.
   b. The tenant shall have the right to enforce the tenancy addendum against the owner. If there is any conflict between the tenancy addendum and any other provisions of the lease, the language of the tenancy addendum shall control.

3. Use of Contract Unit
   a. During the lease term, the family will reside in the contract unit with assistance under the voucher program.
   b. The composition of the household must be approved by the PHA. The family must promptly inform the PHA of the birth, adoption, or court-awarded custody of a child. Other persons may not be added to the household without prior written approval of the owner and the PHA.
   c. The contract unit may be used for residence only by the PHA-approved household members. The unit must be the family's only residence. Members of the household may engage in legal profit-making activities incidental to primary use of the unit for residence by members of the family.
   d. The tenant may not sublease or let the unit.
   e. The tenant may not assign the lease or transfer the unit.
4. Rent to Owner
   a. The initial rent to the owner may not exceed the amount approved by the PHA in accordance with HUD requirements.
   b. Changes in the rent to the owner shall be determined by the provisions of the lease. However, the owner may not raise the rent during the initial term of the lease.
   c. During the term of the lease (including the initial term of the lease and any extension term), the rent to the owner may at no time exceed:
      - The reasonable rent for the unit as most recently determined or redetermined by the PHA in accordance with HUD requirements, or
      - Rent charged by the owner for comparable unassisted units in the premises.
5. Family Payment to Owner
   a. The family is responsible for paying the owner any portion of the rent that is not covered by the PHA housing assistance payment.
   b. Each month, the PHA will make a housing assistance payment to the owner on behalf of the family in accordance with the HAP contract. The amount of the monthly housing assistance payment will be determined by the PHA in accordance with HUD requirements for a tenancy under the Section 8 voucher program.
   c. The monthly housing assistance payment shall be credited against the monthly rent to owner for the contract unit.
   d. The tenant is not responsible for paying the portion of rent to the owner covered by the PHA housing assistance payment under the HAP contract between the owner and the PHA. A PHA failure to pay the housing assistance payment to the owner is not a violation of the lease. The owner may not terminate the tenancy for nonpayment of the PHA housing assistance payment.

e. The owner may not charge or accept, from the family or from any other source, any payment for rent of the unit in addition to the rent to the owner. The rent to the owner includes all housing services, maintenance, utilities, and appliances to be provided and paid by the owner in accordance with the lease.

f. The owner must immediately return any excess rent payment to the tenant.

6. Other Fees and Charges

   a. Rent to the owner does not include the cost of any meals or supportive services or furniture that may be provided by the owner.

   b. The owner may not require the tenant or family members to pay charges for any meals or supportive services or furniture that may be provided by the owner. Nonpayment of any such charges is not grounds for termination of tenancy.

   c. The owner may not charge the tenant extra amounts for items customarily included in rent to the owner in the locality, or provided at no additional cost to unsubsidized tenants in the premises.

7. Maintenance, Utilities, and Other Services

   a. Maintenance

   - The owner must maintain the unit and premises in accordance with the Housing Qualification Statement (HQS).
   - Maintenance and replacement (including redecoration) must be in accordance with the standard practice for the building concerned as established by the owner.

   b. Utilities and appliances

   - The owner must provide all utilities needed to comply with the HQS.
   - The owner is not responsible for a breach of the HQS caused by the tenant's failure to:
     - Pay for any utilities that are to be paid by the tenant.
     - Provide and maintain any appliances that are to be provided by the tenant.

   c. Family damage. The owner is not responsible for a breach of the HQS because of damages beyond normal wear and tear caused by any member of the household or by a guest.

   d. Housing services. The owner must provide all housing services as agreed to in the lease.

8. Termination of Tenancy by Owner

   a. Requirements. The owner may terminate the tenancy only in accordance with the lease and HUD requirements.

   b. Grounds. During the term of the lease (the initial term of the lease or any extension term), the owner may terminate the tenancy only because of:

   - Serious or repeated violation of the lease;

- Violation of federal, state, or local law that imposes obligations on the tenant in connection with the occupancy or use of the unit and the premises;
- Criminal activity or alcohol abuse (as provided in paragraph c); or
- Other good cause (as provided in paragraph d).

c. Criminal activity or alcohol abuse
- The owner may terminate the tenancy during the term of the lease if any member of the household, a guest, or another person under a resident's control commits any of the following types of criminal activity:
  - Any criminal activity that threatens the health or safety of, or the right to peaceful enjoyment of the premises by, other residents (including property management staff residing on the premises);
  - Any criminal activity that threatens the health or safety of, or the right to peaceful enjoyment of their residences by, persons residing in the immediate vicinity of the premises;
  - Any violent criminal activity on or near the premises; or
  - Any drug-related criminal activity on or near the premises.
- The owner may terminate the tenancy during the term of the lease if any member of the household is:
  - Fleeing to avoid prosecution, or custody or confinement after conviction, for a crime, or attempt to commit a crime, that is a felony under the laws of the place from which the individual flees, or that, in the case of the State of New Jersey, is a high misdemeanor; or
  - Violating a condition of probation or parole under Federal or State law.
- The owner may terminate the tenancy for criminal activity by a household member in accordance with this section if the owner determines that the household member has committed the criminal activity, regardless of whether the household member has been arrested or convicted for such activity.
- The owner may terminate the tenancy during the term of the lease if any member of the household has engaged in abuse of alcohol that threatens the health, safety, or right to peaceful enjoyment of the premises by other residents.

d. Other good cause for termination of tenancy
- During the initial lease term, other good cause for termination of tenancy must be something the family did or failed to do.
- During the initial lease term or during any extension term, other good cause includes:
  - Disturbance of neighbors,
  - Destruction of property, or

      – Living or housekeeping habits that cause damage to the unit or premises.
- After the initial lease term, such good cause includes:
  - The tenant's failure to accept the owner's offer of a new lease or revision;
  - The owner's desire to use the unit for personal or family use or for a purpose other than use as a residential rental unit; or
  - A business or economic reason for termination of the tenancy (such as sale of the property, renovation of the unit, the owner's desire to rent the unit for a higher rent).

e. Eviction by court action. The owner may evict the tenant only by a court action.

f. Owner notice of grounds
- At or before the beginning of a court action to evict the tenant, the owner must give the tenant a notice that specifies the grounds for termination of tenancy. The notice may be included in or combined with any owner eviction notice.
- The owner must give the PHA a copy of any owner eviction notice at the same time the owner notifies the tenant.
- Eviction notice means a notice to vacate, or a complaint or other initial pleading used to begin an eviction action under state or local law.

9. Lease: Relation to HAP Contract

If the HAP contract terminates for any reason, the lease terminates automatically.

10. PHA Termination of Assistance

The PHA may terminate program assistance for the family for any grounds authorized in accordance with HUD requirements. If the PHA terminates program assistance for the family, the lease terminates automatically.

11. Family Move Out

The tenant must notify the PHA and the owner before the family moves out of the unit.

12. Security Deposit

a. The owner may collect a security deposit from the tenant. (However, the PHA may prohibit the owner from collecting a security deposit in excess of private market practice, or in excess of amounts charged by the owner to unassisted tenants. Any such PHA-required restriction must be specified in the HAP contract.)

b. When the family moves out of the contract unit, the owner, subject to state and local law, may use the security deposit, including any interest on the deposit, as reimbursement for any unpaid rent payable by the tenant, any damages to the unit, or any other amounts that the tenant owes under the lease.

   c. The owner must give the tenant a list of all items charged against the security deposit and the amount of each item. After deducting the amount, if any, used to reimburse the owner, the owner must promptly refund the full amount of the unused balance to the tenant.
   d. If the security deposit is not sufficient to cover amounts the tenant owes under the lease, the owner may collect the balance from the tenant.
13. Prohibition of Discrimination
   In accordance with applicable equal opportunity statutes, Executive Orders, and regulations, the owner must not discriminate against any person because of race, color, religion, sex, national origin, age, familial status, or disability in connection with the lease.
14. Conflict with Other Provisions of Lease
   a. The terms of the tenancy addendum are prescribed by HUD in accordance with federal law and regulation, as a condition for federal assistance to the tenant and tenant's family under the Section 8 voucher program.
   b. In case of any conflict between the provisions of the tenancy addendum as required by HUD, and any other provisions of the lease or any other agreement between the owner and the tenant, the requirements of the HUD-required tenancy addendum shall control.
15. Changes in Lease or Rent
   a. The tenant and the owner may not make any change in the tenancy addendum. However, if the tenant and the owner agree to any other changes in the lease, such changes must be in writing, and the owner must immediately give the PHA a copy of such changes. The lease, including any changes, must be in accordance with the requirements of the tenancy addendum.
   b. In the following cases, tenant-based assistance shall not be continued unless the PHA has approved a new tenancy in accordance with program requirements and has executed a new HAP contract with the owner:
      ▪ If there are any changes in lease requirements governing tenant or owner responsibilities for utilities or appliances;
      ▪ If there are any changes in lease provisions governing the term of the lease;
      ▪ If the family moves to a new unit, even if the unit is in the same building or complex.
   c. PHA approval of the tenancy and execution of a new HAP contract are not required for agreed changes in the lease other than as specified in paragraph b.
   d. The owner must notify the PHA of any changes in the amount of the rent to owner at least 60 days before any such changes go into effect, and the amount of the rent to owner following any such agreed change may not

exceed the reasonable rent for the unit as most recently determined or redetermined by the PHA in accordance with HUD requirements.

16. Notices

Any notice under the lease by the tenant to the owner or by the owner to the tenant must be in writing.

17. Definitions

Contract unit. The housing unit rented by the tenant with assistance under the program.

Family. The persons who may reside in the unit with assistance under the program.

HAP contract. The housing assistance payments contract between the PHA and the owner. The PHA pays housing assistance payments to the owner in accordance with the HAP contract.

Household. The persons who may reside in the contract unit. The household consists of the family and any PHA-approved live-in aide. (A live-in aide is a person who resides in the unit to provide necessary supportive services for a member of the family who is a person with disabilities.)

Housing quality standards (HQS). The HUD minimum quality standards for housing assisted under the Section 8 tenant-based programs.

HUD. The U.S. Department of Housing and Urban Development.

HUD requirements. HUD requirements for the Section 8 program. HUD requirements are issued by HUD headquarters, as regulations, Federal Register notices, or other binding program directives.

Lease. The written agreement between the owner and the tenant for the lease of the contract unit to the tenant. The lease includes the tenancy addendum prescribed by HUD.

PHA. Public Housing Agency.

Premises. The building or complex in which the contract unit is located, including common areas and grounds.

Program. The Section 8 housing choice voucher program.

Rent to owner. The total monthly rent payable to the owner for the contract unit. The rent to owner is the sum of the portion of rent payable by the tenant plus the PHA housing assistance payment to the owner.

Section 8. Section 8 of the United States Housing Act of 1937 (42 United States Code 1437f).

Tenant. The family member (or members) who leases the unit from the owner.

Voucher program. The Section 8 housing choice voucher program. Under this program, HUD provides funds to the PHA for a rent subsidy on behalf of eligible families. The tenancy under the lease will be assisted with a rent subsidy for a tenancy under the voucher program.

10

Reducing Your Legal Liability as a Landlord

This chapter discusses ways to reduce your legal liability as a landlord or property manager.

Landlord's Responsibilities

As a landlord, you have certain responsibilities to your tenants, the neighbors, and visitors to your properties. Landlords are being sued with increasing frequency by tenants injured by criminals. In addition, landlords are especially likely to be held liable if an assault occurs on property where an assault or another crime occurred in the past. For example, a person who is injured or annoyed by drug dealers—with the other tenants or people in the neighborhood—may sue the landlord on the grounds that the property is a public nuisance that threatens public safety or morals.

The responsibilities of a landlord include the following:

- Protecting their tenants from assailants, thieves, and fellow tenants
- Protecting the neighborhood from their tenants' illegal activities, such as drug dealing
- Protecting visitors to the premises from dangerous conditions on the property

There are steps that a landlord can take to reduce his or her legal liability:

- Screen tenants carefully and choose tenants who are likely to be law-abiding and peaceful citizens. Evict violent or dangerous individuals to the extent allowable under privacy and antidiscrimination laws that may limit questions about a tenant's past criminal activity, drug use, or mental illness.
- Do not tolerate tenants' disruptive behavior. Include a provision in the lease or rental agreement prohibiting drug dealing and other illegal activity and promptly evict tenants who violate that clause.
- Make repairs to rental units as soon as possible. Major problems such as a plumbing or heating problem should be handled within 24 hours.
- Except in cases of emergency, before entering rented premises to make needed repairs, provide advance notice to the tenant (usually 24 hours).
- Take immediate steps to evict tenants who are involved in criminal activities.
- Look for dangerous conditions on the premises and repair or remove them promptly. Be especially vigilant about dangers to children, such as stacks of building materials and other "attractive nuisances."
- Comply with all building codes, ordinances, and statutes.
- Carry liability insurance to prevent financial disaster, including insurance that covers illegal acts by your employees.
- Comply with state and local security laws that apply to the rental property, such as requirements for deadbolt locks on doors, good lighting, and window locks.
- Design a security system that provides reasonable protection for the tenants. Local police departments, your insurance company, and private security professionals can provide useful advice on security measures.
- Post information that makes tenants aware of the crime problems in the neighborhood and the security measures designed to protect them.
- Conduct regular inspections of the property to spot and fix any security problems, such as broken locks and burned-out exterior floodlights.
- Ask tenants for their suggestions as part of an ongoing repair and maintenance system.
- Handle tenant complaints about dangerous situations, suspicious activities, and broken security items immediately.
- Take special precautions in hiring a property manager—a person who interacts with all tenants and has access to master keys.
- Listen to tenants' complaints about any alleged illegal acts by a manager or other employees.
- Educate your rental manager about his or her responsibilities.

Megan's Law

Every state has some form of Megan's Law, which requires that sex offenders register with local law enforcement so that their addresses are publicly available. Never approve a tenant's application without checking to see if that individual is a registered sex offender. If you learn that a current resident is a registered sex offender, terminate the tenancy if possible.

Protecting Tenants from Other Tenants

A landlord has a limited duty to provide a reasonably safe place for his or her tenants. If a landlord determines that another tenant is violent or likely to cause criminal harm to others, the landlord must take reasonable steps to evict the troublesome tenant. If a landlord discovers that a tenant has a tendency to commit violent acts, the landlord is under a duty to take reasonable precautions to safeguard other tenants. If a landlord knows that tenants are keeping vicious or dangerous domestic pets, the landlord probably will be liable if those pets injure another tenant. Although a landlord is generally not liable unless he or she knew that the tenant was likely to cause harm, the landlord must take reasonable steps to ascertain if any tenant has tendencies that may endanger other tenants.

Key Control

A landlord has a duty to safeguard keys to residential units. For example, if a manager who has duplicate keys goes into a tenant's unit and steals property, the landlord generally is liable for the manager's misconduct because the landlord hired the manager and allowed the manager to have access to the residential units. Steps that a landlord should take regarding the control of keys include the following:

- Require tenants to return all keys at move-out.
- Rekey each residential unit when a new tenant moves in or when a tenant reports that a key has been lost.
- Limit access to master keys.
- Use a key system in which keys are difficult to copy or make duplicate keys.
- Provide keys only to people you trust and remember that they could violate that trust.
- Do not label keys with rental unit numbers. Number the keys so that the address or location of the unit is not identifiable.
- Keep a log that indicates every time a master key is used to enter a unit and the individuals who used the key.

Tenant Education Programs

Alert tenants about any crime problems in the neighborhood. Provide signs on the property advising tenants how to protect their property and themselves. If you have professionals evaluate the safety of the property, share the results with the tenants. Schedule safety meetings with the tenants and have local police officers discuss safety precautions with them.

Duty to Warn Tenants

Local and federal regulations require that landlords advise tenants of certain hazards that may exist on the property. The most common of those hazards involve the existence of lead paint in older properties.

Lead Paint

A landlord has a duty to ascertain if lead paint was used in any of his or her buildings. In 1978, the federal government required that levels of lead in paint be reduced. The use of lead pipes in plumbing was banned in 1988, but lead generally is found only in homes built before 1950.

There are professional inspectors who can inspect a property and make a determination of whether the property is lead-free. Before starting a renovation project in a building that may have lead paint and where tenants are residing, the landlord is required to give the EPA pamphlet "Protect Your Family from Lead in Your Home." A copy of the pamphlet is included on the CD with this book. The pamphlets may be obtained from the nearest Environmental Protection Agency (EPA) regional office.

Mold

A recent trend has been to hold landlords responsible for health problems associated with exposure to mold. Mold comes in various colors and shapes. While some mold is easily detected, other types are difficult to detect, especially when hidden between the walls, under floors, and in ceilings. Not all mold is harmful. For example, the mold you commonly see in a shower is not dangerous. Have your properties checked to determine if mold is present, and if it is, take the necessary steps to clean it up. Proper cleanup and maintenance will take care of most mold problems. Focus on early detection and prevention.

Asbestos

Structures built before 1981 may have asbestos. The landlord needs to take affirmative steps not to disturb asbestos when doing remodeling jobs. The U.S. Occupational Safety and Health Administration (OSHA) has a web site—www.osha.gov—that provides updated information on asbestos. OSHA also has an interactive software called "Asbestos Advisor" that may be obtained by an individual before remodeling pre-1981 buildings.

Floods

If your property has a tendency to flood, as a landlord you have a duty to advise tenants of this problem. Failure to warn tenants in this regard and advise tenants about how they can protect their property from floods may open the landlord to liability in this regard.

11

Taxes

Taxes are a necessary evil in doing business as a landlord. The information in this chapter pertains to handling rental income or loss on your federal tax return. Most of the information is taken from IRS Publication 527.

You generally must include in your gross income all the amounts you receive as rent. Rental income is any payment you receive for the use or occupation of property. In addition to amounts you receive as normal rent payments, there are other amounts, discussed later, that may constitute rental income.

When to Report Rental Income

When you report rental income on your return depends on whether you are a cash-basis taxpayer or use an accrual method.

If you are a cash-basis taxpayer, you report rental income on your return for the year in which you actually or constructively receive it. You are a cash-basis taxpayer if you report income in the year you receive it, regardless of when it was earned. You constructively receive income when it is made available to you, for example, by being credited to your bank account.

If you use an accrual method, you generally report income when you earn it rather than when you receive it. You generally deduct your expenses when you incur them rather than when you pay them.

For more information about when you constructively receive income and accrual methods of accounting, see IRS Publication 538, "Accounting Periods and Methods."

Advance Rent

Advance rent is any amount you receive before the period that that payment covers. Include advance rent in your rental income in the year you receive it, regardless of the period covered or the method of accounting you use.

Example. You sign a 10-year lease to rent your property. In the first year, you receive $5,000 for the first year's rent and $5,000 as rent for the last year of the lease. You must include $10,000 in your income in the first year.

Security Deposits

Do not include a security deposit in your income when you receive it if you plan to return it to your tenant at the end of the lease. But, if you keep part or all of the security deposit during any year because your tenant does not live up to the terms of the lease, include the amount you keep in your income for that year.

If an amount called a security deposit is to be used as a final payment of rent, it is advance rent. Include it in your income when you receive it.

Payment for Canceling a Lease

If a tenant pays you to cancel a lease, the amount you receive is rent. Include the payment in your income in the year you receive it regardless of your method of accounting.

Expenses Paid by the Tenant

If a tenant pays any of your expenses, those payments are rental income. You must include them in your income. You can deduct the expenses if they are deductible rental expenses. See "Rental Expenses" later in this chapter, for more information.

Example 1. Your tenant pays the water and sewage bill for your rental property and deducts it from the normal rent payment. Under the terms of the lease, your tenant does not have to pay this bill. Include the utility bill paid by the tenant and any amount received as a rent payment in your rental income. You can deduct the utility payment made by your tenant as a rental expense.

Example 2. While you are out of town, the furnace in your rental property stops working. Your tenant pays for the necessary repairs and deducts the repair bill from the rent payment. Include the repair bill paid by the tenant and any amount received as a rent payment in your rental income. You can deduct the repair payment made by your tenant as a rental expense.

Property or Services

If you receive property or services instead of money as rent, include the fair market value of the property or services in your rental income.

If the services are provided at an agreed-upon or specified price, that price is the fair market value unless there is evidence to the contrary.

Example. Your tenant is a painter. He offers to paint your rental property instead of paying two months' rent. You accept his offer.

Include in your rental income the amount the tenant would have paid for two month' rent. You can deduct the same amount as a rental expense for painting your property.

Lease with Option to Buy

If the rental agreement gives your tenant the right to buy your rental property, the payments you receive under the agreement generally are considered rental income. If your tenant exercises the right to buy the property, the payments you receive for the period after the date of sale are considered part of the selling price.

Rental of Property Also Used as a Home

If you rent property that you also use as your home and rent it fewer than 15 days during the tax year, do not include the rent you receive in your income and do not deduct rental expenses. However, you can deduct on Schedule A (Form 1040) the interest, taxes, and casualty and theft losses that are allowed for non-rental property. See "Personal Use of Dwelling Unit (Including Vacation Home)," later in this chapter.

Part Interest

If you own a part interest in rental property, you must report your part of the rental income from the property.

Rental Expenses

This section discusses the expenses of renting property that you ordinarily can deduct from your rental income. It includes information on the expenses you can deduct if you rent a condominium or cooperative apartment, rent part of your property, or change your property to rental use. Depreciation, which you also can deduct from your rental income, is discussed later in this chapter.

When to Deduct

You generally can deduct your rental expenses in the year in which you pay them.

Vacant Rental Property

If you hold property for rental purposes, you may be able to deduct your ordinary and necessary expenses (including depreciation) for managing, conserving, or maintaining the property while the property is vacant. However, you cannot deduct any loss of rental income for the period in which the property is vacant.

Prerental Expenses

You can deduct your ordinary and necessary expenses for managing, conserving, or maintaining rental property from the time you make it available for rent.

Depreciation

You can begin to depreciate rental property when it is ready and available for rent. See "Placed-in-Service Date under Depreciation," later in this chapter.

Expenses for Rental Property Sold

If you sell property you held for rental purposes, you can deduct the ordinary and necessary expenses for managing, conserving, or maintaining the property until it is sold.

Personal Use of Rental Property

If you sometimes use your rental property for personal purposes, you must divide your expenses between rental and personal use. Also, your rental expense deductions may be limited. See "Personal Use of Dwelling Unit (Including Vacation Home)," later in this chapter.

Part Interest

If you own a part interest in rental property, you can deduct your part of the expenses that you paid.

Repairs and Improvements

You can deduct the cost of repairs to your rental property. You cannot deduct the cost of improvements. You recover the cost of improvements by taking depreciation (explained later).

Separate the costs of repairs and improvements and keep accurate records. You will need to know the cost of improvements when you sell or depreciate your property.

Repairs. A repair keeps your property in good operating condition. It does not materially add to the value of your property or substantially prolong its life. Repainting your property inside or out, fixing gutters or floors, fixing leaks, plastering, and replacing broken windows are examples of repairs.

If you make repairs as part of an extensive remodeling or restoration of your property, the whole job is an improvement.

Improvements. An improvement adds to the value of property, prolongs its useful life, or adapts it to new uses.

If you make an improvement to property, the cost of the improvement must be capitalized. The capitalized cost generally can be depreciated as if the improvement were separate property.

Other Expenses

In addition to depreciation and the cost of repairs, you can deduct the following expenses from your rental income.

- Advertising
- Cleaning and maintenance
- Utilities
- Insurance
- Taxes
- Interest
- Points
- Commissions
- Tax return preparation fees
- Travel expenses
- Rental payments
- Local transportation expenses

Some of these expenses are discussed next.

Rental Payments for Property

You can deduct the rent you pay for property that you use for rental purposes. If you buy a leasehold for rental purposes, you can deduct an equal part of the cost each year over the term of the lease.

Rental of Equipment

You can deduct the rent you pay for equipment that you use for rental purposes. However, in some cases lease contracts are actually purchase contracts. When this is the case, you cannot deduct these payments. You can recover the cost of purchased equipment through depreciation.

Insurance Premiums Paid in Advance

If you pay an insurance premium for more than one year in advance, each year, you can deduct the part of the premium payment that will apply to that year. You cannot deduct the total premium in the year you pay it.

Local Benefit Taxes

Generally, you cannot deduct charges for local benefits that increase the value of your property, such as charges for putting in streets, sidewalks, or water and sewer systems. These charges are nondepreciable capital expenditures. You must add them to the basis of your property. You can deduct local benefit taxes if they are for maintaining, repairing, or paying interest charges for the benefits.

Interest Expense

You can deduct the mortgage interest you pay on your rental property. Chapter 5 of Publication 535 explains mortgage interest in detail.

Expenses paid to obtain a mortgage. Certain expenses you pay to obtain a mortgage on your rental property cannot be deducted as interest. These expenses, which include mortgage commissions, abstract fees, and recording fees, are capital expenses. However, you can amortize them over the life of the mortgage.

Form 1098. If you paid $600 or more in mortgage interest on your rental property to any one person, you should receive a Form 1098, "Mortgage Interest Statement," or a similar statement showing the interest you paid for the year. If you and at least one other person (other than your spouse if you file a joint return) were liable for and paid interest on the mortgage, and the other person received the Form 1098, report your share of the interest on Schedule E (Form 1040), line 13. Attach a statement to your return showing the name and address of the other person. In the left margin of Schedule E, next to line 13, enter "See attached."

Points. The term "points" often is used to describe some of the charges paid by a borrower to take out a loan or a mortgage. These charges also are called loan origination fees, maximum loan charges, and premium charges. If any of these charges (points) are solely for the use of money, they are interest.

Points paid when you take out a loan or mortgage result in original issue discount (OID). In general, the points (OID) are deductible as interest unless they must be capitalized. How you figure the amount of points (OID) you can deduct each year depends on whether your total OID, including the OID resulting from the points, is insignificant or *de minimis*. If the OID is not *de minimis*, you must use the constant-yield method to figure how much you can deduct.

De minimis OID. The OID is *de minimis* if it is less than one-fourth of 1 percent (0.0025 percent) of the stated redemption price at maturity multiplied by the number of full years from the date of original issue to maturity (the term of the loan).

If the OID is *de minimis*, you can choose one of the following ways to figure the amount you can deduct each year:

1. On a constant-yield basis over the term of the loan
2. On a straight-line basis over the term of the loan
3. In proportion to stated interest payments
4. In its entirety at the maturity of the loan

You make this choice by deducting the OID in a manner consistent with the method chosen on your timely filed tax return for the tax year in which the loan is issued.

Loan or Mortgage Ends

If your loan or mortgage ends, you may be able to deduct any remaining points (OID) in the tax year in which the loan or mortgage ends. A loan or mortgage may end because of a refinancing, prepayment, forclosure, or similar event.

However, if the refinancing is with the same lender, the remaining points (OID) generally are not deductible in the year in which the refinancing occurs, but they may be deductible over the term of the new mortgage or loan.

Travel Expenses

You can deduct the ordinary and necessary expenses of traveling away from home, if the primary purpose of the trip was to collect rental income or to manage, conserve, or maintain your rental property. You must properly allocate your expenses between rental and nonrental activities. For informaton on travel expenses, see Chapter 1 of Publication 463.

To deduct travel expenses, you must keep records that follow the rules in Chapter 5 of Publication 463.

Local Transportation Expenses

You can deduct your ordinary and necessary local transportation expenses if you incur them to collect rental income or to manage, conserve, or maintain your rental property.

Generally, if you use your personal car, pickup truck, or light van for rental activities, you can deduct the expenses by using one of two methods: actual expenses or the standard mileage rate. For 2004, the standard mileage rate for all business miles was 37½ cents a mile. For more information, see Chapter 4 of Publication 463.

To deduct car expenses under either method, you must keep records that follow the rules in Chapter 5 of Publication 463. In addition, you must complete Form 4562, Part V, and attach it to your tax return.

Tax Return Preparation

You can deduct as a rental expense the part of tax return preparation fees you paid to prepare Schedule E (Form 1040), Part I. For example, on your 2004 Schedule E you can deduct fees paid in 2005 to prepare Part I of your 2004 Schedule E. You also can deduct, as a rental expense any sum you paid to resolve a tax underpayment related to your rental activities.

Condominiums and Cooperatives

If you rent out a condominium or a cooperative apartment, special rules apply. Condominiums are treated differently from cooperatives.

Condominium

If you own a condominium, you own a dwelling unit in a multiunit building. You also own a share of the common elements of the structure, such as land, lobbies, elevators, and service areas. You and the other condominium owners may pay dues or assessments to a special corporation that is organized to take care of the common elements.

If you rent your condominium to others, you can deduct depreciation, repairs, upkeep, dues, interest and taxes, and assessments for the care of the common parts of the structure. You cannot deduct special assessments you pay to a condominium management corporation for improvements, but you may be able to recover your share of the cost of any improvement by taking depreciation.

Cooperative

If you have a cooperative apartment that you rent to others, you usually can deduct, as a rental expense, all the maintenance fees you pay to the cooperative housing corporation. However, you cannot deduct a payment earmarked for a capital asset or improvement or otherwise charged to the corporation's capital account. For example, you cannot deduct a payment used to pave a community parking lot, install a new roof, or pay the principal on the corporation's mortgage. You must add the payment to the basis of your stock in the corporation.

Treat as a capital cost the amount you were assessed for capital items. This cannot be more than the amount by which your payments to the corporation exceeded your share of the corporation's mortgage interest and real estate taxes.

Your share of interest and taxes is the amount the corporation elected to allocate to you if it reasonably reflects those expenses for your apartment. Otherwise, figure your share in the following way:

1. Divide the number of your shares of stock by the total number of shares outstanding, including any shares held by the corporation.
2. Multiply the corporation's deductible interest by the number you came up with in Step 1. This is your share of the interest.
3. Multiply the corporation's deductible taxes by the number you came up with in Step 1. This is your share of the taxes.

In addition to the maintenance fees paid to the cooperative housing corporation, you can deduct your direct payments for repairs, upkeep, and other rental expenses, including interest paid on a loan used to buy your stock in the corporation. The depreciation deduction allowed for cooperative apartments is discussed below.

Not Rented for Profit

If you do not rent your property to make a profit, you can deduct your rental expenses only up to the amount of your rental income. You cannot carry forward to the next year any rental expenses that are more than your rental income for the year. For more information about the rules for an activity not engaged in for profit, see Chapter 1 of Publication 535.

Where to Report

Report your not-for-profit rental income on Form 1040, line 21. You can include your mortgage interest (if you use the property as your main home or a second home), real estate taxes, and casualty losses on the appropriate lines of Schedule A (Form 1040) if you itemize your deductions.

Claim your other rental expenses, subject to the rules explained in Chapter 1 of Publication 535, as miscellaneous itemized deductions on line 22 of Schedule A (Form 1040). You can deduct these expenses only if they, together with certain other miscellaneous itemized deductions, total more than 2 percent of your adjusted gross income.

Postponing the Decision

If your rental income is more than your rental expenses for at least three years in a period of five consecutive years, you are presumed to be renting your property to make a profit. You may choose to postpone the decision whether the rental is for profit by filing Form 5213.

See Publication 535 for more information.

Property Changed to Rental Use

If you change your home or other property (or a part of it) to rental use at any time other than the beginning of the tax year, you must divide yearly expenses, such as taxes and insurance, between rental use and personal use.

You can deduct as rental expenses only the part of the expense that is for the part of the year in which the property was used or held for rental purposes.

For depreciation purposes, treat the property as having been placed in service on the conversion date.

You cannot deduct depreciation or insurance for the part of the year the property was held for personal use. However, you can include the home mortgage interest and real estate tax expenses for the part of the year the property was held for personal use as an itemized deduction on Schedule A (Form 1040).

Example. Your tax year is the calendar year. You moved from your home in May and started renting it out on June 1. You can deduct as rental expenses seven-twelfths of your yearly expenses, such as taxes and insurance.

Starting with June, you can deduct as rental expenses the amounts you pay for items generally billed monthly, such as utilities.

When figuring depreciation, treat the property as having been placed in service on June 1.

Renting Part of Property

If you rent part of your property, you must divide certain expenses between the part of the property used for rental purposes and the part used for personal purposes, as though you actually had two separate pieces of property.

You can deduct the expenses related to the part of the property used for rental purposes, such as home mortgage interest and real estate taxes, as rental expenses on Schedule E (Form 1040). You also can deduct as a rental expense part of other expenses that normally are nondeductible personal expenses, such as expenses for electricity or for painting the outside of the house.

You can deduct the expenses for the part of the property used for personal purposes, subject to certain limitations, only if you itemize your deductions on Schedule A (Form 1040).

You cannot deduct any part of the cost of the first phone line, even if your tenants have unlimited use of it.

You do not have to divide the expenses that belong only to the rental part of your property. For example, if you paint a room that you rent or if you pay premiums for liability insurance in connection with renting a room in your home, your entire cost is a rental expense. If you install a second phone line strictly for your tenant's use, all the cost of the second line is deductible as a rental expense. You can deduct depreciation, which is discussed later in this chapter, on the part of the property used for rental purposes as well as on the furniture and equipment you use for rental purposes.

How to divide expenses. If an expense is for both rental use and personal use, such as mortgage interest or heat for the entire house, you must divide the expense between rental use and personal use. You can use any reasonable method for dividing the expense. It may be reasonable to divide the cost of some items (for example, water) on the basis of the number of people using them. However, the two most common methods for dividing an expense are one based on the number of rooms in your home and one based on the square footage of the home.

Example. You rent a room in your house. The room is 12 by 15 feet, or 180 square feet. Your entire house has 1,800 square feet of floor space. You can deduct as a rental expense 10 percent of any expense that must be divided between rental use and personal use. If your heating bill for the year for the entire house was $600, $60 ($600 × 10%) is a rental expense. The balance, $540, is a personal expense that you cannot deduct.

Personal Use of Dwelling Unit (Including Vacation Home)

If you have any personal use of a dwelling unit (defined later) (including a vacation home) that you rent, you must divide your expenses between rental use and personal use. See "Figuring Days of Personal Use" and "How to Divide Expense," later in this chapter.

If you used a dwelling unit for personal purposes, it may be considered a "dwelling unit used as a home." If it is, you cannot deduct rental expenses that are more than your rental income for the unit. See "Dwelling Unit Used as Home" and "How to Figure Rental Income and Deductions," later in this chapter. If the dwelling unit is not considered a dwelling unit used as a home, you can deduct rental expenses that are more than your rental income for the unit, subject to certain limits. See "Limits on Rental Losses."

Exception for minimal rental use. If you use the dwelling unit as a home and rent it fewer than 15 days during the year, do not include any of the rent in your income and do not deduct any of the rental expenses. See "Dwelling Unit Used as Home."

Dwelling unit. A dwelling unit is a house, apartment, condominium, mobile home, boat, vacation home, or similar property. A dwelling unit has basic living accommodations such as sleeping space, a toilet, and cooking facilities. A dwelling unit does not include property used solely as a hotel, motel, inn, or similar establishment.

Property is used solely as a hotel, motel, inn, or similar establishment if it is regularly available for occupancy by paying customers and is not used by an owner as a home during the year.

Example. You rent a room in your home that is always available for short-term occupancy by paying customers. You do not use the room yourself, and allow only paying customers to use it. The room is used solely as a hotel, motel, inn, or similar establishment and is not a dwelling unit.

Dwelling Unit Used as Home

The tax treatment of rental income and expenses for a dwelling unit that you also use for personal purposes depends on whether you use it as a home. (See "How to Figure Rental Income and Deduction," later in this chapter).

You use a dwelling unit as a home during the tax year if you use it for personal purposes more than the greater of: (1) 14 days or (2) 10 percent of the total days it is rented to others at a fair rental price. See "Figuring Days of Personal Use."

If a dwelling unit is used for personal purposes on a day it is rented at a fair rental price, do not count that day as a day of rental use in applying condition 2 above. Instead, count it as a day of personal use in applying both condition 1 and condition 2 above. This rule does not apply when one is dividing expenses between rental use and personal use.

Fair rental price. A fair rental price for your property generally is the amount of rent that a person who is not related to you would be willing to pay. The rent you charge is not a fair rental price if it is substantially less than the rents charged for other properties that are similar to your property.

Ask yourself the following questions when comparing another property with yours:

- Is it used for the same purpose?
- Is it approximately the same size?
- Is it in approximately the same condition?
- Does it have similar furnishings?
- Is it in a similar location?

If any of the answers are no, the properties probably are not similar.

Examples

The following examples show how to determine whether you used your rental property as a home.

Example 1. You converted the basement of your home into an apartment with a bedroom, a bathroom, and a small kitchen. You rented the basement apartment at a fair rental price to college students during the regular school year. You rented to them on a nine-month lease (273 days). You figured 10 percent of the total days rented to others at a fair rental price equals 27 days.

During June (30 days), your brothers stayed with you and lived in the basement apartment rent-free.

Your basement apartment was used as a home because you used it for personal purposes for 30 days. Rent-free use by your brothers is considered personal use. Your personal use (30 days) is more than the greater of 14 days or 10 percent of the total days it was rented (27 days).

Example 2. You rented the guest bedroom in your home at a fair rental price during the local college's homecoming, commencement, and football weekends (a total of 27 days). Your sister-in-law stayed in the room, rent-free, for the last three weeks (21 days) in July. You figured 10 percent of the total days rented to others at a fair rental price equals three days.

The room was used as a home because you used it for personal purposes for 21 days. That is more than the greater of 14 days or 10 percent of the 27 days it was rented (3 days).

Example 3. You own a condominium apartment in a resort area. You rented it at a fair rental price for a total of 170 days during the year. For 12 of those days, the tenant was not able to use the apartment and allowed you to use it even though you did not refund any of the rent. Your family actually used the apartment for 10 of those days. Therefore, the apartment is treated as having been rented for 160 (170 − 10) days. You figure 10 percent of the total days rented to others at a fair rental price equals 16 days. Your family also used the apartment for seven other days during the year.

You used the apartment as a home, because you used it for personal purposes for 17 days. That is more than the greater of 14 days or 10 percent of the 160 days it was rented (16 days).

Use as Main Home before or after Renting

For purposes of determining whether a dwelling unit was used as a home, you may not have to count days you used the property as your main home before or after renting it or offering it for rent as days of personal use. Do not count them as days of personal use if:

- You rented or tried to rent the property for 12 or more consecutive months.
- You rented or tried to rent the property for a period of less than 12 consecutive months and the period ended because you sold or exchanged the property.

This special rule does not apply when you are dividing expenses between rental and personal use.

Example 1. On February 28, you moved out of the house you had lived in for six years because you accepted a job in another town. You rented your house at a fair rental price from March 15 of that year to May 14 of the next year (14 months). On the following June 1, you moved back into your old house.

The days you used the house as your main home from January 1 to February 28 and from June 1 to December 31 of the next year are not counted as days of personal use.

Example 2. On January 31, you moved out of the condominium where you had lived for three years. You offered it for rent at a fair rental price beginning on February 1. You were unable to rent it until April. On September 15, you sold the condominium.

The days you used the condominium as your main home from January 1 to January 31 are not counted as days of personal use when determining whether you used it as a home.

Figuring Days of Personal Use

A day of personal use of a dwelling unit is any day that the unit is used by any of the following persons:

1. You or any other person who has an interest in it, unless you rent it to another owner as his or her main home under a shared equity financing agreement (defined later). However, see "Use as Main Home Before or After Renting" under "Dwelling Unit Used As Home," earlier in this chapter.
2. A member of your family or a member of the family of any other person who has an interest in it, unless the family member uses the dwelling unit as his or her main home and pays a fair rental price. Family includes only brothers and sisters, half brothers and half sisters, spouses, ancestors (parents, grandparents, etc.), and lineal descendants (children, grandchildren, etc.).
3. Anyone under an arrangement who lets you use some other dwelling unit.
4. Anyone who rents at less than a fair rental price.

Main home. If the other person or member of the family in condition 1 or condition 2 above has more than one home, his or her main home is ordinarily the one he or she lived in most of the time.

Shared-equity financing agreement. This is an agreement under which two or more persons acquire undivided interests for more than 50 years in an entire dwelling unit, including the land, and one or more of the co-owners is entitled to occupy the unit as his or her main home upon payment of rent to the other co-owner or co-owners.

Donation of use of property. You use a dwelling unit for personal purposes if

- You donate the use of the unit to a charitable organization.
- The organization sells the use of the unit at a fund-raising event.
- The "purchaser" uses the unit.

Examples

The following examples show how to determine days of personal use.

Example 1. You and your neighbor are co-owners of a condominium at the beach. You rent the unit to vacationers whenever possible. The unit is not used as a main home by anyone. Your neighbor uses the unit for two weeks every year.

Because your neighbor has an interest in the unit, both of you are considered to have used the unit for personal purposes during those two weeks.

Example 2. You and your neighbors are co-owners of a house under a shared-equity financing agreement. Your neighbors live in the house and pay you a fair rental price.

Even though your neighbors have an interest in the house, the days your neighbors live there are not counted as days of personal use by you. This is the case because your neighbors rent the house as their main home under a shared equity financing agreement.

Example 3. You own a rental property that you rent to your son. Your son has no interest in this property. He uses it as his main home. He pays you a fair rental price for the property.

Your son's use of the property is not personal use by you, because your son is using it as his main home, he has no interest in the property, and he is paying you a fair rental price.

Example 4. You rent your beach house to Rosa. Rosa rents her house in the mountains to you. You each pay a fair rental price.

You are using your house for personal purposes on the days Rosa uses it, because your house is used by Rosa under an arrangement that allows you to use her house.

Example 5. You rent an apartment to your mother at less than a fair rental price. You are using the apartment for personal purposes on the days your mother rents it, because you rent it for less than a fair rental price.

Days Used for Repairs and Maintenance

Any day you spend working substantially full-time repairing and maintaining your property is not counted as a day of personal use. Do not count such a day as a day of personal use, even if family members use the property for recreational purposes on that day.

Example. You own a cabin in the mountains that you rent during the summer. You spend three days at the cabin each May, working full-time to repair anything that was damaged over the winter and get the cabin ready for the summer. You also spend three days each September working full-time to repair any damage done by renters and getting the cabin ready for the winter.

Those six days do not count as days of personal use, even if your family uses the cabin while you are repairing it.

How to Divide Expenses

If you use a dwelling unit for both rental and personal purposes, divide your expenses between the rental use and the personal use on the basis of the number of days used for each purpose. You can deduct expenses for the rental use of the unit under the rules explained in "How To Figure Rental Income and Deductions," later in this chapter.

When dividing your expenses, follow these rules:

1. Any day the unit is rented at a fair rental price is a day of rental use, even if you used the unit for personal purposes that day. This rule does not apply in determining whether you used the unit as a home.
2. Any day the unit is available for rent but not actually rented is not a day of rental use.

Example. Your beach cottage was available for rent from June 1 through August 31 (92 days). Your family used the cottage during the last two weeks in May (14 days). You were unable to find a renter for the first week in August (seven days). The person who rented the cottage for July allowed you to use it over a weekend (two days) without any reduction in or refund of rent. The cottage was not used at all before May 17 or after August 31.

You figure the part of the cottage expenses to treat as rental expenses by using the following facts:

1. The cottage was used for rental a total of 85 days (92 − 7). The days it was available for rent but not rented (seven days) are not days of rental use. The July weekend (two days) you used it is rental use because you received a fair rental price for the weekend.
2. You used the cottage for personal purposes for 14 days (the last two weeks in May).
3. The total use of the cottage was 99 days (14 days of personal use plus 85 days of rental use).
4. Your rental expenses are 85/99 (86 percent) of the cottage expenses.

When determining whether you used the cottage as a home, the July weekend (two days) you used it is personal use even though you received a fair rental price for that weekend. Therefore, you had 16 days of personal use and 83 days of rental use for this purpose. Because you used the cottage for personal purposes more than 14 days and more than 10 percent of the days of rental use (8 days), you used it as a home. If you have a net loss, you may not be able to deduct all the rental expenses. See "Property Used as a Home," in the following discussion.

How to Figure Rental Income and Deductions

How you figure your rental income and deductions depends on whether you used the dwelling unit as a home (see "Dwelling Unit Used as Home," earlier in this chapter) and, if you used it as a home, how many days the property was rented at a fair rental price.

Property Not Used as a Home

If you do not use a dwelling unit as a home, report all the rental income and deduct all the rental expenses. See "How to Report Rental Income and Expenses," below.

Your deductible rental expenses can be more than your gross rental income. However, see "Limits on Rental Losses," below.

Property Used as a Home

If you use a dwelling unit as a home during the year, how you figure your rental income and deductions depends on how many days the unit was rented at a fair rental price.

Rented fewer than 15 days. If you use a dwelling unit as a home and rent it fewer than 15 days during the year, do not include any rental income in your income. Also, you cannot deduct any expenses as rental expenses.

Rented 15 days or more. If you use a dwelling unit as a home and rent it 15 days or more during the year, include all your rental income in your income. See "How to Report Rental Income and Expenses," below. If you had a net profit from the rental property for the year (that is, your rental income is more than the total of your rental expenses, including depreciation), deduct all your rental expenses. However, if you had a net loss, your deduction for certain rental expenses is limited.

Limit on deductions. If your rental expenses are more than your rental income, you cannot use the excess expenses to offset income from other sources. The excess can be carried forward to the next year and treated as rental expenses for the same property. Any expenses carried forward to next year will be subject to any limits that apply next year. You can deduct the expenses carried over to a year only up to the amount of your rental income for that year even if you do not use the property as your home in that year.

Depreciation

You recover the cost of income-producing property through yearly tax deductions. You do this by depreciating the property; that is, by deducting some of the cost on the tax return each year.

Three basic factors determine how much depreciation you can deduct: (1) your basis in the property, (2) the recovery period for the property, and (3) the depreciation method used. You cannot simply deduct your mortgage or principal payments or the cost of furniture, fixtures, and equipment as an expense.

You can deduct depreciation only on the part of your property used for rental purposes. Depreciation reduces your basis for figuring gain or loss on a later sale or exchange.

You may have to use Form 4562 to figure and report your depreciation. See "How to Report Rental Income and Expenses," below. Also see Publication 946.

Claiming the Correct Amount of Depreciation

You should claim the correct amount of depreciation each tax year. Even if you did not claim depreciation you were entitled to deduct, you still must reduce your basis in the property by the full amount of depreciation that you could have deducted. See "Decreases to Basis," below, for more information. If you did not deduct the correct amount of depreciation for property in any year, you may be able to make a correction for that year by filing Form 1040X, "Amended U.S. Individual Income Tax Return." If you are not allowed to make the correction on an amended return, you can change your accounting method to claim the correct amount of depreciation. See "Changing Your Accounting Method," below.

Filing an amended return. You can file an amended return to correct the amount of depreciation claimed for any property in any of the following situations:

- You claimed the incorrect amount because of a mathematical error made in any year.
- You claimed the incorrect amount because of a posting error made in any year.
- You have not adopted a method of accounting for the property.

If an amended return is allowed, you must file it by the later of the following dates:

- Three years from the date you filed your original return for the year in which you did not deduct the correct amount. (A return filed early is considered filed on the due date.)
- Two years from the time you paid your tax for that year.

Changing your accounting method. To change your accounting method, you must file Form 3115, "Application for Change in Accounting Method," to get the consent of the IRS. In some instances, that consent is automatic. For more information, see "Changing Your Accounting Method" in Publication 946.

What Property Can Be Depreciated

You can depreciate your property if it meets all the following requirements:

- You own the property.
- You use the property in your business or income-producing activity (such as rental property).
- The property has a determinable useful life.
- The property is expected to last more than one year.
- The property is not excepted property (such as property placed in service and disposed of in the same year and Section 197 intangibles).

Property having a determinable useful life. To be depreciable, your property must have a determinable useful life. This means that it must be something that wears out, decays, gets used up, becomes obsolete, or loses its value from natural causes.

Land. You can never depreciate the cost of land because land does not wear out, become obsolete, or get used up. The costs of clearing, grading, planting, and landscaping are usually all part of the cost of land and cannot be depreciated.

Property you own. To claim depreciation, you usually must be the owner of the property. You are considered as owning property even if that property is subject to a debt.

Rented property. Generally, if you pay rent on property, you cannot depreciate that property. Usually, only the owner can depreciate it. If you make permanent improvements to the property, you may be able to depreciate the improvements. See "Additions or Improvements to Property," below.

Cooperative apartments. If you are a tenant-stockholder in a cooperative housing corporation and rent your cooperative apartment to others, you can deduct depreciation for your stock in the corporation.

Compute your depreciation deduction as follows:

1. Figure the depreciation for all the depreciable real property owned by the corporation. (Depreciation methods are discussed later.) If you bought your

cooperative stock after its first offering, compute the depreciable basis of this property as follows:

   a. Multiply your cost per share by the total number of outstanding shares.

   b. Add to the amount figured in Step a any mortgage debt on the property on the date you bought the stock.

   c. Subtract from the amount figured in Step b any mortgage debt that is not for the depreciable real property, such as the part for the land.

2. Subtract from the amount figured in Step 1 any depreciation for space owned by the corporation that can be rented but cannot be lived in by tenant-stock-holders.

3. Divide the number of your shares of stock by the total number of shares outstanding, including any shares held by the corporation.

4. Multiply the result in Step 2 by the percentage you computed in Step 3. This is your depreciation on the stock.

Your depreciation deduction for the year cannot be more than the part of your adjusted basis (defined later) in the stock of the corporation that is allocable to your rental property.

See "Cooperative Apartments" under "What Property Can Be Depreciated?" in Chapter 1 of Publication 946 for more information.

No deduction greater than basis. The total of all your yearly depreciation deductions cannot be more than the cost or other basis of the property. For this purpose, your yearly depreciation deductions include any depreciation that you were allowed to claim, even if you did not claim it.

Depreciation Methods

There are three ways to figure depreciation. The depreciation method you use depends on the type of property and when it was placed in service. For property used in rental activities, use one of the following:

- MACRS (Modified Accelerated Cost Recovery System) for property placed in service after 1986
- ACRS (Accelerated Cost Recovery System) for property placed in service after 1980 but before 1987
- Useful lives and either a straight-line or an accelerated method of depreciation, such as the declining balance method, for property placed in service before 1981

If you need information about depreciating property placed in service before 1987, see Publication 534.

If you placed property in service before 2004, continue to use the same method of figuring depreciation you used in the past.

Section 179 deduction. You cannot claim the Section 179 deduction for property held to produce rental income. See Chapter 2 of Publication 946.

Alternative minimum tax. If you use accelerated depreciation, you may have to file Form 6251, "Alternative Minimum Tax—Individuals." Accelerated depreciation can be determined under MACRS, ACRS, and any other method that allows you to deduct more depreciation than you could deduct using a straight-line method.

Special Depreciation Allowance

You can take a special depreciation allowance (in addition to your regular MACRS depreciation deduction) for qualified property you placed in service in 2004. The allowance is 50 percent of the property's depreciable basis. You compute the special depreciation allowance before you compute your regular MACRS deduction.

Electing to claim a lower or no special allowance. You can elect, for any class of property, to deduct the 30 percent (instead of 50 percent) special allowance for all property in such class placed in service during the tax year. Or, you can elect not to deduct any special allowance for all property in such class placed in service during the tax year.

To make an election, attach a statement to your return indicating what election you are making and the class of property for which you are making the election. See "How Can You Elect Not to Claim an Allowance?" in Publication 946 for more information.

Qualified property. To qualify for the special depreciation allowance, your property must meet the following requirements:

1. It is new property that is depreciated under MACRS with a recovery period of 20 years or less.
2. It meets the following tests:
   a. Acquisition date test
   b. Placed-in-service date test
   c. Original use test

Acquisition date test. Generally, you must have acquired the property after September 10, 2001 (after May 5, 2003, to be eligible for the 50 percent special depreciation allowance).

Placed-in-service date test. Generally, the property must be placed in service for use in your trade or business or for the production of income after September 10, 2001 (after May 5, 2003, to be eligible for the 50 percent special depreciation allowance), and before January 1, 2005.

Original use test. The original use of the property must have begun with you after September 10, 2001 (after May 5, 2003, to be eligible for the 50 percent special depreciation allowance). "Original use" means the first use to which the property is put, whether or not by you.

Example. Dave bought and placed in service a new refrigerator ($700) for one of his residential rental properties in 2004. Dave notes that the refrigerator has a five-year recovery period (see Table 11-1). Dave's refrigerator is qualifying property, and he claims the 50 percent special depreciation allowance.

Dave determines the total depreciable basis of the property to be $700. Next, he multiplies this amount by 50 percent to figure his special depreciation allowance of $350 ($700 × 50 percent). This leaves an adjusted basis of $350 ($700 − $350), which he will use to compute his MACRS deduction.

For more information, see "Claiming the Special Depreciation Allowance (or Liberty Zone Depreciation Allowance)" in Publication 946.

MACRS

Most business and investment property placed in service after 1986 is depreciated by using MACRS.

MACRS consists of two systems that determine how you depreciate your property: the General Depreciation System (GDS) and the Alternative Depreciation System (ADS). GDS is used to figure the depreciation deduction for property used in most rental activities unless you elect to use ADS.

To compute a MACRS deduction, you need to know the following information about your property:

1. Its recovery period
2. Its placed-in-service date
3. Its depreciable basis

Personal home changed to rental use. You must use MACRS to compute the depreciation on property used as your home and changed to rental property in 2004.

Excluded property. You cannot use MACRS for certain personal property placed in service in your rental property in 2004 if it previously had been placed in ser-

Table 11-1 MACRS Recovery Periods for Property Used in Rental Activities

| | MACRS Recovery Period | |
Type of Property	General Depreciation System	Alternative Depreciation System
Computers and their peripheral equipment	5 years	5 years
Office machinery, such as typewriters, calculators, and copiers	5 years	6 years
Automobiles	5 years	5 years
Light trucks	5 years	5 years
Appliances, such as stoves and refrigerators	5 years	9 years
Carpets	5 years	9 years
Furniture used in rental property	5 years	9 years
Office furniture and equipment, such as desks and files	7 years	10 years
Any property that does not have a class life and that has not been designated by law as being in any other class	7 years	12 years
Roads	15 years	20 years
Shrubbery	15 years	20 years
Fences	15 years	20 years
Residential rental property (buildings or structures) and structural components such as furnaces, water pipes, and venting	27.5 years	40 years
Additions and improvements, such as a new roof	The same recovery period as that of the property to which the addition or improvement is made, determined as if the property were placed in service at the same time as the addition or improvement	

vice before MACRS became effective. Generally, personal property is excluded from MACRS if you (or a person related to you) owned or used it in 1986 or if your tenant is a person (or someone related to a person) who owned or used it in 1986. However, the property is not excluded if your 2004 deduction under MACRS (using a half-year convention) is less than the deduction you would have under ACRS. See "Can You Use MACRS to Depreciate Your Property?" in Publication 946 for more information.

Recovery Periods under GDS

Each item of property that can be depreciated is assigned to a property class. The recovery period of the property depends on the class the property is in. Under GDS, the recovery period of an asset is generally the same as its property class. The property classes under GDS are as follows:

- 3-year property
- 5-year property
- 7-year property
- 10-year property
- 15-year property
- 20-year property
- Nonresidential real property
- Residential rental property

The class to which property is assigned is determined by the property's class life. Class lives and recovery periods for most assets are listed in Appendix B in Publication 946.

Under GDS, property that you placed in service during 2004 in your rental activities generally falls into one of the following classes (also see Table 11-1):

1. **Five-year property.** This class includes computers and peripheral equipment, office machinery (typewriters, calculators, copiers, etc.), automobiles, and light trucks. It also includes appliances, carpeting, furniture, and so forth, used in a residential rental real estate activity. Depreciation on automobiles, certain computers, and cellular telephones is limited. See Chapter 5 of Publication 946.
2. **Seven-year property.** This class includes office furniture and equipment (desks, files, etc.). It also includes any property that does not have a class life and that has not been designated by law as being in any other class.
3. **Fifteen-year property.** This class includes roads and shrubbery (if depreciable).
4. **Residential rental property.** This class includes any real property that is a rental building or structure (including a mobile home) for which 80 percent or more of the gross rental income for the tax year is from dwelling units. It does not include a unit in a hotel, motel, inn, or other establishment where more than half the units are used on a transient basis. If you live in any part of the building or structure, the gross rental income includes the fair rental value of the part in which you live. The recovery period for residential rental property is 27.5 years.

The other property classes generally do not apply to property used in rental activities. See Publication 946 for more information.

Qualified Indian reservation property. Shorter recovery periods are provided under MACRS for qualified Indian reservation property placed in service on Indian reservations before 2006. For more information, see Chapter 4 of Publication 946.

Additions or improvements to property. Treat depreciable additions or improvements you make to any property as separate property items for depreciation purposes. The recovery period for an addition or improvement to property begins on the later of:

1. The date the addition or improvement is placed in service
2. The date the property to which the addition or improvement was made is placed in service

The property class and recovery period of the addition or improvement are the ones that would apply to the original property if it were placed in service at the same time as the addition or improvement.

Example. You own a residential rental house that you have been renting since 1986 and are depreciating under ACRS. You put an addition onto the house and placed it in service in 2004. You must use MACRS for the addition. Under GDS, the addition is depreciated as residential rental property over 27.5 years.

Placed-in-Service Date

You can begin to depreciate property when you place it in service in your trade or business or for the production of income. Property is considered placed in service in a rental activity when it is ready and available for a specific use in that activity.

Example 1. On November 22 of last year, you purchased a dishwasher for your rental property. The appliance was delivered on December 7, but was not installed and ready for use until January 3 of this year. Because the dishwasher was not ready for use last year, it is not considered to have been placed in service until this year.

If the appliance had been ready for use when it was delivered in December of last year, it would have been considered placed in service in December even if it actually was not used until this year.

Example 2. On April 6, you purchased a house to use as residential rental property. You made extensive repairs to the house and had it ready for rent on July 5. You began to advertise the house for rent in July and actually rented it beginning

September 1. The house is considered to have been placed in service in July, when it was ready and available for rent. You can begin to depreciate the house in July.

Example 3. You moved from your home in July. During August and September, you made several repairs to the house. On October 1, you listed the property for rent with a real estate company, which rented it on December 1. The property is considered to have been placed in service on October 1, the date when it was available for rent.

Depreciable Basis

The depreciable basis of property used in a rental activity is generally its adjusted basis when you place it in service in that activity. This is its cost or other basis when you acquired it, adjusted for certain items occurring before you place it in service in the rental activity.

If you depreciate your property under MACRS, you also may have to reduce your basis by certain deductions and credits with respect to the property, including any special depreciation allowance (discussed earlier).

Basis and adjusted basis are explained in the following discussions.

If you used the property for personal purposes before changing it to rental use, its depreciable basis is the lesser of its adjusted basis or its fair market value when you change it to rental use. See "Basis of Property Changed to Rental Use," below.

Cost Basis

The basis of property you buy is usually its cost. The cost is the amount you pay for it in cash, debt obligation, other property, or services. Your cost also includes amounts you pay for the following:

- Sales tax charged on the purchase (but see the exception that follows)
- Freight charges to obtain the property
- Installation and testing charges

Exception. For tax years beginning after 2003, you can elect to deduct state and local general sales taxes instead of state and local income taxes as an itemized deduction on Schedule A (Form 1040). If you make that choice, you cannot include those sales taxes as part of your cost basis.

Loans with low or no interest. If you buy property on any time-payment plan that charges little or no interest, the basis of your property is your stated purchase price, minus the amount considered to be unstated interest. See "Unstated Interest and Original Issue Discount" in Publication 537, Installment Sales.

Real property. If you buy real property such as a building and land, certain fees and other expenses you pay are part of your cost basis in the property.

Real estate taxes. If you buy real property and agree to pay real estate taxes on it that were owed by the seller, and the seller did not reimburse you, the taxes you pay are treated as part of your basis in the property. You cannot deduct them as taxes paid.

If you reimburse the seller for real estate taxes the seller paid for you, you usually can deduct that amount. Do not include that amount in your basis in the property.

Settlement fees and other costs. Settlement fees and closing costs that are for buying the property are part of your basis in the property. They include:

- Abstract fees
- Charges for installing utility services
- Legal fees
- Recording fees
- Surveys
- Transfer taxes
- Title insurance
- Any amounts the seller owes that you agree to pay, such as back taxes or interest, recording or mortgage fees, charges for improvements or repairs, and sales commissions

Some settlement fees and closing costs that you cannot include in your basis in the property are as follows:

1. Fire insurance premiums
2. Rent or other charges relating to occupancy of the property before closing
3. Charges connected with getting or refinancing a loan, such as
   a. Points (discount points, loan origination fees)
   b. Mortgage insurance premiums
   c. Loan assumption fees
   d. Cost of a credit report
   e. Fees for an appraisal required by a lender

Also, do not include amounts placed in escrow for the future payment of items such as taxes and insurance.

Assumption of a mortgage. If you buy property and become liable for an existing mortgage on the property, your basis is the amount you pay for the property plus the amount that still must be paid on the mortgage.

Example. You buy a building for $60,000 cash and assume a mortgage of $240,000 on it. Your basis is $300,000.

Land and buildings. If you buy buildings and your cost includes the cost of the land on which they stand, you must divide the cost between the land and the buildings to compute the basis for depreciation of the buildings. The part of the cost you allocate to each asset is the ratio of the fair market value of that asset to the fair market value of the whole property at the time you buy it.

If you are not certain of the fair market values of the land and the buildings, you can divide the cost between them on the basis of their assessed values for real estate tax purposes.

Example. You buy a house and land for $100,000. The purchase contract does not specify how much of the purchase price is for the house and how much is for the land.

The latest real estate tax assessment on the property was based on an assessed value of $80,000, of which $68,000 is for the house and $12,000 is for the land.

You can allocate 85 percent ($68,000 ÷ $80,000) of the purchase price to the house and 15 percent ($12,000 ÷ $80,000) to the land.

Your basis in the house is $85,000 (85 percent of $100,000), and your basis in the land is $15,000 (15 percent of $100,000).

Basis Other Than Cost

There are many times when you cannot use cost as a basis. You cannot use cost as a basis for property that you received

- In return for services you performed
- In an exchange for other property
- As a gift
- From your spouse, or from your former spouse as the result of a divorce
- As an inheritance

If you received property in one of these ways, see Publication 551 for information on how to figure your basis.

Adjusted Basis

Before you can figure allowable depreciation, you may have to make certain adjustments (increases and decreases) to the basis of the property. The result of these adjustments to the basis is the adjusted basis.

Increases to basis. You must increase the basis of any property by the cost of all items properly added to a capital account. This includes the following:

- The cost of any additions or improvements with a useful life of more than one year
- Amounts spent after a casualty to restore the damaged property
- The cost of extending utility service lines to the property
- Legal fees such as the cost of defending and perfecting title

Additions or improvements. Add to the basis of your property the amount an addition or improvement actually cost you, including any amount you borrowed to make that addition or improvement. This includes all direct costs, such as material and labor, but not your own labor. It also includes all expenses related to the addition or improvement.

For example, if you had an architect draw up plans for remodeling your property, the architect's fee is part of the cost of the remodeling. If you had your lot surveyed to put up a fence, the cost of the survey is part of the cost of the fence.

Keep separate accounts for depreciable additions or improvements made after you place the property in service in your rental activity. For information on depreciating additions or improvements, see "Additions or Improvements to Property," above, under "Recovery Periods under GDS."

The cost of landscaping improvements usually is treated as an addition to the basis of the land, which is not depreciable. See "What Property Can Be Depreciated," above.

Assessments for local improvements. Assessments for items that tend to increase the value of property, such as streets and sidewalks, must be added to the basis of the property. For example, if your city installs curbing on the street in front of your house and assesses you and your neighbors for the cost of curbing, you must add the assessment to the basis of your property. Also add the cost of legal fees paid to obtain a decrease in an assessment levied against property to pay for local improvements. You cannot deduct these items as taxes or depreciate them.

Assessments for maintenance or repair or for meeting interest charges are deductible as taxes. Do not add them to your basis in the property.

Deducting versus capitalizing costs. You cannot add to your basis costs that are deductible as current expenses. However, there are certain costs you can choose either to deduct or to capitalize. If you capitalize these costs, include them in your basis. If you deduct them, do not include them.

The costs you may be able to choose to deduct or capitalize include carrying charges, such as interest and taxes, that you must pay to own property.

For more information about deducting or capitalizing costs, see Chapter 8 in Publication 535.

Decreases to basis. You must decrease the basis of your property by any items that represent a return of your cost. These items include the following:

- The amount of any insurance or other payment you receive as the result of a casualty or theft loss.
- Any deductible casualty loss not covered by insurance.
- Any amount you receive for granting an easement.
- Any residential energy credit you were allowed before 1986, if you added the cost of the energy items to the basis of your home.
- The amount of depreciation you could have deducted on your tax returns under the method of depreciation you selected. If you took less depreciation than you could have under the method you selected, you must decrease the basis by the amount you could have taken under that method. If you deducted more depreciation than you should have, you must decrease your basis by the amount you should have deducted, plus the part of the excess you deducted that actually lowered your tax liability for any year.

Basis of Property Changed to Rental Use

When you change property you held for personal use to rental use (for example, you rent your former home), you compute the basis for depreciation by using the lesser of fair market value or adjusted basis.

Fair market value. This is the price at which the property would change hands between a buyer and a seller, with neither having to buy or sell and both having reasonable knowledge of all the relevant facts. Sales of similar property on or about the same date may be helpful in figuring the fair market value of the property.

Figuring the basis. The basis for depreciation is the lesser of:

- The fair market value of the property on the dat, you changed it to rental use
- Your adjusted basis on the date of the change; that is, your original cost or other basis of the property, plus the cost of permanent additions or improve-

ments since you acquired it, minus deductions for any casualty or theft losses claimed on earlier years' income tax returns and other decreases to basis

Example. Several years ago you built your home for $140,000 on a lot that cost you $14,000. Before changing the property to rental use last year, you added $28,000 of permanent improvements to the house and claimed a $3,500 deduction for a casualty loss to the house. Because land is not depreciable, you can include only the cost of the house when figuring the basis for depreciation.

The adjusted basis of the house at the time of the change in use was $164,500 ($140,000 + $28,000 − $3,500).

On the date of the change in use, your property had a fair market value of $168,000, of which $21,000 was for the land and $147,000 was for the house.

The basis for depreciation on the house is the fair market value at the date of the change ($147,000), because it is less than your adjusted basis ($164,500).

MACRS Depreciation under GDS

You can figure your MACRS depreciation deduction under GDS in one of two ways. The deduction is substantially the same both ways (the difference, if any, is slight). You can either:

1. Actually compute the deduction using the depreciation method and convention that apply over the recovery period of the property or,
2. Use the percentage from the optional MACRS tables, shown later

If you actually compute the deduction, the depreciation method you use depends on the class of the property.

Five-, seven-, or fifteen-year property. For property in the five- or seven-year class, use the 200 percent declining balance method and a half-year convention. However, in limited cases you must use the midquarter convention if it applies. These conventions are explained later. For property in the 15-year class, use the 150 percent declining balance method and a half-year convention.

You also can choose to use the 150 percent declining balance method for property in the five- or seven-year class. The choice to use the 150 percent method for one item in a class of property applies to all property in that class that is placed in service during the tax year of the election. You make this election on Form 4562. In Part III, column (f), enter "150 DB."

If you use either the 200 percent or the 150 percent declining balance method, you figure your deduction by using the straight-line method in the first tax year in which the straight-line method gives you an equal or larger deduction.

You also can choose to use the straight-line method with a half-year or midquarter convention for five-, seven-, or fifteen-year property. The choice to use the straight-line method for one item in a class of property applies to all property in that class that is placed in service during the tax year of the election. You elect the straight-line method on Form 4562. In Part III, column (f), enter "S/L." Once you make this election, you cannot change to another method.

Residential Rental Property

You must use the straight-line method and a midmonth convention for residential rental property.

Declining Balance Method

To figure your MACRS deduction, first determine your declining balance rate from the table below. However, if you elect to use the 150 percent declining balance method for five- or seven-year property, determine the declining balance rate by dividing 1.5 (150 percent) by the recovery period for the property.

In the first tax year, multiply the adjusted basis of the property by the declining balance rate and apply the appropriate convention to figure your depreciation. In later years (before the year you switch to the straight-line method), use the following steps to compute your depreciation:

1. Reduce your adjusted basis by the depreciation allowable for the earlier years.
2. Multiply the new adjusted basis in Step 1 by the same rate used in earlier years.

See "Conventions," below, for information on depreciation in the year in which you dispose of property.

Declining balance rates. The following table shows the declining balance rate that applies for each class of property and the first year for which the straight-line method will give an equal or greater deduction. (The rates for five- and seven-year property are based on the 200 percent declining balance method. The rate for 15-year property is based on the 150 percent declining balance method.)

Class	Declining Balance Rate, %	Year
5	40	Fourth
7	28.57	Fifth
15	10	Seventh

Straight-Line Method

To figure your MACRS deduction under the straight-line method, you must apply a different depreciation rate to the adjusted basis of your property for each tax year in the recovery period.

In the first year, multiply the adjusted basis of the property by the straight-line rate. You must figure the depreciation for the first year by using the convention that applies. (See "Conventions," below.)

Straight-line rate. For any tax year, figure the straight-line rate by dividing the number 1 by the years remaining in the recovery period at the beginning of the tax year. When figuring the number of years remaining, you must take into account the convention used in the first year. If the remaining recovery period at the beginning of the tax year is less than one year, the straight-line rate for that tax year is 100 percent.

Example. You place in service property with a basis of $1,000 and a five-year recovery period. You elect not to claim the special depreciation allowance, as discussed earlier. The straight-line rate is 20 percent (1 ÷ 5) for the first tax year. After you apply the half-year convention, the first year's rate is 10 percent (20 percent ÷ 2). Depreciation for the first year is $100.

At the beginning of the second year, the remaining recovery period is 4? years because of the half-year convention. The straight-line rate for the second year is 22.22 percent (1 ÷ 4.5).

To determine your depreciation deduction for the second year:

1. Subtract the depreciation taken in the first year ($100) from the basis of the property ($1,000).
2. Multiply the remaining basis ($900) by 22.22 percent. The depreciation for the second year is $200.

Residential rental property. In the first year in which you claim depreciation for residential rental property, you can claim depreciation only for the number of months the property is in use, and you must use the midmonth convention (explained below).

Conventions

Under MACRS, conventions establish when the recovery period begins and ends. The convention you use determines the number of months for which you can claim depreciation in the year in which you place property in service and in the year in which you dispose of the property.

Midmonth convention. A midmonth convention is used for all residential rental property and nonresidential real property. Under this convention, you treat all property placed in service or disposed of during any month as placed in service or disposed of at the midpoint of that month.

Midquarter convention. A midquarter convention must be used if the midmonth convention does not apply and the total depreciable basis of MACRS property placed in service in the last three months of a tax year (excluding nonresidential real property, residential rental property, and property placed in service and disposed of in the same year) is more than 40 percent of the total basis of all such property you place in service during the year.

Under this convention, you treat all property placed in service or disposed of during any quarter of a tax year as being placed in service or disposed of at the midpoint of the quarter.

Example. During the tax year, Tom Martin purchased the following items to use in his rental property. He elects not to claim the special depreciation allowance discussed earlier:

- A dishwasher for $400 that he placed in service in January
- Used furniture for $100 that he placed in service in September
- A refrigerator for $500 that he placed in service in October

Tom uses the calendar year as his tax year. The total basis of all property placed in service that year is $1,000. The $500 basis of the refrigerator placed in service during the last three months of his tax year exceeds $400 (40 percent × $1,000). Tom must use the midquarter convention instead of the half-year convention for all three items.

Half-year convention. The half-year convention is used if neither the midquarter convention nor the midmonth convention applies. Under this convention, you treat all property placed in service or disposed of during a tax year as being placed in service or disposed of at the midpoint of that tax year.

If this convention applies, you deduct a half year of depreciation for the first year and the last year in which you depreciate the property. You deduct a full year of depreciation for any other year during the recovery period.

Optional Tables

If you elect to use the straight-line method for five-, seven-, or fifteen-year property, or the 150 percent declining balance method for five- or seven-year property, use the tables in Appendix A of Publication 946.

Once you begin using an optional table to figure depreciation, you must continue to use it for the entire recovery period unless there is an adjustment to the basis of your property for a reason other than the following:

1. Depreciation allowed or allowable
2. An addition or improvement that is depreciated as a separate item of property

If there is an adjustment for any reason other than those given above (for example, because of a deductible casualty loss), you can no longer use the table. For the year of the adjustment and for the remaining recovery period, compute depreciation by using the property's adjusted basis at the end of the year and the appropriate depreciation method, as explained under "MACRS Depreciation under ADS."

MACRS Depreciation under ADS

If you choose, you can use the ADS method for most property. Under ADS, you use the straight-line method of depreciation.

Table 11-1 shows the recovery periods for property used in rental activities that you depreciate under ADS.

See Appendix B in Publication 946 for other property. If your property is not listed, it is considered to have no class life. Under ADS, personal property with no class life is depreciated using a recovery period of 12 years.

Use the midmonth convention for residential rental property and nonresidential real property. For all other property, use the half-year or midquarter convention.

Election. For property placed in service during 2004 you choose to use ADS by entering the depreciation on Form 4562, Part III, line 20.

The election of ADS for one item in a class of property generally applies to all property in that class that is placed in service during the tax year of the election. However, the election applies on a property-by-property basis for residential rental property and nonresidential real property.

Once you choose to use ADS, you cannot change your election.

Casualties and Thefts

As a result of a casualty or theft, you may have a loss related to your property. You may be able to deduct the loss on your income tax return. For information on casualty and theft losses (business and nonbusiness), see Publication 547.

Casualty. Damage to, destruction of, or loss of property is a casualty if it results from an identifiable event that is sudden, unexpected, or unusual.

Theft. The unlawful taking and removing of your money or property with the intent to deprive you of it is a theft.

Gain from casualty or theft. When you have a casualty to or theft of your property and you receive money, including insurance, that is more than your adjusted basis in the property, you generally must report the gain. However, under certain circumstances, you may defer paying tax by choosing to postpone reporting the gain. To do this, you generally must buy replacement property within two years after the close of the first tax year in which any part of your gain is realized. The cost of the replacement property must be equal to or more than the net insurance or other payment you received. For more information, see Publication 547.

How to report. If you had a casualty or theft that involved property used in your rental activity, you figure the net gain or loss in Section B of Form 4684, "Casualties and Thefts." Also, you may have to report the net gain or loss from Form 4684 on Form 4797, "Sales of Business Property" (follow the instructions for Form 4684).

Limits on Rental Losses

Rental real estate activities generally are considered passive activities, and the amount of loss you can deduct is limited. Generally, you cannot deduct losses from rental real estate activities unless you have income from other passive activities. However, you may be able to deduct rental losses without regard to whether you have income from other passive activities if you "materially" or "actively" participated in your rental activity. See "Passive Activity Limits," below.

Losses from passive activities are first subject to the at-risk rules. At-risk rules limit the amount of deductible losses from holding most real property placed in service after 1986.

Exception. If your rental losses are less than $25,000, and you actively participated in the rental activity, the passive activity limits probably do not apply to you. See "Losses from Rental Real Estate Activities," below.

Property used as a home. If you used the rental property as a home during the year, the passive activity rules do not apply to that home. Instead, you must follow the rules explained under "Personal Use of Dwelling Unit (Including Vacation Home)," above.

At-Risk Rules

The at-risk rules place a limit on the amount you can deduct as losses from activities often described as tax shelters. Losses from holding real property (other than mineral property) placed in service before 1987 are not subject to the at-risk rules.

Generally, any loss from an activity subject to the at-risk rules is allowed only to the extent of the total amount you have at risk in the activity at the end of the tax year. You are considered at risk in an activity to the extent of cash and the adjusted basis of other property you contributed to the activity and certain amounts borrowed for use in the activity. See Publication 925 for more information.

Passive Activity Limits

In general, all rental activities (except those meeting the exception for real estate professionals, discussed below) are passive activities. For this purpose, a rental activity is an activity from which you receive income mainly for the use of tangible property rather than for services.

Limits on passive activity deductions and credits. Deductions for losses from passive activities are limited. You generally cannot offset income, other than passive income, with losses from passive activities. Nor can you offset taxes on income, other than passive income, with credits resulting from passive activities. Any excess loss or credit is carried forward to the next tax year.

For a detailed discussion of these rules, see Publication 925.

You may have to complete Form 8582 to figure the amount of any passive activity loss for the current tax year for all activities and the amount of the passive activity loss allowed on your tax return. See "Form 8582 Not Required" under "Losses from Rental Real Estate Activities," below, to determine whether you have to complete Form 8582.

Exception for Real Estate Professionals

Rental activities in which you materially participated during the year are not passive activities if for that year you were a real estate professional. Losses from these activities are not limited by the passive activity rules.

For this purpose, each interest you have in a rental real estate activity is a separate activity unless you choose to treat all interests in rental real estate activities as one activity.

If you were a real estate professional for 2004, complete line 43 of Schedule E (Form 1040).

Real estate professional. You qualified as a real estate professional for the tax year if you met both of the following requirements:

1. More than half the personal services you performed in all trades or businesses during the tax year were performed in real property trades or businesses in which you materially participated.
2. You performed more than 750 hours of services during the tax year in real property trades or businesses in which you materially participated.

Do not count personal services you performed as an employee in real property trades or businesses unless you were a 5 percent owner of your employer's business. You were a 5 percent owner if you owned (or are considered to have owned) more than 5 percent of your employer's outstanding stock or capital or profits interest.

If you file a joint return, do not count your spouse's personal services to determine whether you met the preceding requirements. However, you can count your spouse's participation in an activity in determining if you materially participated.

Real property trades or businesses. A real property trade or business is a trade or business that does any of the following with real property:

- Develops or redevelops it
- Constructs or reconstructs it
- Acquires it
- Converts it
- Rents or leases it
- Operates or manages it
- Brokers it

Material participation. Generally, you materially participated in an activity for the tax year if you were involved in its operations on a regular, continuous, and substantial basis during the year. For more information, see Publication 925.

Participating spouse. If you are married, determine whether you materially participated in an activity by also counting any participation in the activity by your spouse during the year. Do this even if your spouse owns no interest in the activity or files a separate return for the year.

Choice to treat all interests as one activity. If you were a real estate professional and had more than one rental real estate interest during the year, you can choose to treat all the interests as one activity. You can make this choice for any year in which you qualify as a real estate professional. If you forgo making the choice for one year, you can still make it for a later year.

If you make the choice, it is binding for the tax year in which you make it and for any later year in which you are a real estate professional. This is true even if you are not a real estate professional in any intervening year. (For that year, the exception for real estate professionals will not apply in determining whether your activity is subject to the passive activity rules.)

See the instructions for Schedule E (Form 1040) for information about making this choice.

Losses from Rental Real Estate Activities

If you or your spouse actively participated in a passive rental real estate activity, you can deduct up to $25,000 of loss from the activity from your nonpassive income. This special allowance is an exception to the general rule disallowing losses in excess of income from passive activities. Similarly, you can offset credits from the activity against the tax on up to $25,000 of nonpassive income after taking into account any losses allowed under this exception.

If you are married, are filing a separate return, and lived apart from your spouse for the entire tax year, your special allowance cannot be more than $12,500. If you lived with your spouse at any time during the year and are filing a separate return, you cannot use the special allowance to reduce your nonpassive income or tax on nonpassive income.

The maximum amount of the special allowance is reduced if your modified adjusted gross income is more than $100,000 ($50,000 if married filing separately).

Example. Jane is single and has $40,000 in wages, $2,000 of passive income from a limited partnership, and $3,500 of passive loss from a rental real estate activity in which she actively participated. In this case $2,000 of Jane's $3,500 loss offsets her passive income. The remaining $1,500 loss can be deducted from her $40,000 wages.

Active participation. You actively participated in a rental real estate activity if you (and your spouse) owned at least 10 percent of the rental property and you made management decisions in a significant and bona fide sense. Management decisions include approving new tenants, deciding on rental terms, approving expenditures, and similar decisions.

Example. Mike is single and had the following income and losses during the tax year:

Salary	$42,300
Dividends	300
Interest	1,400
Rental loss	($4,000)

The rental loss resulted from the rental of a house Mike owned. Mike had advertised and rented the house to the current tenant himself. He also collected the rents, which usually came by mail. All repairs were done or contracted out by Mike.

Even though the rental loss is a loss from a passive activity, because Mike actively participated in the rental property management, he can use the entire $4,000 loss to offset his other income.

Maximum special allowance. If your modified adjusted gross income is $100,000 or less ($50,000 or less if married and filing separately), you can deduct your loss up to $25,000 ($12,500 if married and filing separately). If your modified adjusted gross income is more than $100,000 (more than $50,000 if married and filing separately), this special allowance is limited to 50 percent of the difference between $150,000 ($75,000 if married and filing separately) and your modified adjusted gross income.

Generally, there is no relief from the passive activity loss limits if your modified adjusted gross income is $150,000 or more ($75,000 or more if married and filing separately).

Modified adjusted gross income. This is your adjusted gross income from Form 1040, line 37, figured without taking into account the following:

1. Taxable Social Security or equivalent tier 1 railroad retirement benefits
2. Deductible contributions to an IRA or certain other qualified retirement plans
3. The exclusion allowed for qualified U.S. savings bond interest used to pay higher education expenses
4. The exclusion allowed for employer-provided adoption benefits
5. Any passive activity income or loss included on Form 8582
6. Any passive income or loss or any loss allowable by reason of the exception for real estate professionals discussed earlier
7. Any overall loss from a publicly traded partnership [see "Publicly Traded Partnerships (PTPs)" in the instructions for Form 8582]
8. The deduction for one-half of self-employment tax
9. The deduction allowed for interest on student loans
10. The deduction for qualified tuition and related expenses

Form 8582 not required. Do not complete Form 8582 if you meet all the following conditions:

1. Your only passive activities were rental real estate activities in which you actively participated.
2. Your overall net loss from these activities is $25,000 or less ($12,500 or less if married filing separately).
3. You do not have any prior year unallowed losses from any passive activities.
4. If married and filing separately, you lived apart from your spouse all year.
5. You have no current or prior year unallowed credits from passive activities.
6. Your modified adjusted gross income is $100,000 or less ($50,000 or less if married and filing separately).
7. You do not hold any interest in a rental real estate activity as a limited partner or as a beneficiary of an estate or a trust.

If you meet all these conditions, your rental real estate activities are not limited by the passive activity rules and you do not have to complete Form 8582. Enter each rental real estate loss from line 22 of Schedule E (Form 1040) on line 23 of Schedule E.

If you do not meet all these conditions, see the instructions for Form 8582 to find out if you must complete and attach that form to your tax return.

How to Report Rental Income and Expenses

If you rent buildings, rooms, or apartments, and provide only heat and light, trash collection, and so forth, you normally report your rental income and expenses on Schedule E (Form 1040), Part I. However, do not use that schedule to report a not-for-profit activity. See "Not Rented for Profit," discussed earlier.

If you provide significant services that are primarily for your tenant's convenience, such as regular cleaning, changing linen, or maid service, you report your rental income and expenses on Schedule C (Form 1040), "Profit or Loss from Business," or Schedule C-EZ, "Net Profit from Business." Significant services do not include furnishing heat and light, cleaning public areas, collecting trash, and so on. For information, see Publication 334, "Tax Guide for Small Business (For Individuals Who Use Schedule C or C-EZ)." You also may have to pay self-employment tax on your rental income. See Publication 533, "Self-Employment Tax."

Schedule E (Form 1040)

Use Schedule E (Form 1040), Part I, to report your rental income and expenses. List your total income, expenses, and depreciation for each rental property. Be sure to answer the question on line 2.

If you have more than three rental or royalty properties, complete and attach as many copies of Schedules E as are needed to list the properties. Complete lines 1 and 2 for each property. However, fill in the "Totals" column on only one Schedule E. The figures in the "Totals" column on that Schedule E should be the combined totals of all copies of Schedules E.

Page 2 of Schedule E is used to report income or loss from partnerships, S corporations, estates, trusts, and real estate mortgage investment conduits. If you need to use page 2 of Schedule E, use page 2 of the same Schedule E you used to enter the combined totals in Part I.

On Schedule E, page 1, line 20, enter the depreciation you are claiming. You must complete and attach Form 4562 for rental activities only if you are claiming one of the following:

- Depreciation on property placed in service during 2004
- Depreciation on listed property (such as a car) regardless of when it was placed in service
- Any car expenses reported on a form other than Schedule C or C-EZ (Form 1040) or Form 2106 or Form 2106-EZ

Otherwise, compute your depreciation on your own worksheet. You do not have to attach these computations to your return.

Illustrated Example

In January, Eileen Johnson bought a condominium apartment to live in. Instead of selling the house she had been living in, she decided to change it to a rental property. Eileen selected a tenant and started renting the house on February 1. Eileen charges $750 a month for rent and collects it herself. Eileen received a $750 security deposit from her tenant. Because she plans to return it to her tenant at the end of the lease, she does not include it in her income. Her house expenses for the year are as follows:

Mortgage interest	$1,800
Fire insurance (1-year policy)	100
Miscellaneous repairs (after renting)	297
Real estate taxes imposed and paid	$1,200

Eileen must divide the real estate taxes, mortgage interest, and fire insurance between the personal use of the property and the rental use of the property. She can deduct eleven-twelfths of those expenses as rental expenses. She can include the balance of the allowable taxes and mortgage interest on Schedule A (Form

1040) if she itemizes. She cannot deduct the balance of the fire insurance because it is a personal expense.

Eileen bought this house in 1979 for $35,000. Her property tax was based on assessed values of $10,000 for the land and $25,000 for the house. Before changing it to a rental property, Eileen added several improvements to the house. She determines her adjusted basis as follows:

Improvements	Cost
House	$25,000
Remodeled kitchen	4,200
Recreation room	5,800
New roof	1,600
Patio and deck	2,400
Adjusted basis	$39,000

On February 1, when Eileen changed her house to a rental property, the property had a fair market value of $152,000. Of that amount, $35,000 was for the land and $117,000 was for the house.

Because Eileen's adjusted basis is less than the fair market value on the date of the change, Eileen uses $39,000 as her basis for depreciation.

Because the house is a residential rental property, she must use the straight-line method of depreciation, using either the GDS recovery period or the ADS recovery period. She chooses the GDS recovery period of 27.5 years.

She uses Table 4-D to find her depreciation percentage. Because she placed the property in service in February, she finds the percentage to be 3.182 percent.

On April 1, Eileen bought a new dishwasher for the rental property at a cost of $425. The dishwasher is personal property used in a rental real estate activity, which has a five-year recovery period. The dishwasher qualifies for the 50 percent special depreciation allowance, which she computes first. Next, she uses the percentage under "half-year convention" in Table 4-A to figure her MACRS depreciation deduction for the dishwasher.

On May 1, Eileen paid $4,000 to have a furnace installed in the house. The furnace is residential rental property. Because she placed the property in service in May, she finds the percentage from Table 4-D to be 2.273 percent.

Eileen figures her net rental income or loss for the house as follows:

Total rental income received ($750 × 11)		$8,250
Minus expenses		
Mortgage interest ($1,800 × 11/12)	$1,650	
Fire insurance ($100 × 11/12)	92	
Miscellaneous repairs	297	
Real estate taxes ($1,200 × 11/12)	1,100	
Total expenses		3,139
Balance		$5,111
Minus depreciation		
House ($39,000 × 3.182%)	$1,241	
Dishwasher–special allowance ($425 × 50%)	213	
Dishwasher ($425 − $213 special allowance) × 20%	42	
Furnace ($4,000 × 2.273%)	91	
Total depreciation		1,587
Net rental income for house		$3,524

Eileen uses Schedule E (Form 1040), Part I, to report her rental income and expenses. She enters her income, expenses, and depreciation for the house in the column for Property A. She uses Form 4562 to figure and report her depreciation. See IRS Publication 946 for information on how to prepare Form 4562.

12
Final Observations

This concluding chapter contains some final observations and revisits the most important aspects of being a successful landlord. By purchasing and reading this book, you have indicated a desire to improve as a landlord. Continue to follow this approach by continuing to educate yourself. Be a professional. As one landlord stated: "Being a successful landlord is being a good businessperson coupled with good people skills and knowledge of the rules and regulations of leasing residential property in your state."

Rules for Success

As a guide to success, I recommend the following actions:

- Join a local association of landlords or a real estate association. In addition to the wealth of information that can be obtained from these organizations, you may qualify for special discounts on items or services required in your rental operations.
- Subscribe to the electronic newsletter *Rent For Profit*. Visit the web site www.rentforprofit.com for information on how to subscribe.
- Review the landlord-tenant laws for your state. Become familiar with the local laws and regulations.
- Offer only clean rentals. Never allow a prospective tenant to look at property that is not ready to be shown.

- Take the rental forms that you use, most of which are contained in this book, and personalize them with your name and address. Establish a professional appearance in all your endeavors.
- Do not tolerate any tenant's disruptive behavior. Handle such behavior in a professional manner.
- When you make promises to a tenant, keep them.
- Initiate good management practices and make sure your employees also use them.
- Listen to tenants' complaints. Treat them as a serious matter. Complaints about a dangerous situation or a broken security item need immediate attention.
- Communicate with your tenants in a professional manner.
- Keep your property insured and also carry liability insurance.

Keys to Profit

Many real estate professions think that the key to successful long-term real estate investing is to rent your property for your annual cost. If you do that, the appreciation on the property is your real gain. One investor contends that you make your money in real estate when you buy the property, not when you sell it. Accordingly, if you buy right, you will always be able to rent the property and eventually resell it for good money.

Selecting Rental Property

As was noted earlier, selecting profitable rental property is a prerequisite for success. Some of the general rules for selecting profitable rental property include the following:

- Consider the location of the rental property. Is there a need for rental property in the area, or does the area have too many rentals?
- Consider only newer properties. Older properties have too many problems, such as electrical or plumbing issues and concern regarding lead paint or other hazardous materials in the structure.
- Although this depends on the wishes of the landlord, I prefer to deal in single-family houses. They are easier to keep rented and tend to have fewer problems associated with their rental.
- If your purchase single-family rentals, do not purchase one with more than three bedrooms or less than two bathrooms. Too many bedrooms generally attract large families, and there is a greater chance that the property will be damaged during the tenancy. Homes with only one bathroom are hard to rent, and if the house has only one bathroom, a plumbing problem becomes an emergency.
- Purchase in good neighborhoods, not in poorer neighborhoods. You will get higher rents and have less of a crime problem.

Legal Glossary

Note: For legal terms not listed in this glossary, refer to *Black's Law Dictionary* or *Cochran's Law Dictionary* in the reference section of most libraries.

Abstract of title (abstract). The history of a parcel of real estate compiled from public records; lists transfers of ownership and claims against the property.

Acceleration clause. A provision in a contract or mortgage providing that if a payment is missed or any other provision is violated, the whole debt or requirement to perform becomes immediately due and payable.

Acknowledgment. A formal declaration before a public official that one has signed the document to which the acknowledgment is attached.

Acre. A measure of land that contains 43,560 square feet.

Adjustable-rate mortgage (ARM). A mortgage loan whose interest rate may be changed periodically to keep up with current interest rates.

Adjusted basis. The original cost of property plus any later added improvements and minus a figure for claimed depreciation.

Adjusted sales price. The sale price minus commissions, legal fees, and other costs of selling the property.

Advance rent. Moneys paid to the landlord to be applied to future rent payment periods; does not include rent paid in advance for a current rent payment period.

Adverse impact. Disadvantage to members of the protected class due to a substantially different rate of selection in hiring and/or firing,

Affidavit. A written statement of facts signed and sworn to before an official with the authority to administer oaths.

Affirm. To ratify or approve the judgment of a lower court or an administrative decision.

Agent. A person with the authority to do an act for another.

Alienation clause (also called nonassumption clause). A clause in a mortgage or contract stating that the loan must be paid in full if ownership is transferred or in other contingent occurrences.

Amortization. The gradual payment of a debt through regular installments that cover both principal and interest.

Appeal. A request or application to a higher court to set aside or modify the decision or ruling of a lower court.

Appellant. The party who initiates an appeal.

Appellee. The party to a lawsuit against whom an appeal is taken.

Appraisal. An estimate of the value of a property; generally done by an expert appraiser.

Appreciation. The increase in value of property.

Arbitration. The submission of a dispute to the nonjudicial judgment of one or more disinterested persons called arbitrators.

As is. Refers to the transfer of property with no guaranty or warranty provided by the seller except that the seller had the right to sell the property.

Assessed valuation. The value assigned to property as a basis for determining the property tax on that property; often it is not the property's appraised or market value.

Assign. To transfer rights to another party, who is called the assignee. The party who assigns the rights is called the assignor.

Assignment. A transfer of the rights and/or obligations of a contract from one party to another.

Assumable mortgage. A mortgage loan that may be transferred to the next owner of the property.

Assumption. The takeover of a loan by a qualified or approved buyer.

Automatic renewal clause. A contract provision that allows the renewal of a contract until it is canceled. Often a property sales listing contract with a broker includes a clause renewing the listing contract indefinitely unless it is canceled by the property owner.

Balloon note. A mortgage or loan in which the remaining balance becomes fully due and payable at a predetermined time.

Balloon payment. The final payment on a balloon note.

Bill of sale. A written document transferring ownership of personal property.

Binder. A preliminary agreement for sale of property that usually is accompanied by an earnest money deposit. When used with property insurance, it a document that insures the property until the formal insurance policy is issued.

Bona fide. In good faith, honestly, and without fraud.

Bona fide occupational qualification (BFOQ). A good faith, honest, and without fraud preemployment qualification that is essential to establish the ability of the applicant to perform the necessary and required duties of the position in question.

Bond. A promissory note; a written promise to repay a loan, often with an accompanying mortgage that pledges real estate or other valuable property as security for the performance of an obligation.

Book value. The net worth of a business's assets, minus liabilities, without considering any value for goodwill.

Brief. A prepared statement of a party's position in a legal proceeding.

Broker. An individual licensed by the state to represent another person for a fee in real estate transactions. An individual who represents others in the sale of property.

Building code. The local regulations that establish building requirements and standards for building and construction.

Burden of proof. The duty of a party to present the evidence that establishes that party's contentions or version of the facts. Failure to meet the burden of proof will result in a decision for the opposing party.

Buy-down. In real estate transactions, the payment of additional points to a mortgage lender in return for a lower interest rate on the loan.

Buyers' market. A period when the supply of homes for sale exceeds the demand.

Cap limit. The amount by which an adjustable-rate mortgage may be raised at any one time.

Capital gain. The taxable profit made when an appreciated asset is sold.

Case law. Judicial precedent set forth in prior court opinions that will bind parties in future lawsuits.

Caveat. A warning.

Caveat emptor. A Latin term meaning "let the buyer beware."

Ceiling. The maximum rate beyond which an adjustable-rate mortgage may not be raised.

Certificate of occupancy. A document issued by a local governmental agency stating that a property meets the standards for occupancy.

Chattel. A common law term that now refers to personal property.

Circumstantial evidence. Evidence not directly proving the existence of a fact in question but tending to imply its existence.

Civil Rights Act of 1964. The civil rights act that forms the basis of most equal opportunity requirements. Title 42, U.S. Code, section 1447 et seq.

Civil service commissions. Various groups of local, state, or federal officials that supervise public employees.

Claimant. A person who makes a claim for benefits.

Clayton Act. An act that amended the Sherman Antitrust Act and that prohibits unlawful restraints on trade.

Closing. (Also referred to as the settlement or closing escrow passing papers.) The formal conclusion of a real estate sale, at which time title to the property is transferred and necessary funds are disbursed.

Closing costs. The one-time charges paid by buyer and seller at closing.

Closing statement. The itemized statement prepared for the buyer and seller listing debits and credits for each party; completed by the person in charge of the closing (escrow agent).

Cloud on the title. An indication that there is an outstanding claim or encumbrance that challenges the owner's clear title to a property.

Collective bargaining. The bargaining between management and labor unions regarding the terms and conditions of employment.

Commerce clause. Article I, Section VIII, of the U.S. Constitution; gives the U.S. Congress the authority to regulate trade between the states.

Common areas. The areas of an apartment complex that are used by all tenants. The parts of a condominium development in which each owner holds an interest (swimming pool, etc.).

Common law. An ambiguous term used to describe the concept of law that relies on precedent (i.e., previous court opinions) and traditions.

Comparable property. Property similar to the property being evaluated or assessed in value. Used to estimate the market value of property.

Comparative market analysis. A method used in valuing homes or rental property by using a study of similar properties.

Compensatory damages. The measure of actual damages or losses.

Concurrent jurisdiction. The authority of two or more courts to entertain a particular lawsuit.

Condominium. A type of ownership involving individual ownership of dwelling units and common ownership of shared areas.

Consequential damages. A measure of damages referring to the indirect injuries or losses a party suffers.

Consideration. Something of legal value given to induce another person to enter into a contract.

Contingency. A condition in a contract that must be satisfied before the other party is bound under the contract.

Contract. An enforceable agreement to do or not do a particular thing.

Contract for deed. (Also known as a land contract.) A method of selling property which the buyer receives possession but the seller retains title until the property is paid for.

Conventional mortgage. A mortgage loan arranged between lender and borrower with no governmental guarantee or insurance.

Cost basis. A method of valuing property that includes the original cost of the property plus certain expenses to purchase it and money spent on permanent improvements and other costs, minus any depreciation deduction claimed on previous tax returns.

Curtesy. A common law term still used in some states when a widower obtains a portion of his deceased wife's real property.

Days on market (DOM). The number of days between the time a house or rental property is put on the market and the date of a firm sale contract or the date the property is rented.

De novo. A new, fresh start.

Deed. A formal, written document transferring title to real estate; a new deed is used for each transfer.

Deed of trust. A document by which title to property is held by a neutral third party until a debt is paid. In some states, it may be used instead of a mortgage.

Deed restriction. (Also referred to as a restrictive covenant.) A provision placed in a deed to control use and occupancy of the property by future owners.

Default. The failure to make a mortgage or rent payment or the failure to complete a required contractual duty.

Defendant. The party against whom a lawsuit is initiated.

Deferred maintenance. The act of putting off needed repairs.

Deficiency judgment. The personal claim remaining against a when foreclosed property does not yield enough at sale to pay off loans against the property.

Delivery of a deed. The legal transfer of a deed to the new property owner; the moment at which transfer of title occurs.

Deposit money. Any money held by the landlord on behalf of the tenant, including but not limited to damage deposits, security deposits, advance rent deposit, pet deposit, or any contractual deposit agreed to between landlord and tenant in writing or orally.

Deposition. Oral questions and answers put in writing for possible use in a legal proceeding.

Depreciation. A deduction in the value of property because of deterioration or obsolescence; sometimes an artificial bookkeeping concept.

Dictum. A statement in a judicial opinion that is not necessary to support the decision in that case and therefore is not considered as a precedent.

Direct endorsement. The complete processing of an FHA mortgage application by an authorized local lender.

Documentary tax stamp. A fee by state or local governments imposed when real estate is transferred or mortgaged, evidenced by a tax stamp on the deed.

Dower. The common-law right recognized in some states in which a widow has a right to a portion of her deceased husband's property.

Earnest money. The money deposited by a buyer to show "good faith" accompanying a purchase offer.

Easement. A right to use another person's property: telephone lines, common driveway, footpath, and so on.

Encroachment. An unauthorized intrusion on another person's property; a building or improvement on another person's land.

Encumbrance. A claim against another person's real estate (unpaid tax, mortgage, easement, etc.).

Equal Employment Opportunity Commission (EEOC). A commission established under the Civil Rights Act of 1964 to administer the act.

Equity. The value of a person's interest in property; the money realized when property is sold and all the claims against it are paid.

Escrow. The funds given to a third party to be held pending some occurrence; in real estate, generally refers to earnest money, funds collected by a lender for the payment of taxes and insurance charges, funds withheld at closing to insure uncompleted repairs, or in some states the entire process of closing.

Et seq. Latin term meaning "and following parts."

Exclusive agency. A listing agreement under which only the listing office can sell a property and earn the commission.

Exclusive right to sell. A listing agreement under which the owner promises to pay a commission to a specified broker if the property is sold during the listing period by anyone, even the owner.

Fair Labor Standards Act of 1938. An act designed to establish fair labor standards in employment involved in interstate commerce (Title 29, U.S. Code, section 201 et seq.).

Fee simple. A common law term describing the complete ownership of property.

Fiduciary. A person in a position of trust or responsibility with specific duties to act in the best interest of a client.

First mortgage. A mortgage that takes priority over the claims of other lenders against the same property.

Fixture. Personal property that becomes part of real estate after it is attached to the real estate.

Foreclosure. The legal process of taking and selling mortgaged property for the payment of debt against it.

Good faith. Honesty in conduct or a transaction; an honest and fair purpose without the intent to commit an unjust act.

Grantee. A buyer who receives a deed.

Grantor. A seller who gives a deed.

Hazard insurance. Property insurance covering property against fire and similar risks.

Hearsay evidence. Statements made by witnesses in legal proceedings regarding information obtained from a third person.

Homeowners policy. An insurance policy that puts many kinds of insurance into one package designed to protect a homeowner.

Improvements. Permanent additions that increase the value of a home.

Index. A benchmark measure of current interest levels; used to calculate periodic changes in rates charged on adjustable rate mortgages.

Injunction. A court order directing a party to refrain from certain activity.

Interstate commerce. Any trade, transportation, or communication among the several states or with the District of Columbia. **Note:** Affecting interstate commerce means "involved in," "having an impact on," "burdening," or "obstructing" it.

Job analysis. A detailed statement of work behaviors and other information relevant to a job.

Job description. A general statement of the duties and responsibilities entailed in a job.

Joint tenancy. A type of ownership by two or more persons, each with an undivided ownership; if one dies, the property goes automatically to the survivor(s).

Junior mortgage. A mortgage that is subordinate to another mortgage.

Jurisdiction. The authority of a court or administrative body to hear and decide a dispute.

Labor arbitration. A nonjudicial method to settle disputes between labor and management; governed by the Labor-Management Relations Act of 1947 (LMRA).

Labor dispute. Any dispute under a labor contract between the employer and the labor union concerning the terms, conditions, or tenure of employment or the representation of persons in negotiating, maintaining, or changing the terms or conditions of employment.

Labor-Management Reporting and Disclosure Act of 1959 (LMRDA). An act designed to ensure democratic procedures in labor unions and establish a bill of rights for union members.

Labor organization. Any labor organization, committee, or group that is organized for the benefit of employees and subject to the provisions of the Civil Rights Act of 1964 or the federal labor management acts.

Land contract. A contract plan for buying a house in which a title deed is not issued until the land or a certain portion of the purchase price is paid; a layaway plan.

Landlord. The owner or lessor of a dwelling unit.

Legal holiday. A holiday observed by the clerk of a court.

Les pendens. A notice that is binding on future buyers that litigation is pending on property.

Lien. A claim against property for the payment of a debt: a mechanic's lien, a mortgage, unpaid taxes, and judgments.

Listing agreement. A listing; a written employment agreement between a property owner and a real estate broker that authorizes the broker to find a buyer.

Listing presentation. A presentation submitted orally or in writing by a real estate agent who seeks to put a prospective seller's property on the market.

Loan servicing. Refers to a company that handles the paperwork for collecting loan payments, checking property tax and insurance coverage, and handling delinquencies.

Lock-in interest rate. A guarantee that the borrower will receive the rate in effect at the time of a loan application.

Market value. The most likely price a given property will bring if it is widely exposed on the market, assuming a fully informed buyer and seller.

Marketable title. A title free of liens, clouds, and debts; a title that will be freely accepted by a buyer.

Mechanic's lien. A lien placed against property by unpaid workers or suppliers who provided materials for the property.

Meeting of the minds. A legal term meaning that the parties to a contract formed an agreement on the provisions of the contract.

Mortgage. A lien or claim against real property given as security for a loan; the homeowner "gives" the mortgage and the lender "takes" it.

Mortgagee. A lender.

Mortgagor. A borrower.

Multiple listing service (MLS). An arrangement by which brokers work together on each other's listed homes, with shared commissions.

National Labor Relations Act of 1935 (NLRA). The Wagner Act, which established the NLRB and was designed to support unionism and collective bargaining.

National Labor Relations Board (NLRB). A commission established by the NLRA to enforce the rights of employees under the act.

Nationality. The status acquired by belonging to or being associated with a nation or state; arises by birth or nationalization.

Negative amortization. Arrangement under which the shortfall in a mortgage payment is added to the amount borrowed; gradual raising of a debt on the property.

Net listing. Arrangement under which the seller receives a specific sum from the sale price and the agent keeps the rest as a sales commission.

Norris–LaGuardia Act. An act passed by the U.S. Congress in 1932; designed to stop federal courts from issuing injunctions in labor strikes.

Original jurisdiction. The court with authority to hear a case first; the trial court.

PITT. Abbreviation for principal, interest, taxes, and insurance, which often are lumped together in a monthly mortgage payment.

Plaintiff. The party who initiates a lawsuit.

Plat. A map or chart of a lot, subdivision, or community showing boundary lines, buildings, and easements.

Pleadings. The formal written statements of parties to a lawsuit that establish the basis of each party's contentions before the court.

PMI. Private mortgage insurance.

Point. Used to discount interest; each point equals 1 percent of a new mortgage being placed; paid in a one-time lump sum to the lender.

Portfolio loans. Loans made by a bank that keeps its mortgages as assets in its own portfolio.

Prejudice. A bias that interferes with a person's impartiality and sense of fairness.

Premises. A dwelling unit and the structure of which it is a part; a mobile home lot and the appurtenant facilities and grounds, areas, facilities, and property held for the use of tenants generally.

Prepayment penalty. Charges levied by the lender for paying off a mortgage before its maturity date.

Purchase-money mortgage. A mortgage used to finance the purchase of real property; commonly a mortgage "taken back" by the seller.

Quitclaim deed. A deed that completely transfers whatever ownership the grantor may have had but makes no claim of ownership of the property.

Real property. Land and the improvements on it.

Redlining. The practice of refusing to provide loans or insurance in a certain neighborhood.

Rent. The periodic payments due the landlord from the tenant for occupancy under a rental agreement and any other payments due the landlord from the tenant as may be designated as rent in a written rental agreement.

Rental agreement. Any written agreement or oral agreement if for a duration of less than one year providing for use and occupancy of premises.

RESPA. The Real Estate Settlement Procedures Act; requires advance disclosure to the borrower of information pertinent to a loan.

Restrictive covenant. A deed restriction.

Reverse mortgage. An arrangement under which a homeowner who does not need to meet income or credit requirements can draw against the equity in a home with no immediate repayment.

Right-to-work laws. State anti-union laws that prohibit labor contracts that require all employees to join a union.

Security deposits. Any moneys held by the landlord as security for the performance of the rental agreement, including but not limited to monetary damage to the landlord caused by the tenant's breach of lease before its expiration.

Sellers' market. A time in which demand for homes exceeds the supply offered for sale.

Settlement. The time of closing a real estate transaction.

Sherman Antitrust Act. An act passed in 1890 that was designed to protect trade and commerce by prohibiting certain restraints of trade and monopolies.

Specific performance. A legal remedy requiring that a contractual duty be performed, for example, asking a court to order a seller to convey the property as previously agreed.

Strike. An organized refusal to work by employees that is designed to place economic pressure on the employer.

Survey. A map made by a licensed surveyor who measures the land and charts its boundaries, improvements, and relationship to the property surrounding it.

Taft-Hartley Act. An act that amended the National Labor Relations Act.

Tenant. Any person entitled to occupy a dwelling unit under a rental agreement.

Time is of the essence. A legal phrase in a contract requiring punctual performance of all obligations.

Title insurance. An insurance policy protecting the insured against loss or damage due to defects in title; the "owner's policy" protects the buyer, and the "mortgagee's policy" protects the lender; paid with a one-time premium.

Title search. A check of public records, usually at the local courthouse, to make sure no adverse claims affect the value of a title.

Total disability. A physical disability that prevents a person from performing all the substantial acts necessary for that person's occupation.

Transaction broker. A broker who offers services without owing fiduciary duties to either party as defined by law in various states.

Transient occupancy. Occupancy when it is the intention of the parties that the occupancy will be temporary.

VA. Refers to the Department of Veterans Affairs (formerly The Veterans Administration), which guarantees a veteran's mortgage so that a lender is willing to make the loan with little or no down payment.

Vendee. A buyer.

Vendor. A seller.

Warranty deed. A type of deed in which the grantor makes formal assurance of title.

Zoning ordinances. Laws of local government establishing building codes and regulations on the use of property.

Index

Note: Boldface numbers indicate illustrations; italic *t* indicates a table.

About the Author

Cliff Roberson is authorized to practice law in Texas and California. He also has been admitted to practice before the U.S. Supreme Court and federal courts in Texas and California. Currently, he is a professor at Washburn University, Topeka. Cliff is the author of numerous publications including the following:

- *The Complete Book of Business Forms and Agreements*, McGraw-Hill
- *Fight the IRS and Win: A Self-Defense Guide for Taxpayers*, Liberty House
- *Hire Right—Fire Right: A Manager's Guide to Employment Practices That Avoid Lawsuits*, McGraw-Hill
- *The Businessperson's Legal Advisor*, Tab
- *The Small Business Tax Advisor: Understanding the New Tax Law*, Liberty House
- *The McGraw-Hill Tax Advisor*, McGraw-Hill

His legal experiences include serving as legal counsel for one of the largest property management companies in California. He also has been a property owner and landlord for many years.

Any suggestions for improvements to the book or comments may be forwarded to Cliff at www.rentforprofit.com.